C/C++ Software Quality Tools

Mark L. Murphy

For book and bookstore information

http://www.prenhall.com

Prentice Hall PTR
Upper Saddle River, New Jersey 07458

Library of Congress Cataloging-in-Publication Data

Murphy, Mark L.
C/C++ software quality tools / Mark L. Murphy.
p. cm.
Includes bibliographical references and index.
ISBN 0-13-445123-6 (alk. paper)
1. Computer software--Quality control. 2. C (Computer program language) 3. C++ (Computer program language) I. Title.
QA76.76.Q35M87 1996 95-46749
005.1'4--dc20 CIP

Acquisitions editor: *Gregory G. Doench*
Editorial assistant: *Meg Cowen*
Series editor: *Dr. Lance A. Leventhal*
Editorial/production supervision: *Jane Bonnell*
Cover design director: *Jerry Votta*
Cover design: *Design Source*
Manufacturing manager: *Alexis R. Heydt*

Published by Prentice Hall PTR
Prentice-Hall, Inc.
A Simon & Schuster Company
Upper Saddle River, New Jersey 07458

The publisher offers discounts on this book when ordered in bulk quantities. For more information, contact Corporate Sales Department, Prentice Hall PTR, One Lake Street, Upper Saddle River, NJ 07458. Phone: 800-382-3419; FAX: 201- 236-7141; E-mail: corpsales@prenhall.com

Printed in the United States of America
10 9 8 7 6 5 4 3 2 1

ISBN 0-13-445123-6

Prentice-Hall International (UK) Limited, *London*
Prentice-Hall of Australia Pty. Limited, *Sydney*
Prentice-Hall Canada Inc., *Toronto*
Prentice-Hall Hispanoamericana, S.A., *Mexico*
Prentice-Hall of India Private Limited, *New Delhi*
Prentice-Hall of Japan, Inc., *Tokyo*
Simon & Schuster Asia Pte. Ltd., *Singapore*
Editora Prentice-Hall do Brasil, Ltda., *Rio de Janeiro*

Contents

Preface

Software quality assurance is one of the least discussed aspects of the software development process. This is despite the fact that every project does some form of quality assurance, either organized or ad hoc. Yet a quick inspection of the shelves of a technical bookstore will show many more books on software design and programming techniques.

Part of the problem is that software quality, testing in particular, is not considered to be much fun. People associate testing with grumpy project managers, a continuous series of forms, and a lot of manual work. It is also a "black art," in that many of its techniques are not well explained or justified. So, why write books about something nobody likes to do?

This book tries to make quality assurance more approachable to practitioners in the software development industry. Here, "practitioners" include computer programmers, configuration management specialists, dedicated testing personnel, and anyone else involved, one way or another, in organized quality assurance.

This book is not heavy on methodologies or slogans. Instead, it focuses on the "nuts and bolts" of quality assurance, with an emphasis on tools to assist in the process. Testers cannot test without tools, just as programmers cannot program without editors, compilers, and the like. By explaining the types of tools that are available and showing their use, this book should add a little structure and automation to the readers' future work.

P.1 Goals

This book teaches readers about the software testing process and how tools can accelerate and enhance efforts to achieve better quality. In particular, the book describes tools available to assist in testing and how to construct them.

Learn About Software Testing

Developers typically have varied backgrounds in software quality assurance. Few have received formal training. Many learned it on the job, inheriting the prejudices of more experienced coworkers. Still others were forced by mandate to figure out how to test software on their own.

Like any other computer science discipline, software quality assurance has:

- Methodologies (such as "cleanroom")
- "Classic" texts (e.g., Myers' *The Art of Software Testing* [11])
- Common procedures and techniques used by many professionals (such as structured testing, in the form of unit and system testing)

This book does not provide a complete treatment of all techniques used in software quality assurance. The References section at the back of the book, if read in its entirety, would still not completely cover all known topics. Instead, we wish to give newcomers to software testing an idea of what to do, from a practitioner's point of view. For more experienced testers, this book explains what various tools do and where they fit, thus making their applicability easier to discern.

Learn About Available Tools

There is a lot of focus in the computer industry on tools, especially given the explosion of desktop computing power. Serious attention has been given to analysis and design, with CASE tools, object "stick-and-ball" modelers, etc. There has also been significant work done on development tools, ranging from compilers and editors to profilers and function/class libraries.

Unfortunately, tools for testing and quality assurance have not received the attention they deserve. Software testing is a critical stage in a product's climb to success or fall to failure. As with anything else in this industry, the existence of capable, easily acquired tools will make quality assurance easier to implement.

Readers of this text should gain a working knowledge of the available types of SQA tools. Also, readers should understand where to use different tools in the software development life cycle and which tools to apply when testing specific types of software.

This book provides six tools, with source code on the included disk and descriptions in the text. The tools themselves will be of use to readers on their projects. In addition, trying them out might suggest which types of tools are useful; the project could then invest in a more powerful suite of tools based on experience.

Learn About Test Tool Construction

The final goal is for readers to learn about the construction of the quality assurance tools provided in the book. Some tools have uses in other areas, such as the UTCLang scripting language. Knowing how UTCLang works will help determine its utility for other applications. Still others, such as WinCapT, will highlight interesting techniques for particular types of operations. Many of these will apply to all types of programs, not just testing tools. Finally, the testing tools themselves will also serve as examples of programming techniques related to quality assurance, such as naming conventions.

P.2 About the Tools

Many readers will buy this book primarily for the tools provided. This is certainly reasonable; commercial equivalents of these tools are expensive and tend not to be as portable. Hence, an up-front discussion of what readers will find is in order.

Tools Provided

The disk contains the following six tools:

AssertLib

AssertLib is a library for providing alternative handlers for assertions. Assertions are development-time-only macros used to validate assumptions, such as the state of input parameters (e.g., not expecting a certain pointer to be NULL). These macros log violations, either by stopping the program or writing a message to a file. In production, the macros "evaporate," so they do not affect the shipped application.

Assertions take the knowledge that programmers have about the design and give it to the application itself. Now the program can check itself for violations, helping the developer identify problem areas. Manually checking all this would be impractical, but automation makes it feasible.

ResTrack

ResTrack is a library for tracking the allocation and release of heap memory. It can detect faults related to memory usage, such as overwriting the bounds of an array. It can be extended to track other resources, such as file handles.

Resource mismanagement is one of the banes of programming in C/C++ because the language is so close to the operating system. Developers can frequently spend significant time trying to isolate problems with resources. This job is much easier with a tool like ResTrack.

UTCGen

Given a set of C/C++ function prototypes, UTCGen can suggest unit test conditions to be applied to them. It uses a modifiable catalog as the source of test condition heuristics. Testers can then combine the conditions and other manually identified ones into test cases for a unit test suite.

Experienced developers often can glance at a function and determine what should be tested in it. In most cases, younger programmers lack such insight. This tool ensures that testers try all conditions based on the function's inputs. Even experienced developers will find that it reduces the drudgery of unit test development.

UTCLang

UTCLang is a library for implementing a scripting language, typically attached to a subsystem so unit tests can be written in a higher-level language than C/C++ itself. The resulting scripts can be more resilient to changes than the underlying C/C++ subsystem, resulting in less rewriting of unit test code.

UTCLang is also useful when testers are inexperienced in C/C++. If the developer creates the test driver, the testers then can write scripts. The UTCLang language is far easier to learn than C (let alone C++). The combination can improve testing productivity.

UTCCover

UTCCover is a set of macros and analysis tools that measure "code coverage." Coverage indicates how well a test suite exercises application code. In effect, measuring code coverage is measuring the quality of the testing itself.

Without measuring coverage, one has no idea of the thoroughness of a unit test suite. Although 100% coverage does not guarantee that all the bugs in a subsystem have been found, less coverage will surely find fewer of them.

WinCapT

WinCapT is a tool, similar to the Microsoft Recorder bundled with Microsoft Windows (hereafter referred to simply as "Windows"), that can record a user's session with a Windows application and play it back on demand. Windows can also be captured during recording and playback and compared for changes.

It is comparatively easy to create a regression test suite at the unit test level, particularly with tools like UTCLang. All the test code must do is write a text file indicating state. Comparing the file from run to run under identical circumstances should yield the same file. Doing this with interactive programs is much more difficult. WinCapT provides such functionality for Windows applications.

Availability of Tools

With the exception of WinCapT, these tools are usable on almost any platform providing an ANSI C compiler and, where needed, supporting basic C++ syntax. Neither templates nor C++ exception handling have been used to enhance portability. Table P.1 summarizes the requirements for each tool.

Table P.1 Tools and Compiler/Environment Requirements

Tool	ANSI C	C++	Windows Only
AssertLib	•		
ResTrack	•		
UTCGen	•		
UTCLang		•	
UTCCover	•		
WinCapT	•		•

Table P.2 outlines which platforms and compilers have been tested with the tools.

Table P.2 Compilers and Platforms Tested with Tools

Compiler	16-bit DOS	32-bit DOS	Win16	Win32s	Win NT	OS/2 2.11	OS/2 Warp
Borland C++ 4.05	•	•	•	•	•		
Symantec C++ 6.11	•	•	•	•	•		
Microsoft Visual C++ 1.5	•		•				
Watcom 10.0a	•	•	•	•	•	•	•
Metaware High C++						•	•

In addition, some of the tools have been tested for compatibility with Linux and GCC—see Appendix A for details.

The accompanying disk contains source code for all the tools, plus the Address Lite sample application.

Full instructions for using the disk appear in Appendix A. In addition, the book includes a license agreement for the use of the tools.

P.3 How This Book Is Organized

This book consists of six major sections:

1. The first two chapters introduce the reasoning behind software quality assurance and its importance. In addition, the six tools provided with the book are profiled.
2. Three chapters are then devoted to quality assurance during the development (coding) phase, a period sometimes ignored during SQA. These chapters describe how to prevent or identify faults early and include detailed descriptions of the AssertLib and ResTrack libraries.
3. The next four chapters describe unit and integration testing, perhaps the most important phase in software quality assurance. These chapters go into the goals of unit/integration testing and how to achieve them. In addition, three tools related to this phase are profiled: UTCGen, UTCLang, and UTCCover.
4. Next come two chapters on system testing, with an emphasis on testing graphical user interfaces (GUIs). WinCapT, our tool for regression testing Windows user interfaces, is the main topic of discussion.
5. The final chapter describes SQA activities following system test, emphasizing how to automate them. In addition, the chapter shows how to combine the six tools, and others like them, into a cohesive quality plan.
6. Finally, the appendixes describe the included disk, particularly the libraries and C++ class frameworks provided with the tools.

A theme that pervades the entire book is the idea of continuous improvement. This is the philosophy that quality assurance should not merely solve today's problems but should also try to prevent tomorrow's. While continuous improvement is popular in quality assurance circles, it is not always apparent how to apply it to software development. Each section will discuss continuous improvement and how to incorporate it into each of the main phases of software development.

P.4 Summary

This book will help practitioners of "the software arts" to create quality products, particularly through the use of automation. The tools will give readers a taste of the power that SQA tools can bring to a project. All readers should come away better prepared to tackle the bugs that plague everyone's software.

Acknowledgments

As with any book, this one would have been impossible without the help of many people and organizations. First and foremost, I thank American Management Systems for allowing me to write it and for the opportunity to hone my techniques on several projects. In particular, I thank Tim Taylor, my manager and vice-president for most of my career, for keeping me on interesting projects and always watching out for quality assurance.

I also thank Borland International, Metaware, and Symantec for providing copies of their C/C++ compilers for testing the tools in this book. Without their support, the tools would be less portable than they are.

Thanks also go to the denizens of the Internet, specifically those who frequent the `comp.software.testing` newsgroup, which provided many sources of information and ideas. Particular thanks go to Brian Marick, not only for writing the Generic Coverage Tool and maintaining FAQ lists, but also for teaching me the ways and means of unit testing at the University of Illinois.

Finally, the staff of Prentice Hall Professional Technical Reference has been invaluable in taking this book from random musings to a published work. Meg Cowen, Gregory G. Doench, and Dr. Lance Leventhal are all appreciated for their efforts to put together a quality manuscript. Additional thanks go to the unnamed souls who assembled and produced the book from the original copy.

Trademark Acknowledgments

The following trademarks are referenced within the book and are the property of their respective owners:

Borland C++ and dBASE are registered trademarks of Borland International.

High C++ is a trademark of Metaware, Inc.

Metaware is a registered trademark of Metaware, Inc.

Microsoft, MS-DOS, Visual Basic, and Windows are registered trademarks of Microsoft Corporation, Inc.

Office, Visual C++, and Windows NT are trademarks of Microsoft Corporation, Inc.

OS/2 is a registered trademark of IBM Corporation.

OS/2 Warp is a trademark of IBM Corporation.

Pentium is a trademark of Intel, Inc.

Symantec is a registered trademark of Symantec, Inc.

UNIX is a registered trademark in the United States and other countries, exclusively licensed through X/Open Company, Ltd.

Visual Programmer is a trademark of Blue Sky Software, Inc.

Watcom is a registered trademark of Sybase, Inc.

X Window System is a trademark and product of the Massachusetts Institute of Technology.

All other product names mentioned herein are the trademarks of their respective owners.

Our Sample Application: Address Lite

To properly show how the tools and techniques described in this book work, we need a sample application. This sample should fulfill three main goals:

1. It should have a graphical front end that runs under Windows 3.1. One of the tools, WinCapT, is specifically designed for testing Windows programs, so the sample application must provide a means for demonstrating it.
2. It should have a processing module that is portable across all major platforms. All other tools (except WinCapT) can be used by any C/C++ language implementation, on most platforms. The sample application must provide some source that readers can compile and use on all platforms. Failing to do this would leave some platforms, such as Unix or OS/2, without ready-to-try source code.
3. It should be readily understandable by the reader, without a lot of explanation.

The sample application, Address Lite, is a scaled-down address book, suitable for storing names, addresses, and telephone numbers for individuals or businesses. It uses a Windows multiple-document interface (MDI) for accessing several address databases simultaneously. The address databases themselves are in X-Base format, with a portable C library for manipulating them.

Windows Multiple Document Interface (MDI)

One of the interface paradigms promoted by Microsoft Windows 3.1 is the Multiple Document Interface, or MDI. Applications that manipulate "documents," such as word processors, spreadsheets, and graphics packages, tend to use MDI.

MDI applications have a master (parent) window with several child windows, one per document being modified. The user can have several child windows open at one time, to facilitate moving text between documents, for example. The MDI child windows have a few special properties:

- They exist only within the bounds of the parent window and cannot be dragged outside them.
- When iconized, the icons go to the bottom of the parent window, not to the bottom of the screen as in normal use.

The concept here is that, from the child window's point of view, the parent window is "the known universe," not the entire screen.

X-Base File Format

One of the most popular database programs for PCs starting in the 1980's was dBASE. Due to its success, its file format has been adopted by many other programs. This format is frequently referred to as X-Base (since "dBASE" is trademarked) or DBF, after its traditional file extension.

S.1 Using Address Lite

One can run Address Lite by running ADDRLITE.EXE from the Program Manager (Appendix A shows how to obtain this file from the provided disk). Alternatively, install it as a program in the Windows Program Manager by selecting File|New (meaning "select the New menu option from the File menu") from the Program Manager menu, opting to create a new Program Item, and filling out the dialog.

Address Lite behaves like a typical Windows application. To open a new address database, select File|New from the main menu. This will bring up a Windows file selection dialog box, where the user can choose a directory and specify a filename (Figure S.1).

Figure S.1 Open File Common Dialog

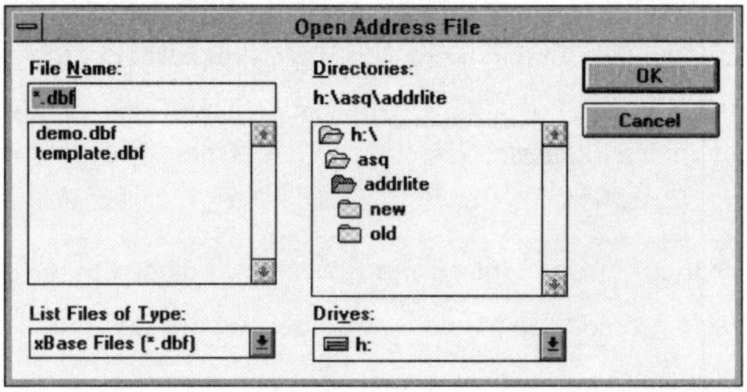

Similarly, to open an existing file, select File|Open from the main menu and select from the ensuing dialog. In either case, once a file has been selected, a window is displayed inside the Address Lite main window. This child window will contain the addresses for this database (Figure S.2).

Figure S.2 Address Lite Database Window

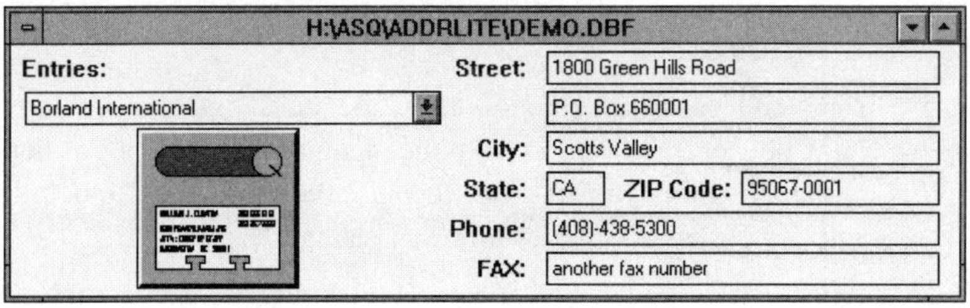

Users can open multiple child windows, all contained within the Address Lite main window. These windows can be moved, minimized, etc., independently. The Window menu provides some common actions that users might wish to apply to all open child windows:

- **Cascade**: Opens all children and sets them up to overlap each other, with all title bars showing.
- **Tile**: Opens all children and arranges them so all are visible at once.
- **Arrange Icons**: If the icons for minimized child windows are scattered around the Address Lite main window, this option will arrange them neatly across the bottom.

Also, the Window menu will contain a list of active windows. One can select windows from this menu, which will bring them to the forefront.

To close a child window, make it the active one (via the mouse or menu) and select File|Close from the main menu. To exit the entire application, select File|Exit or double-click on the system menu box (the upper-left corner of the main window).

Each child window contains a drop-down list of the addresses presently defined in its associated database. Selecting an item from the drop-down list will do two things:

- Save all changes made to the currently displayed listbox to the database.
- Read the selected address from the database and display it in the fields.

The window includes fields for filling in the street (two lines), city, state, ZIP code, telephone number, and fax number.

To add a new entry, select Edit|Add New Entry from the main menu. This will pop up a small dialog, asking for the name to assign to this address. After the new name has been entered, it will appear in the drop-down listbox with associated blank address fields.

To remove an entry, select Edit|Remove Current Entry after selecting it. After confirmation, Address Lite will delete the record from the database and remove it from the drop-down listbox.

One can cut and paste information from the fields by highlighting it and selecting the Cut, Copy, or Paste option from the menu bar. These options behave as in most Windows applications. In fact, since they use the Windows Clipboard, information can be cut and pasted between Windows applications.

S.2 How Address Lite Works

Address Lite consists of two components. One is the graphical front end, containing the windows described above. The other is a Windows dynamic-link library (DLL), which allows access to X-Base files.

GUI Front End

The front end was written with Symantec's C++ compiler, using Visual Programmer and the Microsoft Foundation Classes (MFC). MFC, which comes with both Visual C++ and Symantec C++, provides a class library for creating windows and controls for Windows applications.

Note that Address Lite has only been compiled with the Symantec compiler, whereas the tools have been tried on several compilers. The provided disk includes a compiled version of Address Lite.

X-Base Library

The X-Base access library is derived from public domain C routines originally developed by Mark Sadler and George Sipe. The library allows a developer to open DBF files and read, write, and delete records. The programming interface (API) was rewritten to match the Microsoft/IBM conventions (three-letter function prefixes and Hungarian notation). The source code was also made portable to all supported platforms. Hence, this library will be the main example for testing; the user interface will primarily be tested with WinCapT.

> **Hungarian Notation**
>
> Hungarian notation, developed by Charles Simonyi, is a naming convention for C/C++ variables and function parameters. It divides variable names into two parts: a prefix and a base name. The base name is supposed to reflect the actual meaning and contents of the variable. Hence, a variable holding somebody's first name might have a base name of FirstName.
>
> The prefix represents the data type of the variable. For example, if the first name variable mentioned above is a zero-terminated string, one might have a prefix of "sz", so the full variable name is "szFirstName". This helps in deciphering somebody else's code, since the reader does not have to keep going back to the beginning of the function (or to a separate header file) to determine what sort of data the variable holds. It also helps avoid coding errors based on type incompatibility (such as an equality statement)—the difference in prefixes will catch the developer's eye.
>
> Unfortunately, there are no clear standards on the prefixes for different C types, let alone for developer-defined types. Appendix E lists the prefixes used in the source code that accompanies the text.

Table S.1 outlines the API functions found in this library.

S.3 Address Lite and the Quality Tools

Address Lite is used primarily as an example for demonstrating the tools included in this book. The following sections elaborate on how each tool is applied to Address Lite or the X-Base access library.

AssertLib

AssertLib provides ready means for validating parameters or other values. It also gives C++ classes the ability to check the validity of their internal state on every member function call, an act called invariants checking. AssertLib will be primarily applied to the API functions within the X-Base library.

Table S.1 X-Base API Functions

Function Name	Purpose
XblOpen	Opens a named database file for operations
XblClose	Closes an opened database file
XblFlush	Ensures that all changes to the database file have been written to disk
XblAppend	Adds a blank record at the end of the file
XblBlank	Blanks a database record structure in memory
XblSeek	Moves the database pointer to a specific record, by record number
XblUpdate	Writes changes to a record to disk
XblGetFieldAsString	Returns a field as a C string
XblPutFieldAsString	Sets a field's value from a C string
XblFieldNameFromNum	Given the number of a field (1-n), returns its name
XblFieldNumFromName	Given the name of a field, returns its number
XblFieldType	Returns a letter indicating the type of field (string, numeric, etc.)
XblFieldLength	Returns the length of a field in bytes
XblFieldDecimals	For numeric fields, returns the number of places after the decimal point
XblDelete	Marks the current record as deleted
XblUndelete	Marks the current record as normal (not deleted)
XblIsDeleted	Indicates whether this record is deleted
XblRecordCount	Returns the number of records in the database
XblFieldCount	Returns the number of fields per record in the database
XblGetFieldAsInt	Returns the value of a numeric field as a C integer
XblPutFieldAsInt	Sets the value of a numeric field from a C integer
XblGetFieldAsFloat	Gets the value of a numeric field as a C float
XblPutFieldAsFloat	Puts a C float value into a numeric field

ResTrack

ResTrack offers a means to track heap memory, to make sure allocated buffers are properly released when the application ends. In addition, ResTrack catches mistakes like overwriting or underwriting a buffer. Once again, it will be applied to the X-Base library. It could also track Windows resources (such as graphics contexts) by the user interface, but MFC, through its C++ classes, already handles much of this for the developer.

UTCGen, UTCLang, and UTCCover

These three tools for unit testing will be applied to the unit test of the X-Base library. UTCGen will be used to examine the API and come up with some test conditions for part of a thorough unit test of the library's capabilities.

An interpreted driver, using UTCLang, will be developed to exercise the library without the need for a whole host of C-language stub programs. This makes it possible to write unit tests without having a thorough knowledge of C or C++, thereby expanding the number of people who can assist in unit and integration testing.

Finally, UTCCover will be applied to the test suite, so its thoroughness can be measured. Less than 100% coverage may indicate the need for more test cases.

WinCapT

The WinCapT tool can capture and replay a user's interaction with a Windows GUI application. The user can also indicate windows of importance at various spots. This can be used with Address Lite's user interface.

S.4 Summary

Address Lite is a simple Windows-based application for storing addresses and telephone numbers as an address book does. Its main purpose is to provide example code against which to demonstrate the six testing tools provided in this book. The X-Base database library, which Address Lite uses for data storage, will be exercised by five of the six tools; the Address Lite GUI will be tested by the remaining tool (WinCapT).

CHAPTER 1

Introduction: Why Software Quality Assurance?

A Software Fable:

Sam W. Ramgee was on his first day in his new position as TurboChem project manager and, quite simply, was scared stiff.

One would think that being scared stiff would be the last of his reactions. After all, not every staff programmer gets to move up to project management, especially with only a few years of experience. The upper management at Midearth Chemicals (MeC), however, was concerned about this project and selected Sam out of sheer desperation.

MeC, a chemical-products company, focuses on an area called "designer chemicals." These are low-volume, custom-made chemicals designed to achieve a certain purpose not met by off-the-shelf chemicals. Designing custom chemicals is a tricky business. Not only does it take people trained in chemistry or chemical engineering, but not every such person is good at this type of work. MeC was having difficulty finding, training, and retaining chemical designers.

The Information Systems (IS) group proposed a tool called TurboChem. It would model the interactions between individual chemicals to see how a particular design would work. MeC hoped that using this information technology would allow it to remain highly competitive in the designer chemical industry.

Sam was a member of the TurboChem project from the outset. Initially, things went well. The IS department brought in the latest client/server development tools and assigned the finest developers from all of MeC to the team. After a lengthy design period, the team worked at a rapid pace to assemble the tool. After several months of frenzied activity, the team turned TurboChem 1.0 over to the chemical designers.

At this point, things went downhill.

At first, the only complaints were from the designers, griping about the occasional "hobgoblin" that crashed TurboChem. Later, customers screamed that their custom-designed chemicals were not working. It seems that some designers skipped actual field testing of the chemicals, using the output from TurboChem as the only proof that a chemical would work. However, TurboChem gave incorrect output on occasion, sometimes with disastrous results.

After three more iterations (1.0.1, 1.1, and 1.1.1), the product was sufficiently stable for regular use. Sam, looking back on that release, recognized that they had no real testing plan and no tools to assist in the testing and quality assurance process. The lack of sufficient testing doomed the product.

As one might expect, MeC's executives did not like this situation much, so they replaced the old project manager for release 2.0 of TurboChem. The new manager was enthusiastic, ready to apply all the terms learned in the recent quality assurance course she had attended. That the course was for assuring quality in lawn care products (she had recently been hired from another firm) was no problem.

The new manager took the best programmer the TurboChem project had and the two of them vanished for a week. When they returned, they sent out a seemingly endless stream of memos, telling the development team what to do to have a quality product:

1. *"All global variables must appear after line 5 of the program listing but not after line 45."*
2. *"The power will be cut off to random work cubicles periodically to prove TurboChem can withstand hard system failures."*
3. *"All program source code must contain a header comment identifying the product, version number, developer, and the developer's company ID."*

And so on. They also created a quality plan, outlining what had to be done to achieve their quality goals. The development environment and staff stayed much the same.

During development, the manager was constantly roaming the halls, offering words of encouragement ("What a great bug!") and focusing everybody on the project's goal: "Dead bugs all over the place." She assured everyone that version 2.0 of TurboChem would be a resounding success.

In fact, it was resounding but not successful. Release 2.0 suffered the same problems as did release 1.0. TurboChem could not work on more than four chemicals in a row without crashing. There were several failures where the user-interface team's code used the database-access team's code, causing name-calling and finger-pointing to place the blame.

By release 2.1, things were stable again. While the new manager claimed that this, in effect, was a success ("It only took us ***three*** *releases to get it right this* *time!"), she was sacked by upper management. After some serious head-scratching, they settled on promoting Sam, the lead user-interface team developer, to project manager.*

Before the management gave Sam full authority over TurboChem 3.0 (motto: "Third Time's a Charm!"), they demanded that he find out what went wrong with the first two major releases. He and the rest of the team spent four weeks analyzing what had happened, where the bugs were found, etc. In the end, they came up with two root causes:

1. *Developer apathy toward quality assurance. Most developers felt that testing and related quality tasks were too time-consuming and boring. The second manager's randomly placed directives did little to help.*
2. *Lack of adequate tools for conducting quality analysis and assurance. All of their previous quality work (what little there was) had been scatter-shot in execution and ad hoc in design. There was no commonality between any two developers' testing efforts. Many developers, when asked how they missed a particular bug, simply said "I have no way to find that sort of bug."*

Going into TurboChem Release 3.0, Sam knew what could be done to help with cause #1. In fact, his meeting with the team had gone a long way toward clearing away the apathy. The subsequent meeting with the Vice-President for Information Systems, who spelled out the financial straits that MeC would be in if TurboChem did not live up to its promises, helped as well. With the aid of some management texts on empowerment, Sam felt fairly confident he could eliminate the apathy.

On the other hand, the second cause gave him worries. Nobody on his team had any idea of how to create a more organized testing and quality assurance program, let alone what tools they could use. He only hoped that through continuous research, he and the team could find the tools they needed. The possibility that their efforts would be "too little, too late" is what had him scared stiff.

Sam sighed. He knew that it was going to be a long day.

1.1 Quality and the Software Industry

Quality is a popular mantra today. While Japanese industry, working with the late Dr. W. Edwards Deming, was the early leader in the quality control movement, most other nations have taken interest as well. Quality is applied to both manufacturers and service firms, in companies large and small. Many books have been written on the subject, appearing on shelves in bookstores around the world.

The software development industry has not been untouched. Many firms are touting "zero defects" goals. Others have skipped the slogans but are still highly concerned with the quality of the products they ship. There have been too many examples of software products with "bugs" that have shipped to users; nobody wants to get burned.

Unfortunately, more so than other areas of software engineering, testing and quality assurance have not gotten the attention that designing and programming have. The life-cycle methodologies, such as the "waterfall" and iterative cycles, all have slots for testing. Many delineate different types, separating subsystem (unit) testing from end-user (system) testing. However, testing just has not captured the imagination of the industry like object orientation, graphical interfaces, and kernel-based operating systems have. So, while everybody recognizes the importance of quality, there are few major movements afoot in this crucial area.

Not surprisingly, firms and individual teams have varied attitudes regarding software quality assurance. Many employ it religiously, using all available tools and techniques in a massive effort to eliminate bugs. Others do only the most cursory testing needed to eliminate the obvious bugs. Somewhere between those positions is a "happy medium," where sufficient quality steps are taken to catch the majority of faults. This follows the formula of Dr. Joseph Juran, who argues that quality is not "free" and that there is an optimal point beyond which additional SQA costs more than the bugs themselves.

This chapter frames the discussion of SQA automation, the focus of the rest of the book. In particular, it covers three topics:

1. The reasons why SQA is worthwhile and cost-justified.
2. The concept of continuous improvement and how it can benefit an organization over time.
3. How object orientation affects quality assurance (because there are many concerns and misconceptions in this area).

1.2 Reasons for Software Quality Assurance

As one would expect, there are quite a few good reasons why one bothers with software quality assurance. The following sections outline a few of them.

Software Defect Visibility

Software failures tend to be "high-profile" problems. While documentation may be shoddy, installation impossible, and technical support nonexistent, customers remember the "bugs" most. Even if they are fixed in short order, users will always distrust the product.

Quality Gurus

To understand quality as it is applied to software development, one must also understand the quality movement in general, as it has grown over the past half-century. Readers should read books on general quality assurance programs, such as those listed in the References section.

The quality assurance movement, particularly in America, has been guided by a number of "gurus," including W. Edwards Deming, Joseph Juran, and Philip Crosby.

Deming (4), for whom Japan's top quality award is named, was the first to popularize statistical process control, the concept that process improvement can be attained by first getting it under control (by reducing the variance of key production statistics, like defect rates), then by improving the result while keeping it under control. His most famous book, *Out of the Crisis,* outlines fourteen points for attaining higher product quality, ranging from removing fear in the workplace to continuous improvement.

Juran also believes in process control before process improvement in the effort to improve overall quality. However, whereas some emphasize the worker, he emphasizes management, believing that most quality problems stem from there. Worker empowerment and self-direction are considered ways to overcome the problems.

Crosby (3), author of *Quality Is Free,* is a champion of the "zero defects" goal. Prevention is key to achieving this goal, rather than inspection or other techniques. Like the other gurus, he believes that quality is a process, not a result, and therefore is a continuing effort requiring effective monitoring. He, too, has a fourteen-point plan for quality improvement, including raising overall organizational consciousness of quality and recognizing those who contribute to quality assurance.

While not in the software arena, perhaps the most famous example of shipping flawed product was the 1994 Intel Pentium chip debacle. The original chips had flaws in the floating-point support that could cause significant calculation errors. The resulting publicity surely hurt Intel's reputation, if not its profits.

Marketing

Shipping faults to customers creates difficulties in marketing the firm's products in the future. Some members of a software development project's staff may take a dim view of marketing, looking upon it as a necessary evil. It certainly is necessary—without marketing, there would be no money to pay for programmers. Even projects for government agencies or other non-profit groups require their own form of marketing, in the form of grant proposals, etc.

A poor reputation, stemming from customer dissatisfaction from shipped software faults, will have a noticeable effect on marketing. Everybody has heard people say, "Avoid XXXX; they make a rotten product." While some people may associate this phrase more with computer hardware than software, it is still a significant problem.

Even a string of subsequent successes does not always counteract one bad release. Even after people have forgotten the concrete reasons for disliking a firm, they will still retain unspecified bad feelings. Therefore, even a low rate of defect reports will still have a cascading effect over time on the image the company portrays and its ability to market its products.

Reduced Maintenance Cost

This is one of the largest internal manifestations of a quality problem's effect on "the bottom line." Fixing problems costs time and money, let alone the expense of re-releasing applications to fix the problems. Many firms have faced financial ruin by trying to maintain buggy products.

Even if customers do not encounter problems, later upgrades will run aground if the original product was of poor quality. Developers, who exercise a program more than most users, will be hit by more of the latent bugs, hampering their work efforts. If they are constantly hitting old faults, it will be difficult for them to keep pace with their own work as they try to diagnose and eradicate the faults. Reusing portions of an application in an unintended manner will quickly determine how thorough the unit test was.

Hence, the problem with maintenance cost is not only based on the external influence of customers but also on internal efforts to create new versions of the product.

Programmer Development

Parents always tell children to learn from their mistakes. While programmers certainly are not children, the adage still holds to a degree. In fact, it even extends to learning from the mistakes of others.

New software developers, who have little practical programming experience, can learn from a well-organized testing program. First, they learn about the testing process itself, a topic seldom taught in college. The process of testing and quality assurance will teach them more about coding in general and the techniques used in this area. In effect, this book is a microcosm of the experiences that "rookie" programmers will obtain from a testing program.

Developers will learn from their own mistakes as they uncover bugs in code they and their teammates wrote. In theory, as they recognize improper coding constructs, they will be less likely to use them in the future. Hence, testing and quality control serve as a continuous form of "on-the-job training" that is key to programmer development at all levels.

Morale

Although the psychology of teamwork is sometimes overlooked in technical disciplines, there will be a distinct effect on a team that watches its product fail. Nobody likes to fail; teams wind up coping in various ways with such crises, most of which are negative. Furthermore, the pressure such failures place on the team from others in the organization will certainly not help matters.

Internal Customers

The above sections have focused on external customers, assuming that the project is creating a product to be shipped outside. Many projects are for internal use, and hence the customers are within the firm. One might feel that quality is less of an issue here, since it is much easier to support internal teams than world-wide users.

In terms of real money, this may be true. However, internal customers have political clout that external customers may lack. While such clout will not appear on any project budget, it can have a significant impact on operations. Soon the team may find itself fighting fires for important internal customers, ignoring perhaps more important problems only affecting those with less clout. Also, since projects for internal use are typically funded by the company itself, this clout can translate into "real money" during the budget-setting process, particularly for long-term project development.

1.3 Continuous Improvement

Too many projects look at testing as having one goal: making the application run correctly. That certainly is the top priority. However, there should be a secondary goal of no little importance: continuous improvement. This section outlines the concept, along with its goals and requirements.

What Is Continuous Improvement?

The notion of continuous improvement comes from the teachings of Deming, Juran, et al. The concept behind it is simple. The act of improving the quality of an application should improve the **process** as an intentional side effect. Feedback from testing phases should affect how programming is done. Similarly, results from system testing should impact how developers conduct unit testing. As the SQA process is improved over time, software faults should be prevented or detected earlier. Also, the organization should replace inefficient techniques with more effective ones. The end result: higher-quality systems and lower SQA costs.

Why Bother with Continuous Improvement?

One might wonder why all the fuss about continuous improvement. After all, once one achieves a target quality level, particularly a "zero defects" goal, there seems to be little one can gain by continuing to work on improving quality.

This, of course, assumes that the organization has reached such a target. Few have, so continuous improvement is an important mechanism for reaching that level. Simply adopting a once-and-done quality plan will be insufficient. Too many things will be missed that first time. Just as iterative software development produces more robust designs and systems, iterative quality assurance improvement will bring about a better SQA program.

Even after a firm attains its quality goals, continuous improvement is still needed. Freezing the quality assurance process will work for a while, but eventually it will require changing. This is due to a range of effects, including:

- Changes in technologies or tools that reduce developers' experience levels from those used to reach high quality
- The inevitable entropy that enters into any process, causing rules to be forgotten or misapplied, or possibly becoming irrelevant with no apparent replacement
- New challenges from outside, either clients or competitors, that require the organization to raise the targeted quality levels

Hence, continuous improvement should be applied constantly, not just in short bursts of energy. One can think of it as a form of compound interest: It is only over the long haul, with continuous work, that it will have a large effect.

Requirements for Continuous Improvement

As with everything else in quality assurance, continuous improvement will not merely "fall out" of work being done. Instead, one must plan for it and organize a policy. Three main components are necessary:

- Quality assurance guidelines for use across all projects
- A mechanism for reviewing those guidelines as each project progresses
- A means of measuring the effectiveness of the guidelines in reducing the number of shipped faults

Quality Guidelines

The first criterion is a set of quality assurance guidelines that all developers and testers must follow. Furthermore, the guidelines must be flexible and modifiable over time. They will serve as the means for continuous improvement ideas to be applied to software development.

Guidelines can come in a wide variety of forms, such as:

- Coding style guides
- Structured walkthrough checklists
- Test condition catalogs (such as the one used by UTCGen)

Basically, quality guidelines serve as the source of quality techniques and information for development and testing staff. Everybody should follow the guidelines to the best of their ability; part of the review of a staffer's work should cover adherence to these guidelines.

In summary, the quality guidelines are, in effect, a base and mechanism for knowledge transfer from existing to new development staff and from project to project, based on experiences.

Review Process

Given a set of guidelines, the next step toward continuous improvement is to modify the guidelines as projects find out what is necessary to create quality applications. The project should capture as much information as possible, then have reviews to distill it into useful knowledge that can be embodied in the guidelines.

Information capture is the more difficult task. It implies that during development and testing, extra information is kept regarding the process as it moves along. For example, many projects take the approach that developers should conduct unit testing, fixing the faults as they find them. The end result is a test plan that indicates the subsystem works. This is all well and good, but useful information about the bugs and their likely source is lost.

Given the information from a quality phase, the team must then determine what changes to make to the guidelines for the next project. For example, an organization may not be employing any form of resource tracking. If they find that several bugs are due to resource misuse, some steps for preventing such faults should be added to the guidelines.

Merely adding new guidelines can be insufficient, since over time they may slow the development and testing phases down to a crawl. Part of the review process should also be to see where tools might help. For example, if memory misuse is a problem, a team might recommend anything from using a resource tracking tool (like ResTrack) to switching to a language where memory misuse is less of a problem, such as Visual Basic.

The combination of having guidelines and modifying them over time allows knowledge to be gradually accumulated and applied in future projects.

Measurement Mechanism

Those two steps would be sufficient if one assumes that all the guidelines proposed are worthwhile. This is not necessarily true. For example, one approach to preventing memory misuse is to disallow all C/C++ heap allocation (e.g., malloc()). While this certainly would cut down on memory misuse, it also may greatly reduce programmer productivity. This is a bad guideline, in that the cost of compliance is greater than the benefits accrued.

The only way to determine if guideline changes help is to capture and analyze even more information about how development and testing work. Projects will need metrics, to determine whether particular techniques help. Examples include:

- The number of faults found in each phase
- The number of faults caught by end users, which represent breakdowns in the quality assurance process
- The speed of development, comparing time against the size of the application

If these metrics rise over time, then the continuous improvement program is helping. If the metrics stagnate, or even fall, then the quality assurance process is breaking down somewhere. It may take some investigation to find out why and what to do to fix the problems.

1.4 SQA and Object Orientation

Reusable components have been one of the important selling points of object technology. Organizations can leverage their work by writing sets of object classes once and using them on several projects. The results are faster application development and easier long-term maintenance.

Objects and software reuse are not a panacea for all of the challenges of software development. In reality, object orientation requires changes to standard approaches and methodologies. Testing, in particular, can be affected by attempts to use, and contribute to, reusable components.

Such components divide the focus on testing into two separate areas:

- Testing of components deemed to be reusable
- Testing reusers of other components

Testing Reusable Components

Components are not merely labeled as "reusable." They must go through special design and development to guarantee that they can be reused. This special handling also carries over into testing. A test plan for a reusable component must cover every feature and piece of functionality the component **provides**, not just the ones the initial user will utilize. It is easy for testers to say, "Well, Application X is not using that feature, so we can hold off on testing it for now." Inevitably, to paraphrase Gladstone, "testing delayed is testing denied." One simply cannot trust untested features.

Regression Testing

A strong test implementation for a reusable component must have one feature above and beyond typical test code—regression test capability. One must picture a reusable component as more than a random chunk of code. It takes on a life of its own, like a commercial product. There will always need to be modifications to allow it to be reused on a wider variety of applications. However, since it is a pseudo-product, there will be many projects already using it that will fail if new bugs are introduced. Regression testing, by ensuring that prior functionality still works, is the key to preventing such problems.

Reusable Tests

In addition, a good test implementation for a reusable component will itself be reusable. Some components come in the form of "frameworks," to which users must add a customized set of classes developed via inheritance. Many tests run against the reusable component will, in turn, be valid for the custom implementation. While this does not eliminate the need for a separate test plan for that implementation, it does help certify the correctness of the new classes.

Suppose you are developing a framework for mapping C++ classes to tables in a database. Subclasses will provide specific information about the table-to-class mapping, such as how columns are put into data members. The abstract superclass provides standard behaviors for inserting and updating records in the table, based on an object's data, deleting the record from the table, etc.

When one creates a unit test for this framework, one will write cases that try out all these major actions, using some concrete subclass and table as the benchmark. If, however, the tests themselves are set up **as a framework**, then other custom subclasses can inherit them.

For example, the test for inserting a record might do the following:

1. Create an instance of the class.
2. Fill in the instance with reasonable sample data.
3. Insert the instance into the database.
4. Check (by primary key) if it appears in the table.

The test could rely on the subclass to provide an appropriate sample instance, rather than putting that logic in the test code itself. This test could then be used on **any** subclass that provides such a function. Other users can simply write the "create sample instance" function and automatically be able to test insertions.

Testing Reusers of Components

The reuse of components brings with it a tendency to assume "we are reusing it, so it must be good." This assumption leads teams to cut corners on their testing, leaving gaps in their test plan that might let failures leak through.

The tighter the coupling between the reused component and the code doing the reusing, the more likely it will be for teams to ignore testing. In the case of frameworks, the custom code typically takes the form of scattered object behaviors (e.g., C++ member functions). These are written specifically to plug into the framework as documented to perform custom actions. It is difficult here to picture the "unit" that one should unit test. Since the framework itself is assumed to have been tested properly, projects might give short shrift to testing their usage of it, since their own code is so scattered.

This is dangerous thinking, for several reasons:

- It assumes that the developers plugged the custom behaviors into the framework properly.
- It assumes that the framework was tested for every conceivable means for custom implementations; the framework testers might not have tried the techniques used by the team's developers.
- It presupposes that testing a custom use of a framework is more difficult than testing any other "unit" in the application. If there is a reusable test suite, this is far from the case. Even when there is not, the fact that a unit test for the custom use might also test some framework-only features is far from a crime.

If the framework provides a reusable test suite, then one can use it to help ensure that the reuse is appropriate. A custom suite would be written to test implementation-specific features, while the inherited cases would prove that the framework and the custom subclasses are working well together.

If no test suite is provided, the group must make sure that its code works properly with the framework. This means more unit tests, proving that inherited functionality still works.

In the example above, custom C++ table classes would need to ensure that they can insert records into the table properly, even if the framework failed to provide a reusable test. After all, the author of the subclass might have returned erroneous data to the framework regarding the table-to-class mapping. This might prevent records from inserting properly.

How Object Orientation Aids Testing

Fortunately, object orientation also aids with testing, lest anyone be frightened away by the previous concerns. Two features make testing easier and more effective: encapsulation and inheritance.

Encapsulation

Encapsulation restricts how a set of classes can be used, eliminating most "back doors" to subsystems. While this does not typically make testing easier, it does make it more effective—tests will cover a higher percentage of the real-world situations.

Many C function libraries use structures to pass data to and from the subsystem. Structures are by definition public—any user has full access to their contents. A unit test might do a thorough job of ensuring that subsystem access via the public API works. However, users might manipulate the structure directly, which the tests might not check adequately.

If the functions and structures are replaced by C++ classes, the data can be made protected or private to prevent such illegal access. Tests that provide equivalent coverage of the class member functions will then be more likely to test the way the code will be used, since the "back door" of direct structure modification has been eliminated.

Note that encapsulation can also be done in C. Many C APIs, such as the Windows API, use opaque **handles** to represent data items. The handles map to some basic C type, like a void pointer, whereas inside the library they map to a data structure containing useful information. Users of a handle typically have no documented means of accessing the information inside it.

Inheritance

Inheritance, especially as embodied in the form of frameworks, can provide an infrastructure for testing that makes writing and running tests easier. One of the biggest complaints about testing is the "overhead" involved. One cannot typically write pure test code; instead, one must also write extra code that allows tests to be run.

What a framework can do is abstract common behaviors and allow them to be inherited by subclasses. With a properly designed framework, some overhead in writing test code can be inherited, rather than rewritten. This not only improves productivity during testing but also increases attitudes towards the testing process.

More about the utility of inheritance for testing will be discussed later, as we talk about AssertLib's object invariants and UTCLang's interpreter framework.

1.5 Summary

While most developers realize innately that software testing and quality assurance are important, it is frequently useful to enumerate the reasons to help drive home their criticality. For both internal and external reasons, the quality of the software product is the key to a project's, and frequently the company's, short- and long-term success. Even the advent of object technology has not changed this; if anything, testing is even more important in a world of high-volume reuse. Furthermore, to create a significant continuous improvement program, one must apply SQA techniques during all phases of the software development life cycle.

CHAPTER 2

Types of Software Quality Tools

This chapter discusses why one should use tools to aid in software quality assurance. It also describes the types of tools that are available.

2.1 Why Use Tools?

While many organizations espouse software quality and testing, some ignore or belittle the use of tools to help in the process. Typical reasons for avoiding tools are:

- "They are too expensive."
- "We don't have time to learn new tools—we are behind schedule!"
- "We can do it ourselves just as easily."

This is an unfortunate attitude. Tools for quality and testing are no different from any other software tools. Few teams would fail to use high-level languages (preferring to write in raw machine language) for the above reasons. The same can be said for the other "staples" of software development, such as editors and debuggers. The aforementioned arguments are typically reserved for tools perceived to be "on the fringe" of what is commonly used by a company's projects. Hence, even version control systems and CASE tools might be disregarded by some teams. Software quality and testing tools are also set aside more often than they should be.

Time Savings

A big reason is the savings in development and testing time that tools can offer. While there may be an up-front cost in terms of learning how to use them, most times this is made up for (and more) by the work the tools perform. This is similar to the advantages a symbolic debugger has over embedding print statements in a program to track down problems.

Some tools are geared toward saving time in the short term. Resource leak trackers are an example. These tools, described in greater detail below, determine where resources (such as memory) are allocated but not released. Programs exhibiting serious leaks will crash when the resource is no longer available. A tracking tool will make finding the source of the leaks trivial. Finding them by hand, however, is typically very time consuming, especially for large pools like heap memory. The speed at which the tool can find the root of the problem would far outweigh the time needed to obtain a resource tracking tool and apply it to the application.

Other tools, on the other hand, produce long-term time savings. Regression test support tools are an example. Regression testing is the act of rerunning previously working tests after changes have been made, to ensure that the application is still working properly. If regression testing is not performed, changes in one part of the system might have side effects that break other parts, but the breaks would not be found until much later. Regression testing tools automate the execution of the tests and the comparison of results from the known "good" runs to the most recent runs. Doing all this by hand is time-consuming. An automated version can run in minutes to hours, even as an overnight process. While there is a cost of creating the master copy of the tests and their results, this will be saved many times over as the regression tests are run and rerun.

Thoroughness

Developers can easily get bored when working on tedious tasks, such as validating the syntax of each line of code. Tools, on the other hand, do not get tired or bored. Tools, in many cases, are also faster than developers in identifying problems. Hence, they can be much more thorough than humans in particular tests. For example, a standards-enforcing tool will ensure that a particular set of source code complies with all coding standards used by the sponsoring organization. While manual validation is possible, a tool is much quicker. Also, the tool can have a broader catalog of potential means of violation; a developer reading through the code could only realistically remember and apply a fraction of the applicable rules.

Team Standards

The "we can do it ourselves" attitude can also lead to doing it several different ways. Each developer might create his or her own unit testing harness, for example. This would mean that running each developer's tests would require remembering his or her particular setup. This complicates checkout and regression testing, since there are now several things to remember instead of just one. Also, since testing tools can have bugs like any other piece of software, having multiple tools instead of one increases the probability that a tool will itself be faulty.

Synergies

Also, some testing tools might offer synergies with other work. For example, a project could use a script-based unit test driver as a utility for installing the system or verifying that the installation process succeeded. We would prefer a single tool that could satisfy both needs, rather than having two separate tools.

2.2 Different Tools for Different Phases

Projects divide almost all software development into phases. A typical division, taken from the "waterfall" methodology, consists of the following phases:

1. Requirements analysis
2. Design (high-level and low-level)
3. Development
4. Testing (on various levels, ranging from low-level unit testing to application-wide system testing)

This division serves many purposes, ranging from scheduling and staffing plans to providing milestones for teams to measure their success.

Each phase has tools for quality associated with it. While some tools will be useful in several phases, most are tied to a single one. These phases and the tools involved with them are discussed in the remaining sections of this chapter. Figure 2.1 illustrates the phases used in two popular methodologies: "waterfall" and iterative.

Requirements and Design

Most of the work to date in software quality has focused on products that actually exist (i.e., when programming is under way). There has been far less work done on ensuring quality during requirements analysis and design. This is disappointing, since poor quality in these areas nearly guarantees a low-quality product.

Furthermore, there has been little work done on tools for assisting in this area of quality. This is largely because there are few tools and fewer standards for capturing requirements and designs in computer-readable form. Once the product is being written in source code form, there are means for tools to access the code and assist in ensuring its quality. Without similar means for requirements and designs, tools cannot easily be written or used.

Some tools for requirements analysis and design (e.g., CASE tools) have quality checks built in. For example, some can automatically cross-check that designs

Figure 2.1 Phases in Software Development Methodologies

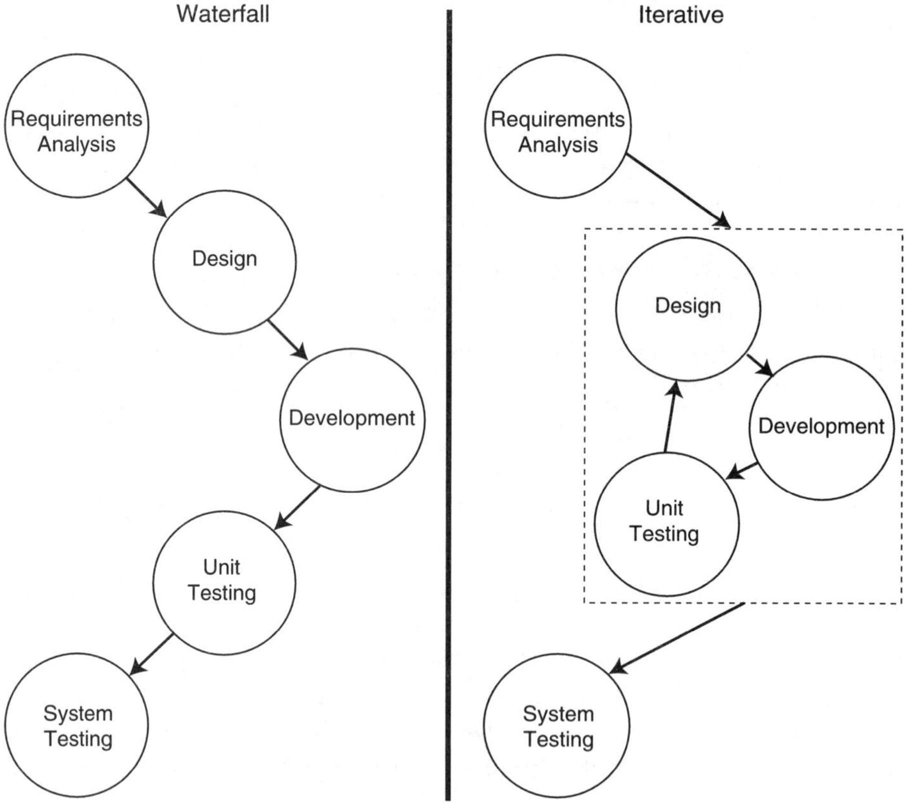

and system tests reference all requirements. These are not stand-alone quality tools, however; they are part of the larger requirements/design tools themselves.

Development

Once development has begun, tools are more readily available, since there are computer files (source code) for them to access. The following types of tools are all useful during development.

Assertion Library

Assertions are tests, embedded in the program itself, that confirm things that are supposed to be true. For example, suppose that the specification for a function requires that its single parameter cannot be zero. The developer can add an assertion to it to confirm this fact. The assertion would be used during development and initial testing. When the system is shipped, the developer would disable the assertions to reduce program size and improve performance. The goal behind assertions is to have active pieces of code confirming that the program meets all assumptions.

An assertion library would provide means of encoding assertions. Mechanisms would be provided for various means of reporting violations (e.g., stopping the program versus logging to a file). AssertLib, included in this book, also provides specialized handling for various platforms, in this case, Windows.

Resource Trackers

Resource leaks can take a useful program and make it useless in practice, as the system fails when a limited resource is exhausted. Since real users often push an application harder than is done during development and testing, a small leak could turn into a big problem in the field.

There are other ways to misuse resources, as well, such as:

- Attempting to release an allocated resource more than once
- In the case of memory, going past the bounds of the allocated block

A resource-tracking tool would watch all allocations and releases of resources, making sure that they match. Better tools would provide built-in tracking for common resources (memory, files) and offer a means for developers to write their own tracking functions for custom resources. ResTrack, provided in this book, handles these situations, as well as watching for overwrites and underwrites of memory blocks.

Parameter Violation Reporter

With the explosion of application programming interfaces (APIs) over the past few years, a popular tool is a parameter violation reporter. It monitors the calls to a particular API (e.g., the Windows API) and confirms that all parameters are valid.

In a sense, this is similar to assertions. Assertions, however, are bound into the implementor of the API, whereas a parameter violation reporter exists outside the API and its implementation. This is useful for third-party APIs that do not ship with assertions enabled; using a parameter violation reporter effectively provides the missing assertions.

The Windows API is very extensive and occasionally confusing. Windows has many types of handles, each pointing to different types of operating system objects, such as:

- Tasks
- Windows
- Instances
- Graphics contexts

It is very easy to make a mistake and provide an instance handle when a task handle is required, for example. This was particularly likely in early versions of the Windows SDK, where many handles were all identified with the HANDLE type. When custom types are used (e.g., HWND versus HTASK), the compiler can catch mistakes.

What a parameter violation reporter does is "hook" into the Windows API functions and inspect the parameters before passing them along to Windows itself. For handles, it can ensure that it has the right type of handle by asking Windows. Windows does not do this itself in the production version, probably for performance reasons. If the wrong type of handle is provided, the parameter violations reporter would take an appropriate action, such as:

- Log a message to a window.
- Pop up a dialog.
- Bring up a debugger on the offending API call.

Using these tools can often help developers home in on certain problems more quickly than manually watching the code in a debugger.

Symbolic Debuggers

One might not think of a debugger as a quality assurance tool. Typically, debuggers are reserved for isolating a problem and determining its cause. After all, that is where they got their name (the act of removing bugs).

However, many developers use symbolic debuggers for quality assurance. They use them as a "live" form of the structured walkthrough often used for code reviews. Developers step their way through the program by using the debugger and examining variables as they go. Often, just watching the program in action will point out a fault, even if the program itself does not crash. This is similar to the "trolling for bugs" approach that developers sometimes take when trying to investigate a given failure, but it does not assume the existence of a bug.

Standards Enforcers

Many programming teams have coding standards. They can be as simple as forcing each function to have a comment or as elaborate as including things such as:

- Function and variable naming schemes
- Indentation and spacing rules
- File, function, variable, and line comment formats

In addition to such explicit standards, others may come as a result of requirements. For example, the requirement of using ANSI C constructs forces the use of function prototypes and ANSI-style function declarations, instead of the "K&R"-style.

K&R versus ANSI C

K&R-style C is the coding style used by Kerninghan and Ritchie (8) in *The C Programming Language*. Since this was the seminal book of its day on C programming, many developers copied their style. Later, the ANSI C standards committee defined another coding style that is widely used today.

Perhaps the most visible difference between the two styles is in function declarations and definitions. The declaration is where the compiler is informed that a function of a certain name will appear in the code (for forward references); the definition is where the function body actually appears.

In K&R C, the function declaration (also called a "prototype") simply defined the name and return type:

```
int some_test_function();
```

K&R also supported indicating the types the function would require:

```
int some_test_function(int, char *);
```

In ANSI C, the function prototype includes both the parameter names and the types:

```
int some_test_function(int iLength, char *pszString);
```

In the function definition, K&R C put the parameter names within the function call parentheses and their type mappings afterward:

```
int some_test_function(iLength, pszString)
int iLength;
char *pszString;
{...
```

In ANSI C, the function prologue is the same as the prototype:

```
int some_test_function(int iLength, char *pszString)
{...
```

The ANSI C standard is typically more readable than K&R, one reason why it has gained so much favor.

A standards enforcer will examine the source code for a subsystem and report where the standards are being violated. Modern compilers can do some of this, notably checking ANSI C compliance. Enforcing other standards can be done by using an enhanced tool, like *lint*, that checks for strange C code. If the team has its own standards, however, it must construct its own enforcement tool. Unfortunately, the work involved in doing this typically prevents its creation and usage.

Complexity Analyzers

An offshoot of the standards enforcer is a tool that measures the complexity of some source code. The basis is usually a metric such as McCabe's cyclomatic complexity. Generally, more complex functions are more difficult to maintain than functionally equivalent but simpler functions. Since maintainability is one aspect of quality, a team might set an upper bound to the complexity allowed for a given function or subsystem. Functions the tool identified as overly complex would need to be rewritten.

Unit-Level Testing

Unit-level testing here is defined as testing that accesses subsystems via their application programming interfaces (API). System testing, discussed below, deals with the application as a whole, with testing being done through its user interfaces. Depending on the testing philosophy one follows, there can be one or several steps in the unit-level testing (e.g., unit, string, integration). The tools described below would be useful for most of these situations.

Test Condition Generators

One of the most time-consuming aspects of testing is figuring out what to test. A test condition generator can help. It will examine the source code of a subsystem and indicate conditions to be included in the unit test. The tester then needs to combine these conditions, along with others determined by the design or implementation, into test cases.

There are many ways in which a test condition generator could select conditions to report. One is to examine the subsystem's interfaces. By examining the parameters used by the various functions, the generator can indicate tests to confirm that they are being used properly. UTCGen, included in this book, takes this approach.

Another means would be to look at the actual implementation of the functions as sources of conditions. One might examine how the data moves through the function or at the structures used (loops, conditional, etc.). Tools that take this approach are more complicated to develop than generators that merely look at function prototypes.

Test Data Generators

Especially for stress testing, which involves large volumes of data, creating test data is also time-consuming. One must choose values that make sense (e.g., no negative numbers for employee salary amounts) and that the subsystem uses. Given a specification, a test data generator will generate as much random data as is desired. The specification will ensure that values and the relationships between them (e.g., a salary and a bonus) are sensible.

The X-Base library provided with this book has three API functions for retrieving the contents of a field:

- XblGetFieldAsString(): Returns a field as a C string.
- XblGetFieldAsInt(): Returns a field as a C integer.
- XblGetFieldAsFloat(): Returns a field as a C float.

One might use a test data generator to create sample values for fields with a variety of lengths, decimal places, etc. This data could then be used to ensure that functions can handle different types of values.

Ideally, the test data generator would create two stores with the same data: a database (DBF) file and a plain flat file, suitable for reading via scanf() or gets(). A test program could read the data from the database and from the file, then compare the two. Any discrepancies indicate a problem in one of the data-reading algorithms.

Test Drivers

For compiled languages like C and C++, code must be written to actually implement the desired tests. For bottom-up programming, this typically takes the form of a test driver. A driver simulates the upper levels of the system not yet implemented. It calls the functions in the subsystem according to the tests to be conducted and also captures the results. There are two main approaches to writing test drivers.

One approach is to implement tests in the product's language (C or C++) as a single function or object. A main routine then executes each function or object in turn. This is simple to implement; with the support of a test framework, it is easy to capture the results and indicate progress.

The alternative is to create a script-based driver that has its own interpreted language. The language provides sufficient expressive power to implement any reasonable test. The test cases are then implemented in the script language, not C/C++. Not only does this allow testing by individuals who are not C literate, but it may also be useful in other ways, such as for the installation utility mentioned above. UTC-Lang provides a framework for implementing script-based drivers.

Coverage Analyzers

A coverage analyzer watches subsystems as they are being executed and records what portions of them are run. After the entire test suite has been executed in one shot, the coverage analyzer can point out areas that were inadequately tested (e.g., a function that is never called). This indicates where the test suite needs improving. UTCCover, provided in this book, offers basic coverage analysis.

Profilers

One might tend to lump profilers, which report on how many times different functions or statements were executed, with coverage analyzers. As will be seen in Chapter 9 on UTCCover, profilers can indeed measure some types of coverage metrics, though not all. There are performance-related reasons to employ a profiler. It can indicate where the "hot spots" in the subsystem are (i.e., where the program spends a lot of time). These areas would be candidates for optimization, particularly if the overall application runs more slowly than desired.

System Testing

System testing, as mentioned above, is testing the entire application by using the applicable interfaces. Most times, this will be the user interface. However, some applications also have programming interfaces, macro languages, or other programmatic means of control. For them, other unit testing tools may prove useful in addition to those described below.

Session Capture Tools

The problem with testing at the user interface level is that it typically involves a user—a person. Somebody must sit at the application and put it through its paces, examining fields and values at various points to determine if it is running properly. This makes regression testing nearly impossible, because every time there is a change to the application, a user must go through the whole test suite again.

A session capture tool can change that. It hides in the background while the user goes through the test suite. It records all keystrokes, mouse movements, and screen states. Then, quality assurance staff can replay the session at any time. The tool will produce the same keystrokes and mouse movements and capture the screens at the same points. By comparing screen to screen, one can see the differences. Nobody needs to sit and watch the tool; it can run during off-hours. This makes regression testing at the user interface level possible.

WinCapT, described later in this book, is a session capture tool for Windows applications.

Coverage Analyzers

Coverage analyzers were discussed in the unit-level testing section for determining what functions, etc., were not tried. One can also use them during system test to make sure it is sufficiently thorough. The biggest difficulty is that frequently there are parts of the code, such as error handlers, that cannot be conveniently executed from the user interface. In this case, testers need to measure coverage at a higher level. Ideally, there would be user interface "coverage" metrics. A group of radio buttons should be tried in each position, while checkboxes should be tried in the on and off settings, etc.

Bug-Tracking Tools

Many people think of bug-tracking databases as being a management device rather than a quality assurance tool. However, such a database can have important uses within a system testing (or even unit testing) environment:

- Bugs can be easily forgotten, especially by developers who get swamped with reports. If there is no means of tracking outstanding bugs, ones that are found may get lost again. Everyone, possibly even the tester who found it, will forget where it was, how it was invoked, etc.
- For projects that have multiple versions of an application (e.g,. 1.1, 2.0, and 2.1 are all being used), a bug-tracking database is essential for keeping all versions in sync with respect to fixes. If a bug is found in the latest version, one must go back to earlier ones that are still in use and ensure that it either did not exist then or gets fixed. Frequently, due to the difficulty of switching between application releases, a team may periodically apply bug fixes to prior releases rather than doing them every time a fix is determined. Without a bug-tracking database, one can easily lose track of what fixes need to be applied where and to what releases.

2.3 Summary

Tools to assist with quality assurance are the key to a project's success, both to extend developers' abilities and to help prevent mistakes. Most tools available today are for the later stages in the development life cycle: programming, unit testing, and system testing. Unfortunately, few tools for quality assurance in requirements analysis and design are presently available.

CHAPTER 3

Quality Control During Development

Many developers or projects do not begin to focus on quality until they start testing. This ignores many ways in which one can start improving quality during coding. Such approaches can prevent faults by giving the developer hints as to how to avoid them. At the very least, they make it easier to catch faults.

Some of these steps, like using proper compiler warning settings or resource-tracking tools, are well known. However, all too frequently they are considered to be nuisances, in that they require extra work. Few developers realize that these techniques are sometimes trivial to incorporate.

This approach also ignores the many benefits to incorporating quality control during development. Finding faults up front means fewer to find during unit and system testing, making those phases less painful. Since it also tends to find faults soon after they were made, repair is likely to be easier than at a later stage.

3.1 Outcomes of Quality Control During Development

The following sections outline some of the outcomes one can expect from a solid quality control program during software development.

Fault Prevention

The common attitude is that code is "innocent until proven guilty," meaning that there are no faults unless they are found to exist. This flies in the face of conventional wisdom, which declares that all programmers make mistakes. Taking steps to prevent faults in the first place will help reduce the fault rate.

Providing More Information

Developers can better prevent mistakes if they have more information at their disposal. This sort of knowledge can range from simple training on the tools being used (so developers no longer misuse them) to a better understanding of the problem domain and the end users' wishes.

Preventing Categories of Errors

Many errors that developers make are well known, either because others around the world make the same mistakes or those errors have happened to this group before. In either case, given that one knows about a type of error, one may be able to devise ways to prevent it from happening.

For example, some projects might have a big problem with developers misusing other developers' subsystems. One way to counteract this is by better API documentation. Another way is to design the interface in such a way that developers are less likely to misunderstand its usage, perhaps by selecting better function and variable names.

As Crosby [3] points out in *Quality Is Free*, fault prevention is vastly preferable to fault detection later on.

Fewer Shipped Faults

Despite our best efforts to prevent, identify, and eliminate faults in programs, some will be shipped. Quality control simply reduces the "leak rate" of faults making it past our defenses and going out with the completed product. The more effective such efforts are, the lower the leak rate will be.

Emphasizing bug prevention during development will help reduce the number of faults that make it into the testing phases. This can be thought of as constricting the flow of bugs at the source, whereas testing works on filtering out ones that have made it into the program.

Cheaper Fault Repair

As with nearly every development process (from software to automobiles), finding and repairing faults earlier is cheaper than fixing them later. There can be significant differences in costs between fixing faults at development time versus in a unit testing phase, such as avoiding work-arounds or identifying serious design flaws earlier.

In addition, the developer is much closer to the code and the faults when they are detected early. The more time between when a programmer works on a module and when he or she must repair something in it, the more difficult the repair will be.

3.2 Continuous Improvement

As quality assurance continues to affect the way in which firms do business, it is important to have a clearly visible program for continuous improvement. A firm's quality programs may be assessed by certification boards (such as the ISO-9000 reviewers) or awards panels (such as the Baldridge National Quality Award in the United States). These groups emphasize not only how high the quality is now, but also whether the firm is working on improving it down the road.

Continuous improvement in software development primarily means improved procedures, methodologies, and techniques to prevent faults from reaching the end product. As bugs are found in shipped products, it is important to be able to repair both them and process that allowed them to ship in the first place. This feedback will almost invariably involve development-time changes. Testing and other quality approaches (e.g., code reviews) may not offer a means for preventing certain types of faults, such as resource leaks. As part of a demonstration of continuous improvement, firms need documentation describing both existing quality measures and how they are augmented over time.

There should be an organized effort to take information from development and use it to upgrade the process itself for later projects.

3.3 Techniques for Interface Quality

One can divide a subsystem into interfaces and implementations. The interfaces are the function definitions and prototypes, often called an application programming interface (API). They are the public functions others will use when requesting services of this subsystem. The implementations are the bodies of the interface functions, including private functions.

Microsoft Windows offers a large API to perform operating system functions, ranging from opening windows to accessing files. Each function is defined by an interface, in the form of a C function, with a prototype in the WINDOWS.H file that accompanies all Windows-supporting C compilers.

The implementations of the API functions are embedded in the various DLLs that make up Windows. The code for the functions is **not** supplied with C compilers. This code might well include other C functions, used internally, that are not publicly exposed and therefore do not have an API function exported and defined in WINDOWS.H.

Figure 3.1 illustrates the relationship between a subsystem's interface, its implementation, and partner subsystems. The partners only interact with the API of the subsystem, not its implementation directly.

Figure 3.1 Division between Interface and Implementation

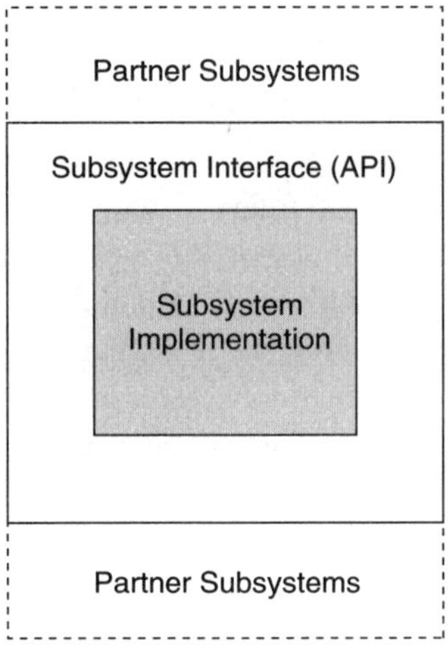

The following sections describe tips for ensuring quality through the interfaces.

Intuitive Parameters

One of the biggest problems for developers when writing C/C++ programs is determining what parameters to pass to interface functions. Confusion can stem from many causes, including the following:

- No comments or other documentation describing how to call the function
- Parameters with multiple uses (e.g., a pointer that could point to a string or to a function, depending on some other value)
- Cryptic parameter names
- Obscure structures

The first two of these are described in the following sections.

No Developer Documentation

Poorly documented interfaces are typically the result of laziness on the programmer's part. Documentation not only takes the form of comments about the function but also an intelligent, consistent naming scheme for functions and parameters. Some projects use data dictionaries and similar tools to ensure common names. Even without such formality, one can make sure names make sense via code reviews and similar mechanisms.

The first function shown below is from the original source code behind the X-Base library's XblGetFieldAsString() function. Note the short function and parameter names, which make it difficult to read.

```
char d_getfld(d, f, buff)
struct DBF *d;
unsigned int f;
char *buff;
{
    struct FIELD_RECORD *fp;
    if (f > 0 && f <= d->num_fields) {
        fp = d->fields_ptr + (f - 1);
        memcpy(buff, fp->field_data_address, fp->len);
        buff[fp->len] = '\0';
        return (fp->typ);
    } else {
        buff[0] = '\0';
        return ('\0');
    }
}
```

Below is the X-Base library version, using the Xbl function prefix, Hungarian notation, and fuller function and parameter names.

```
int EXPORT XblGetFieldAsString(XBL_HANDLE hHandle,
                               unsigned int uiFieldNum,
                               char *pszBuffer)
{
    XBL_FLDINFO *prField;
    XBL_DBINFO *prDbf=(XBL_DBINFO *)hHandle;
    Assert(hHandle!=(XBL_HANDLE)0);
    Assert(pszBuffer!=(char *)0);
    if (uiFieldNum>0 && uiFieldNum<=prDbf->usFields)
    {
        prField=prDbf->prFields+(uiFieldNum-1);
        memcpy(pszBuffer, prField->pszLocation, prField->ucLen);
        pszBuffer[prField->ucLen]='\0';
        return(XBL_NO_ERROR);
    }
    return(XBL_ILLEGAL_FLDNUM);
}
```

Multiple-Use Parameters

A multiple-use parameter is overloaded to serve several purposes. An example is the string versus function pointer scenario mentioned above. Since passing parameters to a function takes time and space, developers create multiple-use parameters to improve performance. From a quality perspective, however, it is better to have well-documented, intuitive parameters to function calls.

The following function has a single void * parameter that could be a pointer to an integer, a C string, or a structure.

```
typedef struct { int iParm,
                 char szValue[16]
               } SAMP_STRUCT;

void SampMultiUseParm(int iType, void *pParm)
{
    SAMP_STRUCT *prStruct = (SAMP_STRUCT *)pParm;
    switch(iType)
    {
        case SAMP_INT:
            printf("An integer was supplied: %d\n",
                   *((int *)pParm);
            break;
        case SAMP_STRING:
            printf("A string was supplied: %s\n", (char *)pParm);
            break;
        case SAMP_STRUCT:
            printf("A structure was supplied: %d, %s\n",
                   prStruct->iParm, prStruct->szValue);
            break;
    }
    return;
}
```

Obviously, if one mismatches the iType and the type of the pParm parameters, the SampMultiUseParm() function will give erroneous results or will crash. It would be better to write three separate functions, one for each type of parameter. Then the C/C++ type checking features could help prevent illegal values from being passed.

Note that in C++, one could have separate API functions for each type, thanks to the function overloading feature. Several functions can have the same name so long as they differ in a parameter type. Hence, one could have two functions with prototypes as follows:

```
void SampMultiUseParm(int iParm)
void SampMultiUseParm(char *pszValue)
```

Confusing interfaces cause programmers to either make assumptions (based on incomplete documentation) or choose incorrectly (forgetting how to use the multiple-use parameter). While the proper use of assertions can sometimes detect mistakes, they will not work everywhere.

In the example above, assertions cannot help the situation. There is no universal test to ensure that a pointer points to a certain type of data. Therefore, there is no way to confirm that the iType and pParm values match properly.

Consistent Return Values

A related problem is the inconsistent definition of function return values. Many functions use integer error codes to indicate success or failure. However, some programmers use zero to indicate success and non-zero to indicate an error. Others return a boolean value for the result (true = success); extended error information is available via another function call.

Even the ANSI C library suffers from inconsistent return values. The malloc() function returns a valid pointer to heap memory on success and a NULL pointer on failure (e.g., out of memory). Here, "success" is a non-zero value.

On the other hand, the remove() function, which deletes a file given its name, returns 0 on success and -1 on failure, with the errno global holding a more detailed error code. In this case, "success" is a zero value.

Many developers, expecting zero to mean success and non-zero to be an error code, take a simple approach to handling errors: Simply surround the function call with an if() statement, as in:

```
if (iResult=SampZeroSuccess())
{
    // do some error-handling here, with iResult=error code
}
```

This mechanism fails outright for functions where zero indicates failure, such as malloc(). This means that developers must pay attention to what return values a function provides. Having consistent values for a project's code at least simplifies this a little—the developer only needs to worry about third-party libraries having different semantics.

Single-Purpose Functions

While it may be convenient to write a single function that performs several types of actions, it can wind up being confusing.

A classic example of a multipurpose ANSI C function is strtok(). It is frequently used in parsing strings, as it returns a substring using a provided set of delimiters. What makes strtok() multipurpose is that a non-NULL input string causes it to begin parsing from the beginning of the string; a NULL input string causes it to continue parsing after the end of the last substring returned:

```
pszField=strtok(pszLine, ",");      // parse comma-delimited line
while (pszField)
{
    // do something with the field here
    pszField=strtok(NULL, ",");
}
```

The problem here is the same as with multiple-use parameters: Developers will forget which way to use the function. It takes just a few extra lines of code to create separate functions for each action.

Here are two functions that wrap around strtok() to provide a clearer interface to its functionality:

```
char *UtlGetFirstSubstring(char *pszString, char *pszDelimiters)
{
    return(strtok(pszString, pszDelimiters));
}

char *UtlGetNextSubstring(char *pszDelimiters)
{
    return(strtok(NULL, pszDelimiters));
}
```

Developers will be less likely to misuse these functions, since their purpose is clear from their names and parameter lists. Accidentally substituting one function for the other will cause a compiler warning because the parameter lists are different. Alternatively, one can replace the functions shown above by macros that expand into the strtok() function calls.

Information Hiding

One powerful concept from object orientation that is related to the quality effort is encapsulation. As noted in the last chapter, encapsulation is the notion that there are "public" and "private" parts to a subsystem (in the case of C++, a class). Only the public parts are available to users; only the class itself can access private areas.

This is not just available through C++. Information hiding, as encapsulation is sometimes called, can be done in C as well. The trick is to use handles. A handle is a piece of data that, to the user, has no inherent meaning—it is just a "black box" passed to various functions. The FILE * pointer used for the ANSI standard I/O library is a good example. While FILE is a structure, few developers use the members; they merely pass the FILE * around to fopen(), fclose(), etc. An even better example is the Windows HWND window handle, which maps to an opaque 4-byte value and cannot be used directly to manipulate information about a window.

The steps to creating a subsystem using information hiding are as follows:

- Instead of having public structures that are manually manipulated by developers, use handles and provide access functions instead.

The X-Base library provides handles for its main data structure, the database file. The XblOpen() function fills in an XBL_HANDLE; this handle is passed into all other API functions to perform operations on the file.

The XBL_HANDLE is a void pointer (void *). In reality, the pointer points to a dynamically allocated XBL_DBINFO structure, containing information about the database file as read from its header. This structure has fields that would be useful to the application programmer (e.g., the number of records in the file). Instead of giving the programmer full access to the data structure, access functions (e.g., XblRecordCount()) return selected values given a handle.

- Instead of having a single header file for the subsystem, have two: a public one (containing the handle type definition and public access function prototypes) and a private one (containing the handle structure definition and any internal function prototypes). The public header file would be distributed with the subsystem; only the subsystem developer uses the private header.

The X-Base library has two header files: DBF.H and DBFAPI.H. The latter is the public API header, the one that would be included by any application wishing to use the X-Base subsystem (e.g., Address Lite). DBF.H is a private header file, where XBL_DBINFO is defined. This file is only used to create the X-Base library itself and is not meant for public use.

Obviously, information hiding can be done in a C++ class by declaring the data to be private members and the accessing functions to be public members.

3.4 Techniques for Implementation Quality

Having a well-designed interface will help prevent **others** from having problems with a given author's subsystem. The following ideas can help a developer prevent or detect faults in his or her **own** code.

Syntactic Tricks

The C and C++ languages are very expressive, allowing one to implement a given action in many ways. Some may be more error-proof than others. Especially when they are equivalent from a performance perspective, one should use the implementation least likely to result in an error.

One trick relates to the common problem of typing = when == is required. = is used solely for variable assignment, whereas == is used in logical tests for equality. While many compilers raise a warning when there is an = without a logical test in an if() statement, this is not always the case. If an = was used, the result would be to update a variable that probably was not meant to be updated. This would cause the branch to be taken, when in reality it should not be:

```
if (iServerCrashCode=TstUpdateRecord())     // maybe wanted ==
{
      ...
}
```

The trick is to note that = only works with a variable on the left-hand side. Therefore, the rule of thumb is always to put variables on the right-hand side when writing an equality test in an if() statement, as shown below:

```
if (TstUpdateRecord()==iServerCrashCode)
{
      ...
}
```

If the developer had = in the above sample, even if the compiler would not normally complain about the lack of ==, it would certainly complain that TstUpdateRecord() is not a variable and therefore cannot have anything assigned to it.

Syntax Checking

Unfortunately, despite the best of intentions, programmers will invariably make syntax errors. While many of these are true errors, preventing the code from compiling, others are valid C/C++ statements in their own right, just not the intended ones. The = versus == example shown above is perhaps the archetype for this kind of problem.

The first step in combatting such problems is to heed the compiler warnings. Not only should these be read and compared against the source code, but they should be actively solicited, typically by setting a warning level to its maximum setting.

Some warnings are truly benign. Others cannot be fixed, if for example, the source code is from a third party. To help in these cases, some compilers allow selected categories of warnings to be disabled. Giving the Borland compilers the -w-pro switch will disable warnings about function prototypes, for example. Use these instead of disabling or limiting all warnings, and only on the files that need them.

Compilers may have other helpful options. For example, if the intent is to use pure ANSI-compatible code (e.g., requiring function prototypes), the compiler might have a switch that issues warnings or errors for non-ANSI constructs.

Finally, external utilities can provide even more information about syntax. Typically, these programs are called *lint* (or related trademarked names), after the progenitor of the species. Their sole purpose is to detect and report on problems in C/C++ code.

Project Coding Standards

Syntax checkers like lint use rules set forth by their authors. Projects might also want to create their own rules, such as eliminating global variables, employing function name prefixes, or using Hungarian notation. Many of these rules will not be checked by either the compiler or a third-party lint program.

One could write a program to try to check for violations of a project's rules. However, this is probably difficult to do, since the tool will need to parse and understand C/C++ code. It is easier to roll this type of standards enforcement into a code review. Code reviews and standards enforcement are described later.

Appendix E contains a list of sample style rules and their justification for use.

Global Variables

Global variables are popular in some circles. They eliminate extra parameter passing, thereby improving performance and simplifying function calls. Therefore, many programs, particularly for Unix, have dozens of global variables scattered throughout the code.

Globals, however, can be dangerous and can lead to software faults. Here are a few reasons why:

- Globals can be touched by many pieces of a program, including separate subsystems. It is easy for developers to get confused as to how to use them if their use is poorly documented. However, since globals are variables and not functions, the original subsystem author cannot use assertions or other checks to confirm proper usage. Encapsulating globals, so they are accessed only by subsystem functions, is one solution.
- For Windows 3.x (and optionally on OS/2 and Win32), each DLL has its own data segment, so it owns any global variables in its code. However, the DLL might be used by more than one executable program if two programs share it or the same program is opened twice. The executables, therefore, share the globals in the DLL, rather than having their own copy. Since this is not how one expects globals to behave (i.e., one copy per executable), it can lead to faults.
- For multithreaded operating systems, such as OS/2 and Windows NT, several threads will all have independent access to the globals. Two threads might try to change the same one at the same time, with uncertain results. While this can be prevented by using semaphores or critical sections, these techniques add overhead. If the globals were used for performance, the overhead may make matters worse. Also, the added code will wreck any hoped-for simplicity.

Typically, a better solution will be to use handles instead. All API functions for a subsystem can take a handle as input, which will represent a structure that holds all the data that would otherwise be put into globals. For the last two cases above, each user (thread) of the subsystem would have its own handle. The only globals would then be ones containing information needed across multiple handles.

3.5 Code Reviews and Standards Enforcement

Code reviews frequently bridge the gap between development-time quality assurance and testing. Such reviews can range from casual meetings to peruse code to highly formal affairs with forms and specific procedures. Any code review, however, has the goal of using human inspection to identify problem areas in a subsystem or module.

The concept is obvious. There are always aspects of programming that tools cannot automatically audit. Rather than leave those areas alone, projects can employ code reviews to use human experience and analysis to supplement the tools. The goals of a code review include:

- Identifying sections in a subsystem that fail to comply with the programming standards set forth by the group.
- Pointing out potential flaws, either in design, interface, or implementation. These flaws might have short-term effects or merely pose a maintenance problem.
- Making suggestions for improving algorithms, from a performance or readability perspective.

What underlies all these goals is that code reviews provide knowledge transfer from more-experienced staff to junior developers. Here, "junior" does not necessarily reflect overall experience; one can be expert in many areas but unfamiliar with a new technology. SQA tools will be less effective than people in making this transfer.

The biggest concern with code reviews is the time they take. Not only are there meetings to discuss the subsystem, but the reviewers need time to review the code to make recommendations. For projects on a tight time budget, code reviews seem expensive. However, this assumes that all developers can write solid code and follow coding standards. Only code reviews can determine this for certain. Also, one can take steps to minimize the effort needed for code reviews.

Implementing Code Reviews

Traditional code reviews typically occur late in the development phase, either just before or in parallel with unit testing. In an iterative methodology, one could conduct reviews after each phase or after all phases are complete. Assuming one can keep them from being too time-consuming, holding iteration-level reviews will help catch problems earlier. Moreover, the experience of the first review will help developers in writing the code for later iterations.

One key issue for code reviews is staffing: Who should participate? Most teams have the subsystem developer present to receive comments and explain confusing sections of the code. One also needs reviewers. Many projects make code reviews a team-wide affair, with everyone reviewing everybody else's code. This, of course, is very time-consuming. So long as goals are set forth and are met, the number of reviewers makes little difference. While two reviewers will catch more problems than one, diminishing returns arrive quickly. In fact, one could get by with a single reviewer (sometimes called a peer review).

The key to staffing reviews is ensuring one solid reviewer for each critical subsystem. As with any development activity, outstanding staff members can have a great impact. Given that each project has only a few such people and recognizing that they are probably overworked, one must leverage them appropriately. If they have the time, they could review everything—since they do not, have them review the components deemed crucial for the application's success. If possible, hold those reviews early, so other reviewers can learn from them.

Some SQA and methodology experts have identified roles that should be included in code reviews. Ed Yourdon [16], for example, recommends identifying reviewers responsible for standards enforcement, usability, maintainability, etc. The problem is that naming these areas as "roles" suggests heavy staffing. In reality, these are goals of the review: It must ensure that standards have been met, usability is on par, etc. The project must determine how many people are required to reach the goals.

Formality is another issue in code reviews. Some projects prefer significant documentation (memos, etc.), to maintain a "paper trail" on the proceedings. Other projects are more apt to do a review over pizza and beer on a Friday night. This, again, is a matter of style. The key is ensuring that goals are met and positive action is taken. Making recommendations on code changes that are not implemented greatly diminishes the effectiveness of a review. Documentation can help management ensure that the team does such follow-up work, but this increases overall code review cost. Ideally, project management will have other ways of incorporating review comments that require less staff time.

The actual review itself is typically anticlimactic. Reviewers will have read the code before the meeting. Their comments will be discussed in turn, by going through the subsystem a piece at a time and discussing each function or class. Somebody keeps track of the comments that are generally agreed upon, so the developer has a reference for later revisions. Occasionally, a review will unearth issues that transcend the subsystem being reviewed, such as a major design flaw. The project as a whole needs to deal with these, so they should be discussed separately.

One challenge in the review itself is to keep it moving. Code reviews are looked upon as a bore by many developers, as they can drag on interminably. Part of the problem is that reviewers spend too much time arguing. To some extent, team-level coding standards can control this, as style issues tend to be "religious" and heavily debated in code reviews. Other time-wasters, such as spending too much time discussing solutions, need to be controlled by the chairperson. Things that are better dealt with "off-line" (i.e., outside the meeting) should be tabled promptly, so the review can continue.

Based on comments received from the review, the developer will make changes to the subsystem. Some projects have a checkout procedure to ensure that the changes are made. Assuming that developers are properly motivated, such procedures may be superfluous.

Standards Enforcement Before Reviews

One problem with code reviews is that side issues are often simply tossed into them for convenience. One is enforcing coding standards. Having standards that all team members follow will improve both short-term quality and long-term maintenance. However, standards work only if developers use them. Hence, there typically needs to be some means of enforcing them.

Code reviews will obviously identify violations, as each line of code will get reviewed by at least one reviewer. The problem is in the timing: If reviews happen late in the development cycle, there will not be a lot of time to go back and fix coding style. This leads to one of two bad results:

- Standards are ignored, at least in part, due to lack of time.
- The developer fixes the subsystem but delays overall progress into system test.

It would be better to check standards earlier during development. If an iterative development methodology is used and code reviews occur during every cycle, the problem will be solved. In single-review projects, however, standards enforcement must be done earlier.

The best way would be for an automated oracle to determine violations, as *lint* does for unusual C structures. In lieu of such a tool, a quick review of selected functions or classes may suffice. A peer or a central QA staff member should conduct it. The random selection hopefully will be a representative sample of the developer's work and will identify the most frequent violations of the standards. Should the developer fix only the cited places and leave the rest of it as it was, then the problem becomes one for management to handle.

Relationship to Continuous Improvement

Style guides and code reviews may be part of the overall quality plan for a project. Ideally, the plan will have been honed over several prior projects to identify the most efficient approaches. If the quality plan stipulates certain procedures, follow them—that is the purpose of the plan!

However, code reviews must not only help to fix the application but also the overall SQA process. A code review might highlight a standard that, while beneficial, costs more to implement than it will ever provide in value. This should be reflected in later editions of the quality plan, so other projects do not make the same mistake.

3.6 Quality Assurance Concerns

One reason why development-time quality assurance is not more popular is the perceived impact on the project and team. The two most-cited concerns are application performance and team productivity.

Performance

In today's era of high-volume data transfer and information processing, applications must run as fast as possible. Performance, therefore, is a key concern of project managers. Anything that might negatively impact it, given broad parameters (e.g., the language used for development), is frowned upon.

Because development-time quality assurance affects the way the code is written, some worry that it will lead to poorer-performing systems. Fortunately, this concern is usually unfounded. Most coding style conventions, such as intelligent variable names, have no impact whatsoever on speed. Similarly, tools like AssertLib and ResTrack have options to disable their extensions when creating a production executable. Even though they will slow down the code during development and testing, they will not affect the speed seen by end users.

There are some situations, however, in which writing code for quality will cause worse performance. Highly optimized code tends to be difficult to maintain, and some coding style rules run counter to optimization techniques. The rule of thumb here is to optimize only where it is worthwhile, where profilers indicate slow modules. The remaining code should be written with maintainability and quality in mind.

Productivity

Not only is the performance of the application in question when using quality techniques, but so is the "performance" of the development team. Many projects are faced with tight deadlines and rapid turnaround times, so the team does not have time to spare.

The key to reconciling quality assurance with team productivity is knowing what the goals are and how much it will cost to reach them. Presumably, one wants applications with zero defects; faults found by end users will have real short-term and long-term costs. One must weigh the effectiveness of quality techniques in preventing or eliminating faults versus the cost to employ them.

That is why a continuous improvement program is so important. Not only must it identify new ways to prevent faults, it must do so with effectiveness and efficiency in mind. Adding new rules whose implementation costs outweigh their fault-finding benefit will not do an organization any good. The continuous improvement program must also evaluate existing rules and see whether they are still necessary or can be made more efficient. Removing a rule because it does not seem to be worth the effort is reasonable, so long as it is a rational and justifiable decision rather than a desperate response to tightening deadlines.

3.7 Summary

By tackling quality issues during development rather than waiting until testing time, one can have a serious impact on the number of faults created and, eventually, shipped to users. Usually the impact is positive, because many techniques are cheap to implement and fairly effective in fault prevention. This is particularly true when techniques can be automated through tools, like the AssertLib and ResTrack tools described in the next two chapters.

However, one should not "go overboard" and wind up harming either application performance or team productivity. A solid continuous improvement program, modifying the techniques over time based on usefulness, will help prevent this from occurring.

CHAPTER 4

Validations: AssertLib

One result of a team meeting to discuss quality was that a few TurboChem developers got energized about quality assurance. They, along with Sam, kept trying to improve their quality efforts. Sometimes, however, the results were not quite what they intended.

One example was an incident that occurred three weeks into the TurboChem 3.0 programming effort. Sam was chatting with Linda and Sean, two developers working on the database-access subsystems. All of a sudden, George, one of the other programmers, stuck his head in the door and bellowed, "You two—get over here! Your code's broken!" Sam, Linda, and Sean followed George back to his office.

"See, look at that!" George exclaimed, pointing at some text at the bottom of his screen that read:

"Assertion failed: NULL name pointer provided. Abnormal program termination."

Sean quickly asked, "Well, are you passing in a NULL pointer for the name?"

"Maybe. But you shouldn't just trash the program like that!"

Linda then pointed out that, according to the detailed design, all strings passed to functions must not be null unless specifically allowed.

George retorted, "OK, I made a mistake. Maybe. But you wrecked the screen with those messages!"

George was right. The text output had overwritten the graphical user interface. In fact, George was now trying to get a response out of his computer.

"See—now the machine's locked up!" he grumbled as he started the slow operating system start-up sequence.

Sean and Linda explained that they had read about assertions—statements that checked things that were guaranteed (such as non-NULL strings as input). They were using an ANSI C function, assert(), to implement them.

"We need another way to do assertions that is as easy to use as assert(), but will not have quite the effect on George's machine," said Sam.

"Or on George," Linda chuckled.

4.1 Introduction

One popular adage is that "anything that can go wrong, will." One can divide "things that can go wrong" with software into two major categories: exceptions and faults.

External events that cause software failures, termed exceptions, can happen at any time and must be watched for constantly. An example is running out of memory or disk space. Exceptions can occur in a perfectly written program, such as when a network file server crashes, damaging a link or corrupting program data. There is nothing one can do, in general, to prevent them. One must simply deal with them in the best possible way.

The other type of problem, faulty programming, is preventable. Obviously, software testing will catch and remove faults before a program is released to unsuspecting users. The key is that the team can catch many faults during development itself, before formal testing begins.

Partitioning Software Development

Some projects require only a single developer. This is the simple case of the more general (and more typical) situation involving several developers. Over the past decades of software development, various techniques of partitioning development have arisen that help manage the "multiple developer to single application" situation. Under one such scheme, one divides the application into several pieces. Developers are assigned pieces, but no two work directly on a single piece.

The nature of the division is largely up to the team. Some prefer dividing by functional area, so an accounting system would have pieces such as the general ledger, subsidiary ledgers, account posting, etc. This technique is called vertical slicing. Some prefer dividing by technical function, so the same accounting system splits into the user interface, domain model/business logic, and database interaction subsystems. This approach is called horizontal slicing.

Figure 4.1 shows how the three forms of partitioning (vertical, horizontal, and "random") work. It illustrates a simple accounting system, with general ledger, accounts payable, accounts receivable, and inventory functions. There are also three technical layers: user interface, business logic, and database access.

Figure 4.1 Partitioning an Application

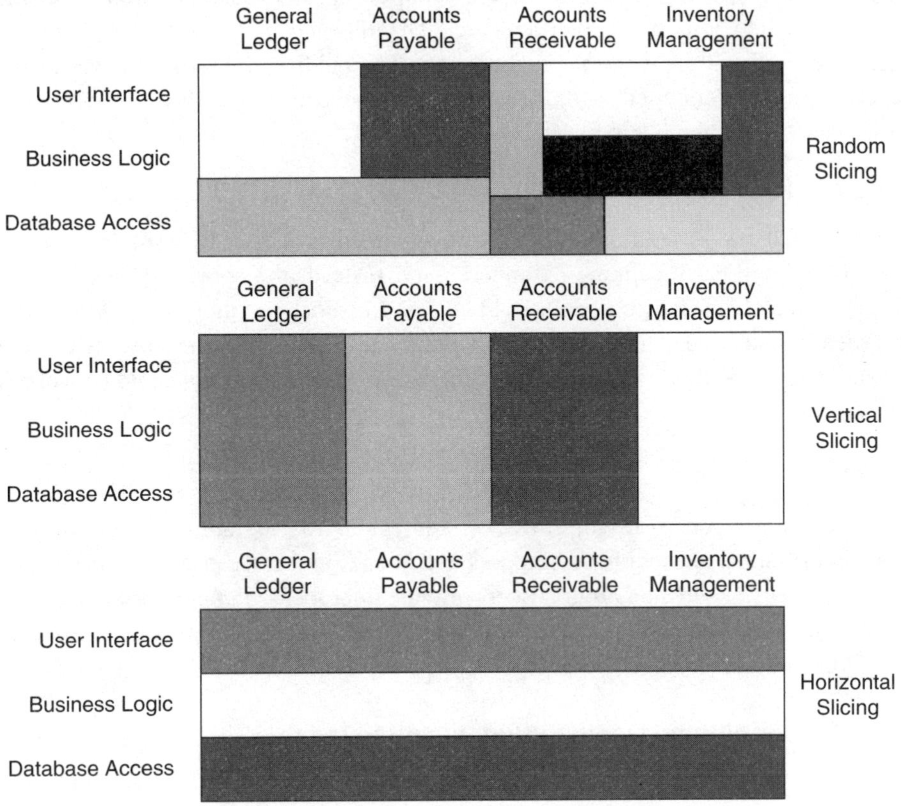

In either case, the physical form is largely identical: C function libraries with a defined application programming interface (API) or C++ class libraries.

In this book, the prime example of partitioning comes in the sample application. The graphical front end to Address Lite was separated from the database engine, in the form of the X-Base access library. Arguably, these could have been combined without affecting the sample application's functionality. Keeping them separate allowed for them to be worked on under separate schedules, in theory by separate individuals.

One extension to this technique is the "software contract." Here, developers create a detailed design of their particular components and decide, up front, what the interface will look like. The interfaces are then published and provided to other team members who will be using the components. The published interface serves as the specification or "contract"—the developer must build it as specified, and the users must access the component through it.

With the X-Base library, since the development was done by a single person, a formal written specification was unnecessary. Instead, the specification consisted solely of the planned API, as defined in DBFAPI.H. Each function in the API is prototyped in that header file. So long as Address Lite used only the functions in the header and the X-Base library provided them, the two components could be worked on separately.

What this does is divide software failures due to programmer error into two major categories: ones within a component and ones in the use of a component. The latter typically arise when programmers provide improper parameters to an interface or use functions out of order. The former will occur within a component, when the developer makes a syntactical or logic error.

Preconditions, Postconditions, and Invariants

The goal, of course, is to have fault-free components before the application is released. Testing will assist in reaching that goal. One can, however, work on guaranteeing fault-free components before testing even begins. If a project uses the software contract model described above, then one has a powerful technique available: giving the components working knowledge of the specifications in the contract.

A software contract or specification is simply a set of rules. They state how one should use the interface (e.g., "the filename provided must point to an existing file" or "the XblOpen() function must be called before other library functions can be called"). The rules also state what the interface does (e.g., "XblOpen() will initialize the database handle") and what results, if any, it provides (e.g., "XblOpen() will return an integer, with zero indicating success").

For example, below are the function prototypes of two X-Base library API functions for getting and setting the value of a field, using a C string as the source/destination of the field's value:

```
int XblGetFieldAsString(XBL_HANDLE hHandle, unsigned int uiField,
char *pszBuffer);
int XblPutFieldAsString(XBL_HANDLE hHandle, unsigned int uiField,
char *pszBuffer);
```

Both have a rule that a zero return code indicates success and a non-zero code indicates an error, using an enumerated set of error codes (found in DBFAPI.H). XblGetFieldAsString() places the field's contents in pszBuffer; similarly, XblPutFieldAsString() puts the string's contents in the field.

Both have additional rules regarding the parameters to each function:

- The database handle must have been properly initialized and the file must still be open.
- The field number must be valid (i.e., greater than zero and less than or equal to the number of fields in the record).
- The string must point to valid storage (e.g., not NULL) of the appropriate length.

Many of these rules can be defined programmatically in the component itself. Encoding the rules in the component allows it to validate both itself and its users, with respect to the particular interfaces used. These rules serve as ever-present "guards," watching for the slightest mistake. If properly implemented, they will alert developers when a fault has crept into the system that violates the rules defined in the contract.

There are three major categories of rules:

- Preconditions, rules that define what the state of the component should be before an interface is actually executed. Preconditions can check both component state (e.g., "do I have a valid storage buffer?") and parameter validity (e.g., "does the named file exist?").
- Postconditions, rules that define what the state of the component and results should be after an interface is through executing.
- Invariants, rules that should be true at all times for a given component. Whereas postconditions deal primarily with the workings of a given action

provided by an interface, invariants are rules that should be true before and after **every** action.

Preconditions for the two X-Base library API functions include the parameter rules outlined above. Other content rules might also be included. For example, on XblPutFieldAsString(), the string must point to something valid to put in the database field (e.g., no embedded NULLs or control characters).

Postconditions for these functions include:

- The database file is still open and has not been modified.
- The same record that was modified is still being pointed to by the database handle.
- On XblPutFieldAsString(), the memory buffer for this record has been updated with the new field contents.

The invariants for the X-Base library all deal with the database handles, since they contain the only information that persists from call to call. The following invariants should be true for handles:

- They should always correctly indicate if they point to an open or closed file.
- For open files, the handle should always be pointing to a valid database record.
- For open files, the handle should always have database header information that is up-to-date.

The means for checking whether these rules hold true is through an assertion. An assertion merely executes some statement and verifies that it is true (e.g., pszFileName!=(char *)0). An assertion library, such as AssertLib, provides a response when the assertion fails. One might halt the program immediately or continue processing after logging the failure in a file.

Assertions in C/C++

Some languages, such as Eiffel, provide built-in capabilities for employing assertions and invariants. C and C++, however, have no such logic built into the language itself. Most implementations provide an assert() function or macro, which evaluates an expression and halts the application if it is false. However, there is no automatic means of having particular assertions used for C functions or C++ classes. Developers must embed the assertions into each interface. Moreover, they must either settle for the standard assert() behavior, use a third-party library (such as AssertLib), or write their own handlers.

The assert() macro is passed, as a parameter, a logical expression like ones used in if() statements. If the expression evaluates to true, nothing happens and processing continues. If, however, it evaluates to false, assert() writes a message to standard output identifying the failure, then terminates the application (via abort()).

For example, to assert that a particular string is non-NULL, one would use an assertion like:

```
assert(pszName!=(char *)0);
```

The advantage of creating one's own assertion handler, as opposed to its being built into the language, is control of when the assertions are used. One certainly wants them to be fired during software development, since this is when the faults that they detect enter the code. One probably wants to enable them during at least some of the testing, in case developers failed to try particular cases that cause them to fail. However, due to the performance penalty, one should not include assertions in distributed applications, relying on the fact that the faults will have been found before shipping. Languages with built-in assertions, such as Eiffel, suffer because assertions are forced everywhere, all the time.

Benefits of Using Assertions

To summarize, there are several benefits to littering your code with assertions.

Standards Enforcement

Assertions help prove, before testing begins, that everybody is "playing the game" properly, based on the specification. Attempts to misuse a subsystem governed by assertions will be detected. Obviously, since assertions cannot be everywhere, there will still be places where a subsystem may not be properly used. Assertions can reduce the odds of this significantly, however.

Early Fault Detection

Assertions tend to catch faults fairly soon after they are introduced, which helps make them easier to find. The developers will be more familiar with the affected area because assertions are built into the application itself and therefore will raise a flag as soon as the application is run after making a coding error.

Rapid Fault Identification

Assertions take you right to where the problem is first manifested. Other diagnostics, such as Unix core dumps, emit semi-intelligible CPU and memory information. An assertion will tell you the precise location (file and line) where it failed, along with the text of the failed logical expression. This makes diagnosis and repair much easier.

Warnings about Assertions

As with any other subsystem, assertions themselves can be misused. First of all, they should be unobtrusive—they cannot be allowed to change anything. An assertion should not change a program's state, for example, by changing variable values. Otherwise, it might wind up inserting a bug instead of detecting one.

A common mistake of this kind in an assertion macro is to use the ++ or - - operators, particularly in prefix mode. The fact that they increment (or decrement) a tested value may make the assertion logic work, but then the value is decremented for the rest of the code. The following C fragment makes sure that an empty string was not provided by testing the first character for NULL; however, it also moves up the string pointer by one slot:

```
assert(*(pszString++)!='\0');
```

There are two possible outcomes to writing an assertion in this way. If the code following it is expecting the string pointer to be at its original spot, the assertion will cause that code to fail. If the code is expecting the pointer to have been incremented by one, it will work so long as the assertion is executed. In production mode, assertions are frequently turned off (see below); the code would then fail, since the pointer would no longer be incremented.

Also, assertions should be managed and removed for production releases. One reason, speed degradation, was mentioned above. There is a similar space issue, based on the assertion logic and message text. However, three other reasons are even more important:

- Assertions themselves are just lines of code, like anything else written for the application. There is nothing magical about them that prevents them from introducing bugs. By having them automatically removed for the production release (typically by using the preprocessor #ifdef statement), one leaves fewer potential sources of trouble.

- Assertions could wind up masking bugs, if they fail the rule mentioned above that they cannot change a program's state. If one changes the assertion later, all of a sudden a fault will crop up in seemingly perfect code. Soon, certain assertions will be left turned on in production code to prevent these bugs from recurring. This is not improving quality—it is burying mistakes.
- Suppose, due to a missed mistake, an assertion were to fire in a production application. Typically, assertions emit error information that is useful to a developer but unlikely to be helpful for an end user. An alternative to removing the assertions would be to replace the standard development-time output mechanism with one that provides a more user-friendly message (e.g., "An anomaly was detected in the program. Please pass the following information on to the Technical Support Staff...").

What Should Be Asserted?

Several conditions should be asserted in any C function or C++ member function:

- Input Parameters: Based on the software contract, they typically will have rules they must follow (e.g., no NULL pointers). Assertions should prove that users are calling the function properly.
- Output Values: Again, the contract should stipulate what type of result should come back. Assertions cannot validate every result (e.g., "any integer value"). Watch that an assertion does not test something that should be handled by exception handling, such as an out-of-memory condition.
- Invariants: These are conditions that should always be true. For C++ classes, place them in a common function, called from every other member function. They should prove that the object is in a proper state after each member function is through. One can take a similar approach with C subsystems, especially ones that use handles or other data structures as a common parameter.
- Impossible Situations: If you consider adding exception handling logic and then say "That can never happen," add an assertion to prove, over time, that it truly **is** impossible. If the assertion later catches an occurrence of the impossible event, then either there is a fault somewhere or the event is possible and should be handled by exception logic.

As important as what should be asserted is what should **not** be, which is any situation that is really an exception. Recall that exceptions are things that might happen even in a production application, such as running out of memory. This is not impossible, so occurrences of it should be detected and managed, using proper exception handlers.

One might write an assertion like:

```
assert((pszString=(char *)malloc(uiSize))!=(char *)0);
```

This will allocate memory, holding on to the pointer to it, and checking said pointer for NULL to indicate a failed access.

The problem here is that out-of-memory conditions do happen, even in the best of applications. Probably the system should not "fall over and die" in such cases, but inform the user of the situation and exit as gracefully as possible. Also, if assertions are removed when the production version is compiled, there would be no memory checking, and the application might try using a NULL pointer.

Instead of using an assertion, an application should take other steps to handle out-of-memory conditions by using exception handling:

```
if ((pszString=(char *)malloc(uiSize))==(char *)0)
{
    longjmp(rSafePlace, SAMP_OUT_OF_MEMORY); // bail out of here
}
...
```

Another rule regarding assertions is: "Do not assert anything you cannot solve." For example, the ANSI C library function memcpy() is supposed to return the destination pointer for the memory copy. One could include an assertion to prove that this is the case. But why? One should not need that return value, since one already has it. And if memcpy() for some reason returned something else, there is little a C developer can do about it. Placing such an assertion in a test suite for a C compiler makes sense—the compiler writer can fix a mistake that caused the erroneous result. Everyone else can only use the library, not fix it. There is no point in wasting effort to check something that cannot be repaired.

It is easy to go too far with adding assertions. Proving that every divisor is non-zero may be excessive. On the other hand, if it is cheap to add an assertion that is fired a lot, do so. For example, if one has a C++ class for multiprecision arithmetic that overrides the division operator, adding an assertion in the division member function that checks for a zero divisor is an excellent idea.

4.2 Using AssertLib's Assertions

AssertLib provides an Assert() macro that mimics (and sometimes utilizes) the ANSI C assert() macro. One can wrap the macro around a logical statement that is supposed to be true. If the statement is actually false, a report will be presented to the user. The developer can use it to help track down the source of the problem.

Adding Assertions to C/C++ Source

The first step to using AssertLib is to #include the _ASSERT.H header file in any source file that uses assertions. This file defines the Assert() macro, using a definition dependent on the type of assertion desired (described in the next section). Since _ASSERT.H defends against nested inclusion, its placement does not matter (in source files, header files, or both).

Nested Inclusion Protection

Complex C/C++ programs frequently employ quite a few header files: those for the application itself, and the standard C library, plus ones for third-party libraries. Unfortunately, compilers frequently dislike having header files multiply included in a source file. So, if a source file includes both DBF.H and DBFAPI.H, and DBF.H also includes DBFAPI.H, then the compiler might complain about duplicated type definitions, etc.

There is an easy way to prevent this from occurring. An entire header file can be bracketed in an #ifndef/#endif construct that checks whether it has already been included. The following code fragment does the job:

```
#ifndef DBFAPI_H
#define DBFAPI_H
// rest of header goes here
#endif
```

The first time DBFAPI.H is included for a given source file, DBFAPI_H will not be defined. Therefore, the #ifndef evaluates to true and the rest of the header is executed, which, among other things, defines DBFAPI_H. The second (and subsequent) times the header file is included for a given source file, DBFAPI_H **will** be defined, so the header file is largely ignored (the #ifndef test evaluates to false).

This assumes that nobody else is using DBFAPI_H as a defined constant. Basically, the rule of thumb is that defined constants ending in _H are reserved for nested header inclusion protection and should not be used elsewhere.

Given that this file has been included, one can then place Assert() calls in the source code, following the above guidelines for selecting conditions. In the X-Base library that forms the basis for the Address Lite demo, assertions were used primarily to validate input parameters contracted to meet specific conditions. Usually, the contracts disallowed NULL values (for database handles, character buffers, etc.). The assertions check for such conditions.

The following is an implementation of XblGetFieldAsString() from the X-Base library:

```
int EXPORT XblGetFieldAsString(XBL_HANDLE hHandle,
                               unsigned int uiFieldNum,
                               char *pszBuffer)
{
    XBL_FLDINFO *prField;
    XBL_DBINFO *prDbf=(XBL_DBINFO *)hHandle;
    Assert(hHandle!=(XBL_HANDLE)0);
    Assert(pszBuffer!=(char *)0);
    if (uiFieldNum>0 && uiFieldNum<=prDbf->usFields)
    {
        prField=prDbf->prFields+(uiFieldNum-1);
        memcpy(pszBuffer, prField->pszLocation, prField->ucLen);
        pszBuffer[prField->ucLen]='\0';
        return(XBL_NO_ERROR);
    }
    return(XBL_ILLEGAL_FLDNUM);
}
```

This function uses two Assert() macros, one to check for a NULL handle and one to check for a NULL buffer. The Assert() macro is used just like the assert() macro in ANSI C, save for the different header file.

Ensuring that the field number is in the proper range is handled not by an assertion but by normal error processing (e.g., a non-zero return code). This was a judgment call, based on how the library could be used (e.g., to create a database language interpreter). NULL values for the handle and buffer are certain to be system-programmer errors, while an illegal field value could conceivably be an end-user error. Since assertions vanish at run-time, the field value check was placed in normal C code.

There are three useful variants on the Assert() macro:

- AssertMsg() takes two parameters, the assertion logical expression (like Assert()) and a string indicating what the assertion is about. The string replaces the normal output of the text of the logical expression.

To log a custom assertion failure message rather than the default (the expression that failed), the Assert() macros shown from XblGetFieldAsString() replace AssertMsg() macros:

```
AssertMsg(hHandle!=(XBL_HANDLE)0, "NULL database handle!");
AssertMsg(pszBuffer!=(char *)0, "NULL field character buffer");
```

- AssertAction() takes a C keyword or function call in addition to the logical expression. If the assertion is triggered and it would not cause the program to halt (e.g., assertions are being quietly logged to a file), the provided code fragment will be executed. This is frequently used to return from a function that cannot proceed if the assertion fails.

To exit the function called if the assertions fail, replace the Assert() macros by AssertAction() macros:.

```
AssertAction(hHandle!=(XBL_HANDLE)0, return(XBL_ASSERTION););
AssertAction(pszBuffer!=(char *)0, return(XBL_ASSERTION););
```

- AssertMsgAction() takes three parameters: the logical expression, a string to be included in the assertion output, and an action like the one used in AssertAction(). This version combines the behavior of AssertMsg() and AssertAction().

Compiling and Linking with Assertions

By default, the Assert() macros map to the normal ANSI C assert() macro, which dumps a message to standard output and terminates the program. For many programs, such as command-line driven tools, the default is satisfactory. However, in other situations, this is not desirable, typically when the display cannot use standard output, such as in a graphical interface.

There are four other options one can use to control the behavior of Assert():

- Have the assertion output sent to a file, ASSERT.LOG, instead of standard output. The program, like assert(), will terminate on an assertion failure.
- Send the output to a file and continue processing the application without stopping. If multiple assertions fail, the ASSERT.LOG output file will contain information about all of them.
- Under Windows, bring up a dialog box displaying the assertion output information, asking the user if processing is to continue. The user can halt the program, if desired.
- Turn off assertions, causing the Assert() macro calls to have no effect. This option is typically used when creating the production version to ship to end users.

One selects an option via #ifdefs in the _ASSERT.H include file. Each option is associated with a different constant. Table 4.1 lists the available values.

Table 4.1 AssertLib Constants and Resulting Assertion Types

Macro	Resulting Assertion Type
NO_ASSERTS	None (assertions turned into no-operations)
ASSERT_LOG	AssertToFile(), will continue past failures
ASSERT_LOG_AND_QUIT	AssertToFile(), will stop on failure
ASSERT_DIALOG	AssertToDialog()
None of the above	Uses compiler's assert() macro

Typically, one can define constants on the compiler's command line by using a switch, such as /D.

The following command line builds the test executable for ResTrack, and uses /D to enable ASSERT_LOG style assertions:

```
bcc -DASSERT_LOG -I..\assert test.c restrack.c ..\assert\assert.c
```

Also, if one uses the file or dialog assertion modes, the ASSERT.C file must be compiled and linked with the application. It contains the source for the routines that actually perform the file- and dialog-based assertions.

Testing with Assertions

Given that one has created an executable or library containing assertions, it is now merely a matter of exercising the code and seeing what assertions, if any, fail. Hence, use AssertLib not only during development, but also during unit and system testing. If the testers and developers are different people, show the testers how to watch for and record assertion failures, as these are sure signs of something being wrong.

Also, if the application to be shipped will not contain the assertion code (i.e., NO_ASSERTS is defined), then as much of the testing as possible should be rerun in regression test format. This is necessary to prove that the assertions themselves did not affect the code. It is unsafe to assume that the program, which ran properly with assertions in place, will continue to be correct without them. Assertions can have faults like any other code.

4.3 Using AssertLib's Invariants

AssertLib also provides a mechanism to allow C++ classes to define a function that performs invariant checking. This function, courtesy of some special macros, will be executed at the end of every member function (except constructors and destructors). Hence, it should use assertions to ensure that the object is in a legal state.

What to Test

As mentioned above for assertions, the invariants should always be true (hence the name "invariant"). A failure indicates either a direct programming error (e.g., forgetting to update a state flag) or damaged memory. Damaged memory could have many causes, including overwriting arrays in a memcpy()-style function or using a pointer to a stack-allocated object after it has been released.

Note that the invariants checked must **always** be true, not just most of the time. If, for example, a pointer to an allocated buffer must always be non-NULL, that is a good invariant to check. However, if it can legally be NULL in certain situations, then the invariant must take them into account. If there is a state flag that indicates when a NULL pointer would be legal, it could be added to the invariant check:

```
Assert(pBuffer!=NULL || iState==NULL_BUFFER_LEGAL);
```

The fact that the invariant-checking code is not called from a constructor or destructor will help. Most of the time, the constructor sets up a legal situation; the object should then remain legal throughout its lifetime. By waiting until after the constructor to start utilizing the invariant code, one avoids the danger of an invariant failing because the constructor has not been fired.

Implementing Invariants

The AssertLib code contains ASSTCPPE.H, a C++ header file that defines a class named AssertBase. AssertBase is a base class for all C++ classes that use the invariant logic. Note that not every C++ class in an application **must** use invariants. If a particular class has nothing that can properly be tested by using invariants, it can be left alone.

Below is the definition of AssertBase from ASSTCPPE.H:

```
class AssertBase /* base class for invariant checks */
{
public:
    virtual void CheckInvariants() = 0;
};
```

AssertBase contains a single public member function, CheckInvariants(). It is a pure virtual function, meaning that it has no definition, so AssertBase is abstract and cannot directly be instantiated. Any class that subclasses from AssertBase must implement CheckInvariants(), or else it, too, will be abstract.

To turn an existing C++ class into one that uses invariant checking, do the following:

- Separate all member function implementations into source files that will use invariants. One cannot mix pure C and C++ code within a source file. Also, one cannot mix code from C++ classes that do and do not inherit from AssertBase. These restrictions are due to the macro "trick" used to automatically fire the assertion code.
- Add a #include statement to include ASSTCPPE.H into the files containing C++ class declarations and definitions that will use invariants. ASSTCPPE.H is protected against nested #includes, so there is no harm in having it in both an include file and the corresponding source file, for example.
- For all C++ classes that will use invariants, have them inherit from AssertBase, in addition to any classes they already inherit from. Thanks to C++'s multiple inheritance, this is not only possible but very easy.

If we have class DbHandle that inherits from class GenericHandle, and we want to add invariant checking to it, simply have the class declaration begin like:

```
class DbHandle : public GenericHandle, AssertBase
```

- For all concrete classes that inherit from AssertBase, implement the CheckInvariants() function. It must execute assertions (using the assertion techniques described above) to check for failures in invariants. The function is declared as void and hence does not need to return any special values.

Below is a sample partial class definition that implements a CheckInvariants() member function:

```
class SampClass: public AssertBase
{
public:
    virtual void CheckInvariants();
    // other member functions here
private:
    int bStateFlag;
};

void SampClass::CheckInvariants()
{
    Assert(bStateFlag==0 || bStateFlag==1);
}
```

Note that the CheckInvariants() function lacks an explicit return statement. Many compilers allow this for void functions, and it prevents an infinite loop of CheckInvariants() recursively calling CheckInvariants(). For compilers that do not support this feature, the CheckInvariants() function should either be inlined in the class declaration or put into a source file that does not include ASSTCPPE.H.

- Deal with static member functions in the class. They will not be able to use the normal CheckInvariants() function, as it is a regular member function, not a static one. Since invariants are typically useless on a static member function, it is best to move such functions into a separate C++ source file. Alternatively, one can create a separate static CheckInvariants() function for them to use.

Compiling and Testing with Invariants

AssertBase has no source file, since it does not define any member functions. All one must do is link with the assertion code, as described above. If the assertion checks use the ANSI C assert() instead of AssertLib's Assert() macro, then one can skip linking in the assertion code. The compilation must also define any flags needed by AssertLib, as noted above.

Once compiled and linked, the application should run as before with one exception: the CheckInvariants() function will be called by every other member function of classes that employ invariant checking. These may trip assertions, which will cause the standard reporting mechanism to be invoked (e.g., a Windows dialog box). The report will indicate which invariant failed; one will then need to use a debugger or other tool to determine exactly why this invariant no longer is true.

4.4 AssertLib and the Sample Code

The X-Base library uses assertions to catch violations in input parameters, such as disallowing NULL database handles in most functions. Assertions were not used for checking anything else, as there was little else that warranted them.

Although Address Lite employs C++ classes in its GUI implementation, these are unfortunately not candidates for invariant testing. The source and header files generated by Visual Programmer provide only limited hooks for developers to add their own code without its being overwritten by future code generations. In particular, Visual Programmer does not support adding new classes to the inheritance list of a particular interface class, which makes the use of invariants-checking problematic.

4.5 How AssertLib Works

For the six tools and libraries presented in this book, we will examine their underlying implementation to show how they work. Not only will this help in better using them, but it will also highlight interesting techniques that help make them easier to use or to accomplish their basic purpose.

Assert() Macro Mapping

The _ASSERT.H header provides five definitions of the Assert() macros, each controlled by defined constants (#define). These are presumably set via a command-line switch or similar mechanism.

Below are the macro definitions for the ASSERT_LOG case from _ASSERT.H:

```
#define Assert(a)    AssertToFile(#a, a, 0, __FILE__, __LINE__)
#define AssertMsg(a, b) AssertToFile(b, a, 0, __FILE__, __LINE__)
#define AssertAction(a, b)   if (!AssertToFile(#a, a, 0, __FILE__, __LINE__)) b
#define AssertMsgAction(a, b, c)   if (!AssertToFile(b, a, 0, __FILE__, __LINE__)) c
```

Two of the five mappings are simple. If NO_ASSERTS is defined, then Assert() expands into the number zero. Since Assert() is typically used in a statement, this mapping creates a no-op statement that will be removed by an optimizing compiler. If no recognized constants are defined, then Assert() maps to the ANSI C assert() macro to use the normal processing defined by the language.

Three others use two C preprocessor tricks worthy of explanation. If either ASSERT_LOG or ASSERT_LOG_AND_QUIT are defined, Assert() maps to AssertToFile(). Similarly, if ASSERT_DIALOG is defined (and a Windows application is being compiled, as determined by the existence of the _Windows manifest constant), Assert() maps to AssertToDialog(). However, these functions take five and four parameters, respectively, while the Assert() macro only takes one.

Both functions have, as their first parameter, the token #a, where 'a' is the name of the parameter in the Assert() macro. The preprocessor translates this into the literal string representation of the 'a' expression. This is how the assertion reporting functions can show the exact text of the assertion that failed—the preprocessor provides it.

Suppose we have a macro definition as follows:

```
#define PrintAnInt(a) printf("%s = %d\n", #a, a)
```

This macro prints the text string and integer value of the expression. The results of calling the macro with:

```
PrintAnInt(rand());
```

would be:

```
rand() = 19403
```

depending on the random number generated.

Also, the final two parameters of both functions are __FILE__ and __LINE__. They are manifest constants mandated by the ANSI specification that expand to the filename and line number where the constants are used. Since these are contained in a macro definition, they provide to the assertion reporting functions the file and line where the assertion is located. If the assertion fails, these are reported to the developer to further assist in determining what went wrong.

Finally, AssertToFile() takes a boolean (zero or one) parameter to indicate whether processing is to continue (zero) or halt (one) if the assertion failed.

The AssertMsg() and AssertMsgAction() macros replace the #a with the string provided in the macro. The AssertAction() and AssertMsgAction() macros watch the return value from the assertion function, which is the value of the assertion itself. If the assertion failed and execution reaches this point (i.e., abort() was not called), then the code fragment supplied to the macro will be executed. Note that this is not done for the default use of the ANSI assert(), since it always halts execution.

Assertion Reporting Functions

As mentioned above, the Assert() macro is typically mapped to either AssertToFile() or AssertToDialog(), with the result of the assertion along with diagnostic information. ASSERT.C contains these functions, which is why it must be linked to applications that use AssertLib.

AssertToFile()

AssertToFile() writes the assertion failure to a file named ASSERT.LOG. It produces one of two actions: Either operation continues past the failure, or the program halts. The bAssertion parameter, set to zero or one by the Assert() macro mapping, determines which happens.

Below is the source for the AssertToFile() function:

```
int AssertToFile(char *pszAssertion, int bAssertion, int bQuit,
                 char *pszFile, unsigned long ulLine)
{
    if (!bAssertion) /* if assertion failed...                    */
    {
        if (pLogFile==(FILE *)0) /* ...if log file is not open */
        {
    /* open the log file and register function to close it      */
            pLogFile=fopen("assert.log", "w");
            atexit(AssertCloseFile);
        }
        if (pLogFile) /* if the file is opened...                */
        {
    /* write the info out to the file & flush buffers           */
            fprintf(pLogFile,
                    "Assertion %s in %s at line %lu failed!\n",
                    pszAssertion, pszFile, ulLine);
            fflush(pLogFile);
        }
        if (bQuit) /* if we are to exit, do so                    */
        {
            abort();
        }
    }

    return(bAssertion);
}
```

Handling the case where processing is to terminate is simple. All one must do is open the file, write the assertion failure message, close the file, and terminate the program. Here, the ANSI C abort() function is used to terminate abnormally.

Handling the situation where processing is to continue is more complicated. Developers need not call any initialization or termination functions to use the assertion library. This decision was made to simplify the usage of AssertLib; all one must do is insert Assert() statements—nothing more. It does add a challenge to maintain information from failure to failure, so they all work together.

The means of communication between assertion failures is a global variable, pLogFile. This variable, a FILE pointer, holds the handle to the opened ASSERT.LOG file, or NULL if it has not yet been opened. Global variables are dangerous to use in many circumstances and should be avoided wherever possible.

The first time through the AssertToFile() function, if pLogFile is NULL, the file is opened and an atexit() function is registered. The ANSI C function atexit() takes as a parameter the pointer of a function to call (represented by its name) when the program terminates. In this case, the AssertCloseFile() function is provided. AssertCloseFile() will simply close the open ASSERT.LOG file. By registering the atexit() function, there is no need for an explicit termination request by the developer—the compiler will call the cleanup function when needed. If the application crashes, however, it is quite likely that AssertCloseFile() will not be called.

When writing the assertion failure message to the file, the fflush() standard I/O function is also called to flush the file buffer before continuing. Under some operating systems, this will help ensure that the ASSERT.LOG file will contain some or all the assertion messages, even if the application crashes without calling AssertCloseFile().

AssertToDialog()

AssertToDialog(), available only under Windows, uses the Windows API MessageBox() function to display a dialog alerting the user of the assertion failure. Based on the user's response, the program will either continue or be halted.

Here is the source to AssertToDialog():

```
int AssertToDialog(char *pszAssertion, int bAssertion, char *pszFile,
                   unsigned long ulLine)
{
    int iResult;

    if (!bAssertion) /* if assertion failed...          */
    {
    /* build message string and pop up dialog box */
        sprintf(szAssertMessage,
                "Assertion %s\n(%s:%lu)\nDo you wish to continue?",
                pszAssertion, pszFile, ulLine);
        iResult=MessageBox(NULL, szAssertMessage,
                           "Assertion failure",
                           MB_TASKMODAL | MB_YESNO | MB_ICONEXCLAMATION);
        if (iResult==IDNO) /* if user does not want to go on    */
        {
            abort(); /* halt the application              */
        }
    }

    return(bAssertion);
}
```

The message buffer used for the assertion message is a global, szAssertMessage. Here, the global is not for failure-to-failure communication. Instead, it helps prevent stack problems. When writing programs, developers will often try to tune the stack to occupy as little memory as possible. Hence, the assertion handlers may have very little stack to operate from. Rather than allocate the 160-byte buffer on the stack, the buffer is placed in global memory instead.

The other interesting feature of AssertToDialog() is the use of the newline escape ('\n') in the message sent to MessageBox(). It is not well advertised, but MessageBox() can print several lines of text, not just one. The newline delineates the division between lines, making the assertion text more readable.

Automatic Invariants Checking

One might suppose that AssertBase, the base class for invariant-based C++ classes, has special logic to have all member functions call CheckInvariants() as they return. However, it has no associated code and only defines the protocol for invariant checking.

Instead, ASSRTCPP.H contains a line that performs the requisite "magic":

```
#define return CheckInvariants(); return
```

This highlights a powerful, and occasionally dangerous, technique of using macros to redefine C constructs. Here, the macro is changing the definition of the return statement to call CheckInvariants(). This macro works for both void returns (return;) and parameter returns (return(iValue);). It does not work for functions that lack return statements, such as constructors and destructors.

If we have a member function that looks like:

```
int SampClass::Sample1()
{
    // do something worthwhile here
    return(0);
}
```

the expanded source code will look like:

```
int SampClass::Sample1()
{
    // do something worthwhile here
    CheckInvariants(); return(0);
}
```

The beauty of this technique is that it requires no coding by the programmer. By merely having this #define in the source file, all return statements also check invariants. The danger is that **all** return statements do so. This explains why C and non-invariant-checking C++ code cannot be in the same file as the #define statement. If they were, they too would have their return statements expanded; since they would not have access to a CheckInvariants() function, the compiler would complain and refuse to create the program.

The UTCCover library also uses this technique.

4.6 AssertLib Enhancements

AssertLib could be extended in several ways to make it even easier to use and more powerful.

Additional Assertion Handlers

Presently, all handlers simply dump a message, aimed at the developer, to a file or the current display device. Dumping to a file is passive—the developer does not realize assertions were fired until after the run. Using the current display device disrupts the normal program's output. There are two major alternatives. One would be to use a debugger, with the assertion logic effectively inserting a breakpoint where the assertion failed. Another option would be to send the assertion information to another device, such as a printer or second monitor. The latter is sometimes used by developers for debugging messages, anyway.

Tool Support

Presently, the only way to place assertions in code is to inspect the program and the software contract manually and determine what assertions should be placed where. This is similar to the task of creating unit test conditions; this book later presents a tool (UTCGen) for assisting in that process. A similar tool could help identify missing assertions. It would scan a function and report any **conceivable** assertions. For example, if it saw a pointer as an input parameter, it would list a potential assertion to prove that the pointer is not NULL.

Invariants on Member Function Entry

Presently, the return macro causes the CheckInvariants() function to be called when a member function exits. Ideally, it would also check before the member function body begins. This would help track down wild memory overwrites, since the state of an object is likely to be damaged when this happens.

Track CheckInvariants() Callers

The name (or file/line number) of the CheckInvariants() that triggered an assertion failure could be reported. Presently, when an invariant fails, all that is known is what class and which invariant failed, not what member function reported the failure.

4.7 Summary

Assertions are a powerful technique for allowing the computer to audit software contracts between developers. Each rule will be checked every time, yet they can be removed for production versions to eliminate their effect on application performance.

AssertLib is an enhanced library for using assertions. It provides alternatives to the typical "standard-output-and-abort" assertions provided by the ANSI C macro. It allows assertions to be sent to a file or (under Windows) a dialog, with optional halting of the application.

AssertLib also comes with a C++ base class and associated macro for providing object invariants checking on each member function call. These check for "truths" about objects that should be correct all the time. Applying invariants checking allows assertions to reside in a single member function and to be checked on each and every member function call, except for constructors and destructors.

CHAPTER 5

Resource Management: ResTrack

Sam leaned into Chuck's doorway just in time to be greeted by a string of expletives.

"Out of memory again! I can't believe it!" Chuck screamed into his monitor, which seemed to be blithely ignoring the outburst.

Sam asked, "What's the matter?"

"I have a serious memory leak," said Chuck.

"Should I fetch a mop?" asked Sean, happening by at the time. Sean then immediately ducked the wadded-up printout Chuck threw his way.

"Why don't you cook up one of those fancy assertions to make my leak go away?" asked Chuck.

Sean said, "Maybe I can. Where's the problem?"

Chuck exclaimed, "How should I know? If I knew where it was, I would have fixed it." He then began muttering more expletives under his breath, while beginning to clean up from the program failure.

Sam and Sean left Chuck fuming over his PC. Sean explained that a "memory leak" occurs when a program, over time, allocates more memory than it releases. Eventually, the application can no longer allocate any new memory, so it crashes.

Sean had heard of tools that would watch for memory leaks and report where the memory had been allocated. Unfortunately, he had not found one that worked on the unusual operating system and compiler they were using for TurboChem.

Sam inquired, "Can you write one? Just something simple to keep Chuck from blowing his fuse again."

"Possibly," Sean replied, "I'm not quite sure how to catch every place where memory is allocated and freed. With my luck, I'll introduce a memory leak into the memory leak detection code!"

The two of them laughed as Sam went back into his office.

"Leaking memory," Sam chuckled to himself. "Next they'll want to order some spare file handles or graphics contexts or something."

5.1 Introduction

A few useful C/C++ programs are entirely self-contained and use nothing outside the C language itself. For better or worse, however, most real-world applications need external resources. These resources either provide storage (such as allocated memory), interaction (such as windows and graphics contexts), or data (such as a bitmap handle in Windows).

What makes dealing with resources difficult is that they are not magical. They do not come into existence just when we need them and evaporate when we are done with them. Actually, with C++ classes and proper use of constructors and destructors, some resources can actually be endowed with such behavior. Not all resources fit a nice C++ wrapper model, however. Moreover, dynamically allocated C++ objects themselves are resources that can be misused.

Common Problems with Resources

Common problems with external resources should be eliminated proactively, rather than waiting for them to occur. Figure 5.1 illustrates the normal flow of resources and where problems can arise.

Figure 5.1 An Application's Use of External Resources

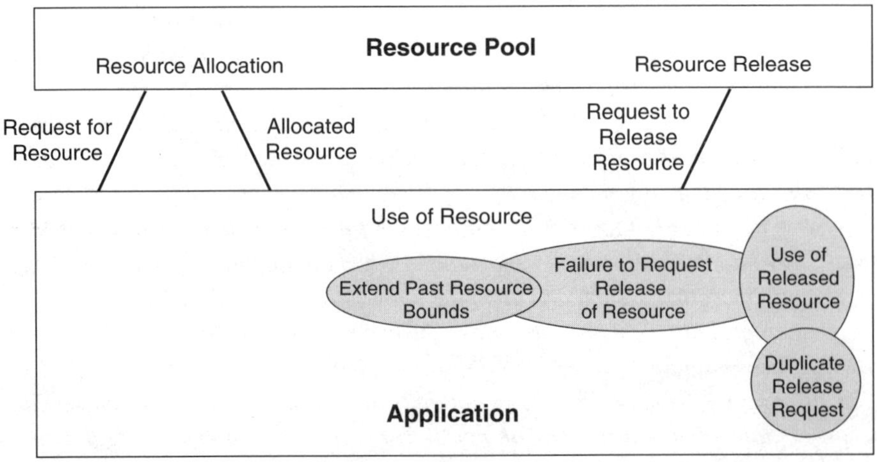

Leaks

A resource "leak" occurs when one allocates a resource and never releases it. Typically, each individual allocation is matched by an identical release later. In a leak situation, some allocations do not get freed. The result is a slow overallocation. For example, not matching ANSI C malloc() and free() calls will cause a leak of heap memory.

Typically, what eventually happens is that an attempt to allocate more of the resource fails. Some examples include:

- A call to malloc() might return the NULL pointer due to insufficient (or overly fragmented) heap space.
- A call to write()/fwrite() might return fewer bytes written than requested because of being out of drive space.
- A call to GetDC() in Windows might fail because too many graphics contexts are presently in use.

What happens next depends on the application. Some developers never bother checking whether the action succeeded. In this case, the result of the allocation failure will range from an immediate crash (such as trying to use the NULL pointer) to unusable data much later (when trying to read data unwritten due to lack of drive space).

Other developers include error handling. Then the application still terminates, but with a warning message and with some semblance of grace. Also, this guarantees that the allocation failure will be detected at its first occurrence.

There is another possibility: reduced performance. This is often the case in virtual memory systems when a memory leak occurs. Since the application uses virtual memory, it would take quite a while for the leak to exhaust the physically available room. However, since most virtual memory systems use disk space as a "swapfile" for on-chip memory, performance will degrade as extra swapping occurs. Also, the swapfile will grow, which may, in turn, lead to running out of disk space, triggering a seemingly unrelated resource allocation failure on a disk write.

Sometimes a leak may occur because one does not realize that memory was, in fact, allocated. Consider the following code fragment:

```
// TstPrintFields() prints each field in a comma-delimited record
void TstPrintFields(char *pszRecord)
{
    char *pszTemp=strdup(pszRecord); // strtok() changes string
    char *pszField=strtok(pszTemp, ", \t"); // get first field

    while (pszField)
    {
        puts(pszField);
        pszField=strtok(NULL, ", \t");
    }

    return;
}
```

This function should work nicely, especially in keeping pszRecord intact, since the strtok() function changes the input string (by placing NULLs to denote ends of tokens). However, it never frees the duplicated string (held by pszTemp). It may not be apparent, but strdup() actually returns heap memory, just like malloc() does. All it does, in effect, is a malloc() and a strcpy() to duplicate the string. Since this function fails to free the duplicated string, it has introduced a memory leak. It will work fine, but eventually the application will run out of heap space.

Duplicate Release

Sometimes, a developer will be overzealous in freeing allocated resources. It is quite easy to litter a program with release calls, figuring that leaks will be impossible. However, frequently this will lead to freeing the same resource (e.g., a memory block) more than once. A related problem is releasing something that was never allocated, such as trying to use free() on a pointer from the stack.

These are particularly subtle bugs, in that many resource management subsystems will prevent such an act from damaging their data structures. Some implementations of ANSI C's free(), for example, make sure that the pointer passed to them actually points to allocated memory before freeing it. Other implementations, however, may just go ahead and try to free the already-released pointer, which may corrupt the heap structure.

Even for resources where the subsystems have been fortified to defend against duplicate release, there is a threat of damage. The handle to the resource, which was freed earlier by the application, may have been **reallocated** already. Here, the second request to free the resource seems perfectly legitimate, in that the handle or pointer is valid. However, since the resource is actually in use by another piece of code, bugs may crop up there.

A duplicate release probably occurs because the resource was released from two different places. Most programmers would easily recognize the resource being freed twice in the same function. A variant on this is when resource release is nicely encapsulated in a single function, but then the application calls it from several spots, as demonstrated below:

```
class TstObject
{
public:
    TstObject(char *pszName);
    ~TstObject();
    void FreeResources();
private:
    char *pszObjName;
};

TstObject::TstObject(char *pszName)
{
    pszObjName=strdup(pszName); // copy; could be from anywhere
}

TstObject::~TstObject()
{
    FreeResources();
}

void TstObject::FreeResources()
{
    free(pszObjName);
    return;
}
```

Since FreeResources() is a public member function, an overzealous programmer (typically not the author) may call it before destroying the object, thereby releasing the object name (pszObjName) twice. If FreeResources() were private, this would be less likely.

Using Released Resources

Another resource management problem is a program retaining a handle to a released resource and trying to use it. For example, a pointer to heap memory might already have been freed, but the application might still try to write more data out to it.

Some types of resources have built-in defenses against such occurrences. For example, protected-memory systems **may** be able to detect somebody trying to write to released memory. However, in some places, the C kernel may provide another layer of memory management that might defeat such protections. For example, many C implementations for Windows use a single global handle for all memory allocated via malloc(); they parcel out memory held by it by using DOS-style heap managers. Here, freed memory (with respect to the application) is still owned by the C kernel, so there will not be a protected memory fault if one accesses it, as shown in Figure 5.2.

Figure 5.2 Protected Memory and Illegal Heap Access

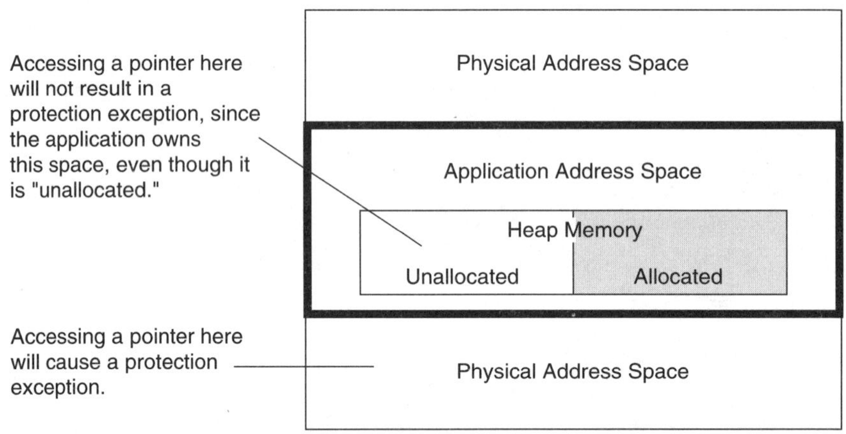

One frequent culprit in such problems is the C stack. Many variables are allocated local to a function and therefore go onto the stack. When the function returns, those variables are no longer accessible. However, if a pointer to one of them were passed to a subsystem that holds on to it and uses it later, there will be a problem. The data is released once the original function returns. However, the pointer, from a physical memory perspective, will still be valid. In fact, the proper data may be visible for quite a while, until the stack gets used again and the data is overwritten. Then the pointer will be pointing to garbage.

Suppose we rewrite the comma-delimited record printing function as follows:

```
// TstPrintFields() prints each field in a comma-delimited record
void TstPrintFields(char *pszRecord)
{
    char *pszField=TstGetFirstField(pszRecord);

    while (pszField)
    {
        puts(pszField);
        pszField=TstGetNextField();
    }

    return;
}

char *TstGetFirstField(char *pszRecord)
{
    char szScrap[256]; // used for copy instead of strdup()

    strncpy(szScrap, pszRecord, 255);
    szScrap[255]='\0'; // make sure it is NULL-delimited
    return(strtok(pszRecord, ", \t"));
}

char *TstGetNextField()
{
    return(strtok(NULL, ", \t"));
}
```

The problem here is that the buffer passed to strtok() is allocated on the stack. The strtok() function holds on to the buffer in a global variable; this is how it can return the next token when passed NULL as a string. When TstGetFirstField() returns, however, that buffer will no longer be valid, since it was stack-allocated. Now strtok() is holding on to a pointer to invalid stack space. Not only might strtok() return garbage strings (when the buffer gets overwritten with other function parameters, etc.), but since it actually modifies the buffer by inserting NULLs for string terminals, it might damage parameters or return addresses placed on the stack.

Extending Past Resource Bounds

A related danger is in using more resource than was allocated. Memory buffers are particularly prone to this problem. Especially because of the many cases where developers misuse memory in this manner, two terms have come into play to describe the types of boundary failures: underwriting and overwriting. Overwriting, that is, writing past the end of an allocated resource, is more common.

String copying and concatenation can frequently cause overwriting of a character array:

```
char szFileName[12];

strcpy(szFileName, "eightchr");
strcat(szFileName, ".ext");
```

In this case, the trailing NULL character was forgotten when the string buffer was allocated. A DOS "8.3"-style filename requires 13 characters (8 + 3 + 1 for the period + 1 for the trailing NULL). If the above code were executed, the byte after szFileName would be overwritten with a NULL.

Underwriting, while less frequent, is no less a problem. An underwrite is when one tries to work ahead of the beginning of the allocated resource. An example is writing to a memory address that precedes the first byte of the allocated block. This can sometimes happen with improper array indexes or mistakes in pointer arithmetic.

Suppose we have a situation where we are parsing a string, breaking it up into chunks. Our rule is that an exclamation point ('!') marks the beginning of the chunk, and so we want to replace the character before it with a NULL. Here is one implementation:

```
char *TstGetChunk(char *pszString)
{
    char *pszExclam;

    pszExclam=strchr(pszString, '!');
    if (pszExclam)
    {
        *(pszExclam-1)='\0';
    }

    return(pszString);
```

The problem is that a string with a leading exclamation point (e.g., "!chunk") will result in an underwrite. The strchr() function will return the beginning of the string (where the exclamation point is). The NULL-replacement statement will then back up one from the beginning of the string into unallocated space.

Sometimes, as noted above, a protection system might detect this failure. In cases where that detection fails, the effects of the overwrite or underwrite may persist. Sometimes the resource allocation infrastructure will be damaged by the action, such as a corruption of the heap nodes maintained by malloc() and free(). Sometimes the overwrite will destroy other data in the system, causing improper variable values or similar problems. If a buffer allocated on the stack is overwritten or underwritten, it might destroy return addresses or other control information. Later on, some function will wander off into the void as a result.

5.2 Dealing with Resources

Given all the above problems, the biggest challenge with respect to external resources is to manage them properly and avoid the potential dangers. There is little in standard C and C++ implementations to help. However, several techniques can help one take better care of resources.

Wrapping in Classes

One technique that was mentioned above is wrapping resource usage into C++ classes. The constructor would allocate the resource, and the destructor would free it. Member functions can provide access to the resource, using state flags to guarantee that it has been properly allocated. Also, the member functions can use parameter checking to validate that the requested actions do not violate any rules, such as writing past the end of an allocated memory block.

There are caveats, though, to using this technique. C++ objects allocated off the heap (using new) must be expressly released; this saves little over releasing the underlying resource. C++ objects allocated off the stack as local variables will automatically clean up after themselves but have a finite lifetime.

In addition, classes are only available in C++. ANSI C-only systems must use alternate measures. One approach is to use a library that mimics the ANSI C resource usage functions (e.g., malloc() and free()), while providing "sanity checking" on actions to prevent duplicate freeing, report on leaks, etc. ResTrack falls into this category.

Exception Handling and Resource Managers

One area that frequently causes resource misuse is exception handling. Typically, a function or operation will first gain access to needed data and resources, then utilize them. If there is an exception late in the resource-access phase or during actual computation, the challenge is to make sure that all allocated resources are released before returning. Since exceptions can occur almost anywhere, there are many places where the application must try to release resources. Often developers will forget this step in at least a few areas.

One solution is to create an overall resource manager that handles all allocation and release requests. If operations could log who they are when they access resources, the manager could keep track of who owns what. If an exception occurs, the operation could ask the manager to release all allocated resources. This gives the resource manager the knowledge that the developer may be forgetting—what resources were allocated. In effect, the operation is asking the manager to "roll back" the allocations, similar to asking a database manager to roll back a set of database operations.

A resource manager allocates and releases all resources used locally by a function. When the function terminates, at any point during its execution, it simply tells the resource manager to release its resources. This allows the manager to know precisely what to free. The following sample function illustrates the technique:

```
int TstUseResMgr(char *pszFile)
{
    FILE *pFile;
    char *pszInBuf, char *pszOutBur;
    unsigned long ulResUseID; // generated by resource manager

    ulResUseID=ResGetID(); // uniquely identifies resources
    pFile=(FILE *)ResGetResource(ulResUseID, RES_FILE, pszFile);
    if (!pFile)
    {
        return(TST_NO_FILE);
    }

    pszInBuf=(char *)ResGetResource(ulResUseID, RES_MEM, 1024);
    if (!pszInBuf)
    {
        ResFreeResources(ulResUseID);
        return(TST_NO_MEM);
    }

    pszOutBuf=(char *)ResGetResource(ulResUseID, RES_MEM, 1024);
    if (!pszOutBuf)
    {
        ResFreeResources(ulResUseID);
        return(TST_NO_MEM);
    }
// rest of function here
```

Similarly, when the function ends successfully, it would release the resources via ResFreeResources(). Developers do not need to keep tabs on which resources they need to free to safely exit the function—the resource manager keeps track of this instead.

5.3 Using ResTrack

ResTrack can track memory usage and problems associated with it. The following sections outline how to add it to existing C/C++ code and how to interpret the results.

Instrumenting Code

Typically, one wants to keep using the standard memory allocation functions: malloc/free, new/delete, etc. The alternative is to use memory-tracking functions directly, by replacing all calls to malloc(), etc., by their resource-tracking equivalents. Since memory tracking is frequently added after some code has been written, it is usually easier to stick with the original functions.

By including the _ALLOC.H file that ResTrack provides, the three main ANSI C memory allocation functions (malloc(), free(), and strdup()) will be redirected, via macros, to use memory-tracking versions. No other modifications are required—the C preprocessor handles the details. Note, however, that some compilers may be a bit finicky about where you include _ALLOC.H. Borland's compiler (version 4.02), for example, requires applications to include it **after** both stdlib.h and string.h.

Also note that not all memory allocation functions are automatically instrumented by _ALLOC.H—only malloc(), free(), and strdup(). The new and delete operators are discussed below. If other functions are used, such as calloc(), one must write support code to instrument them as well, using malloc() as an example. Making macro replacements for memory functions will be discussed later in this chapter.

Replacing the new and delete operators takes a little more work. The simplest approach is to add MemBase as a base class of any of the application's C++ classes. MemBase provides implementations of new and delete that use the memory-tracking functions.

Below is a sample class definition with MemBase as one of two superclasses:

```
class DbHandle : public GenericHandle, MemBase
{
public:
// rest of class here -- no other changes needed for MemBase
// however, do not re-override new and delete!
};
```

An alternative would have new and delete definitions from MemBase copied into each of the application's classes. This may seem suboptimal; after all, avoiding such reuse by "cut and paste" is why inheritance (particularly C++'s multiple inheritance) is so important. However, as will be noted below, this approach has advantages when obtaining results.

Below is a sample class definition with new and delete pasted in from the code found in MemBase:

```
class DbHandle : public GenericHandle
{
public:
// other member functions here
    void * operator new(unsigned uSize)
        { return(MemMalloc(uSize)); }
    void operator delete(void *pValue)
        { MemFree(pValue); }
};
```

Also, ResTrack uses AssertLib to register problems at runtime (e.g., detecting an overwritten buffer). By default, it will use the ANSI assert() macro, which normally prints a message and aborts the application. One of the other assertion options discussed earlier may be preferable.

In addition, the RESTRACK.C file must become part of source files for this project. Also, depending on which assertion policy one uses, ASSERT.C might be needed.

The simplest way to set up a subsystem to use ResTrack for memory tracking, therefore, is to proceed as follows:

- Include _ALLOC.H in all source files (or header files that perform memory allocation in inline functions).
- Override the global new and delete as shown previously.
- Modify the source code, if needed, to always use malloc()/free() or new/delete, rather than other functions such as calloc().
- Add RESTRACK.C to the source files for this subsystem.
- Add a call to MemDumpUnfreed() (described in the next section) as the application is ending.

The result of these steps is to track all memory allocations and releases for the subsystem. Any violations detected as the application is running will cause the program to stop immediately with an assertion violation. Also, ResTrack will report all unfreed memory blocks when the application terminates (via the MemDumpUnfreed() function).

Getting Results

Once ResTrack is monitoring memory allocation, there are several ways in which it will assist in diagnosing and debugging memory problems.

Memory Leaks

The most frequent problems detected by ResTrack are memory leaks: memory that was allocated but not freed. To list such blocks, call MemDumpUnfreed(), which writes the list to a file, RESTRACK.OUT, in the current working directory.

RESTRACK.OUT will list each item's ID number (assigned sequentially on each memory allocation), size, and allocation location, as shown below:

```
Did not free item #47 (19 bytes, from   objref.cpp line 71)
Did not free item #46 (14 bytes, from til\_alloc.h line 22)
Did not free item #4 (7 bytes, from   objref.cpp line 71)
Did not free item #3 (14 bytes, from til\_alloc.h line 22)
```

It is best to call MemDumpUnfreed() just before terminating the application. That way, one can be certain that all memory is released. MemDumpUnfreed() can be registered as an atexit() function and hence can be one of the last things called when the application terminates.

Registering an atexit() function is simply a matter of calling atexit() with the function as a parameter:

```
int main(int argc, char **argv)
{
    atexit(MemDumpUnfreed);

// rest of application goes here

    return(0);
}
```

Memory allocated by using malloc() or strdup() that was not freed is shown in RESTRACK.OUT, along with the file and line number where the offending function was called. This makes it easy to see where the block was allocated and can help identify who should be freeing it.

Memory allocated by using new and delete, however, will use the file/line number location where the new operator was implemented. For classes inheriting from MemBase, this will be a line in RESTRACK.H. This information is less useful, since it does not indicate which class was being allocated, let alone the exact line where the allocation occurred.

If one uses the included MemBase class to provide the overridden new and delete for C++ classes, all undeleted objects will reference _ALLOC.H as their location in the MemDumpUnfreed() output:

```
Did not free item #46 (14 bytes, from _alloc.h line 22)
```

This is not terribly helpful, since line 22 in _ALLOC.H is in the code for MemBase. Many different classes will inherit from MemBase, so this does not indicate exactly what was not released. The size may serve as a clue, but it is difficult to determine the precise size of a class by looking at the code.

Another approach is to copy the new and delete operators from _ALLOC.H's implementation of MemBase into each individual class. Then the RESTRACK.OUT file will show the actual location of the new operator, which should uniquely identify the class. Hence, one has a choice: simpler coding and more difficult diagnosis by using MemBase or more coding with pinpoint leak identification via the cut/paste mechanism.

Another technique for identifying memory problems is to use the ID number for each block, which is provided in the unfreed pointers log. If the program is deterministic (i.e., it always runs the same way for a given set of inputs), each block's ID number should remain constant from run to run. One can use a debugger to set a watchpoint on the line where ID numbers are assigned (in _MemMalloc() in RESTRACK.C). When the watchpoint is triggered, one can use the debugger to reach the code where that block was allocated.

Overwrite/Underwrite

When a block is freed, ResTrack checks it to ensure that the buffer was not overwritten or underwritten. If either situation is detected, an assertion will be triggered. Depending on the policy set using AssertLib, the program might continue or stop immediately.

If a block is severely underwritten (i.e., by more than two bytes), the program will always terminate, since the data for this block has been totally corrupted, which breaks the overall resource list and will prevent ResTrack from operating properly.

Using Freed Memory

ResTrack does not automatically have a means of halting a program when it utilizes a buffer that has already been freed. However, it fills all released buffers with the hexadecimal value 0xF0. If, when debugging a program, one finds a block filled with 0xF0, it is probably a released buffer. 0xF0 was selected because it is a relatively unlikely value, as opposed to NULLs or spaces.

Freeing Memory Twice

If a memory block is freed more than once, another assertion will be triggered. As with overwrites and underwrites, whether the program continues depends on the AssertLib policy.

Other ResTrack API Functions

Two other ResTrack API functions may prove useful.

MemIsValidPointer() returns true (one) or false (zero) to indicate if the provided pointer represents an allocated block. It returns false under any of these conditions:

- The pointer passed in is NULL.
- The line number for the block is the magic value 0xFEFEFEFE.
- The underwrite guard bytes are incorrect due to damage or the block's not having been allocated by ResTrack.
- The ResTrack block header is damaged.

MemCheckListIntegrity() will scan through all unfreed resources in the resource list and confirm that the ResTrack block headers are undamaged. An assertion will be triggered if this is not the case. Calls to this function can be sprinkled throughout a section of code that appears to be severely underwriting a block or otherwise damaging the ResTrack resource list.

5.4 ResTrack and the Sample Code

ResTrack was applied to the X-Base library to track memory access. Since very little heap memory is used in this library, ResTrack failed to uncover any violations. One could also extend the tool to track database handles as resources, since they are allocated and released like memory.

ResTrack was also applied to the Address Lite C++ classes. Since they could not be modified to use MemBase (because of Visual Programmer's code generation scheme), the modified versions of new and delete were pasted into them directly. This code was then removed after development and testing to create the "production" version. They could have been left in and logically removed via #ifdef constructs.

5.5 How ResTrack Works

ResTrack is a simple package, consisting only of two include files and one source file. It employs a few tricks to wring the most functionality out of the existing C framework. These tricks are described below, along with discussions of how ResTrack works as a whole.

Macros

As noted earlier, ResTrack must support the existing memory allocation mechanisms (e.g., malloc() & free()). This is done in a two-step process:

- Functions are written that do the same jobs but also enter the blocks into ResTrack's resource list. Hence, there are _MemMalloc(), _MemFree(), and _MemStrDup() to match malloc(), free(), and strdup(), respectively.
- Macros are provided that map the standard function names into the ResTrack versions.

ResTrack actually has two layers of macros. malloc(), for instance, is mapped to MemMalloc(). MemMalloc() itself is a macro that maps to _MemMalloc(). The MemMalloc() macro also includes the __LINE__ and __FILE__ manifest constants to provide the location of the allocation. This allows one to use either malloc() or MemMalloc() as memory allocation routines. Some teams may prefer the latter, to emphasize that ResTrack is being used.

Here are the macro definitions that replace the standard ANSI malloc() and related functions:

```
#define malloc(x)     MemMalloc(x)
#define free(x)       MemFree(x)
#define strdup(x)     MemStrDup(x)
```

Here are the macro definitions for MemMalloc() and friends:

```
#define MemMalloc(a) _MemMalloc(__FILE__, __LINE__, a)
#define MemStrDup(a) _MemStrDup(__FILE__, __LINE__, a)
#define MemFree(a) _MemRelease(a)
```

Memory Blocks

Most of the logic for working with memory blocks resides in _MemMalloc() and _MemFree(). _MemStrDup() simply uses _MemMalloc() and copies over the string.

When _MemMalloc() is asked to allocate a block, it actually gets a little more than the requested size. It effectively adds some room onto both sides of the "result" block, the one that was requested. This is illustrated in Figure 5.3.

Figure 5.3 Allocated Block and "Extra" Bytes

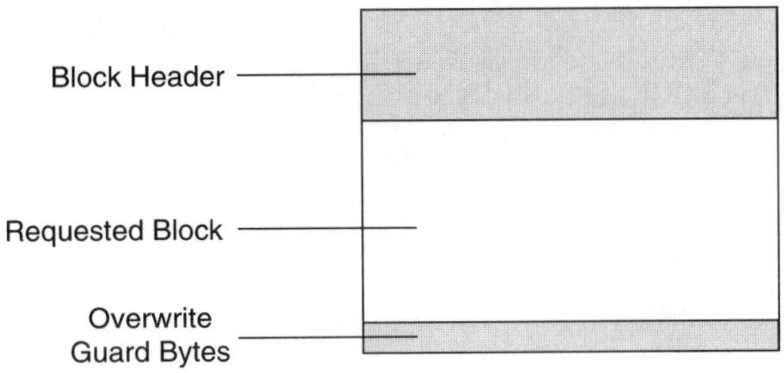

The space before the requested block is a RESTRACK_INFO structure. It tracks the information about the resource. By allocating a little more than the requested size, one can store the ResTrack information in memory, associated with the requested block, without a second allocation. In addition, there are four bytes after the requested block, which serve as an overwrite guard (described below).

The following structure (RESTRACK_INFO) defines the extra header information included with every block by ResTrack:

```
typedef struct _ResTrack {
    unsigned int uiSize; /* size of buffer          */
    unsigned long ulID;  /* ID # of buffer          */
    char szFilename[12]; /* filename of allocator   */
    unsigned long ulLine;    /* line # of allocator  */
    struct _ResTrack *pNext; /* linked list chain    */
    struct _ResTrack *pPrev;
    unsigned int uiChecksum; /* header checksum      */
    char szGuard[4]; /* underwrite guard bytes       */
} RESTRACK_INFO;
```

This block appears before the actual section of memory returned to the caller of MemMalloc(). The four overwrite guard bytes appear after it.

Guard Bytes

In a protected memory scheme, one can detect writing past owned memory via the CPU, which raises an exception when this occurs. ResTrack does not perform such an "active" overwrite/underwrite detection. Instead, it is "passive," looking for damage when the block is released and reporting on it then.

Four bytes on either side of the requested block serve as "guard bytes." When the block is allocated, they are set to known values ("AZAZ" for the underwrite guard, and the ASCII values 13 and 12 (doubled) for the overwrite guard). When the block is released, the guard bytes are checked. If the values changed, the overwrite or underwrite is reported via an assertion.

Figure 5.4 Overwrite/Underwrite Detection

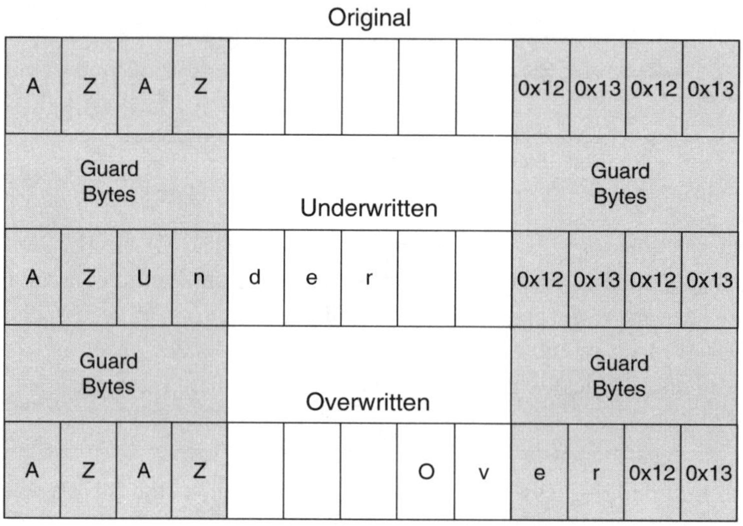

What happens if the application overwrites or underwrites with the exact values the guard bytes use? This is improbable and should not be a serious concern. At worst, an overwrite or underwrite will go undetected.

Location Tracking

Part of the RESTRACK_INFO structure is a 12-byte buffer for a filename and an unsigned long for a line number. These are provided by the __FILE__ and __LINE__ manifest constants, respectively, as supplied by the MemMalloc() macro. Twelve bytes are sufficient to hold a standard DOS filename (without the trailing NULL). Some compilers provide a fully qualified pathname in __FILE__; in this case, the last 12 characters are all ResTrack keeps.

The fact that the file and line numbers are supplied by the MemMalloc() macro explains the problem with using MemBase as an abstract class. The macro expansion occurs in RESTRACK.H, not in the application where new or delete is used.

Checksum

Many implementations of this type of memory tracking subsystem include an identifying (ID) value in the block header. It identifies the block as being one that the resource tracker manages.

If a pointer provided by the application lacks the proper ID value, then one of two things has happened:

- The application provided a pointer to storage not managed by the resource tracker (e.g., a pointer to something on the stack).
- Something has damaged memory and changed the ID value.

ResTrack works similarly, with a slight twist: Its ID value is not a constant but a checksum of the first part of the RESTRACK_INFO structure. Specifically, the checksum covers the following pieces of data:

- block size
- block ID number
- the location of the block's allocation (file and line number)

A checksum is more expensive than a constant, in that it takes extra time to compute. The advantage is that ResTrack can detect damage to more of the block header. A damaged header can still corrupt the resource list by altering the linked-list pointers.

Resource List

All blocks are stored in a doubly linked list. Each RESTRACK_INFO structure contains pointers to the previous and next blocks. A global (pHead) contains the head to the list. The list is used primarily when reporting unfreed pointers: Anything still on the list is not yet freed.

Actions

The following section describes what happens on the three major actions in ResTrack: memory allocation, memory release, and listing of unfreed pointers.

Allocate

When an allocation is requested, ResTrack uses the standard malloc() function to allocate the requested block plus the extra room needed for RESTRACK_INFO and the overwrite guard bytes. If the allocation fails, an assertion is triggered. The header is then filled out, including the checksum, with the block being added to the end of the linked list. Finally, a pointer to the requested block is returned to the application.

The following is a pseudocode outline of all actions taken during memory allocation:

```
Allocate a memory block for application use plus control header/guard bytes
Assert the allocation success
Fill in control header with block size, location, and ID number
Perform a checksum on the monitored areas and add it to the header
Fill in the guard byte values for overwrites and underwrites
Add the block to a linked list of allocated blocks
Return a pointer to the application's sub-block within the block
```

Free

When a pointer is provided with a request to free the block, a series of checks are done to confirm that it is safe, specifically:

- Is the pointer NULL?
- Was this block already freed (line number == 0xFEFEFEFE)?
- Has there been damage to the header?

Assuming that all those check out fine, the block is removed from the linked list. The requested block is filled with 0xF0, so any attempts to use it afterward will encounter erroneous yet identifiable data. Finally, the block itself is released by free().

The following is a pseudocode outline of all actions taken during memory release:

```
Assert that the pointer to be released is non-NULL
Assert that pointer does not point to a released block
Compute the checksum of the header
Assert that the computed checksum matches the header value
Assert that neither an overwrite nor an underwrite occurred
Remove the block from the linked list of allocated blocks
Set the contents of the application block to 0xF0
Set block's location (line) to 0xFEFEFEFE to indicate it is freed
Free the entire block
```

List

When a list of unfreed pointers is requested, ResTrack merely spins through the linked list and reports its contents. Blocks are added to the list on allocations and removed when released. Hence, anything still in the list when the application terminates represents leaks.

The following is a pseudocode outline of all actions taken during the process of listing unfreed memory blocks:

```
Open the output file RESTRACK.OUT
Assert the file's availability
For each entry in the linked list of pointers
    If the item is marked as freed
        Log to RESTRACK.OUT that entry is not removed from list
    Else
        Log to RESTRACK.OUT that block is not freed
    EndIf
EndFor
Close the file
```

MemBase Abstract Class

The MemBase abstract class, defined in RESTRACK.H, simply overloads the new and delete operators that use MemMalloc() and MemFree().

Here is the class definition for the MemBase C++ class:

```
class MemBase /* Base class for C++ obj tracking  */
{
public:

    /* MemMalloc() instead of malloc()   */
    void * operator new(unsigned uSize)
        { return(MemMalloc(uSize)); }

    /* MemFree() instead of free()       */
    void operator delete(void *pValue)
        { MemFree(pValue); }
};
```

The new and delete operator code, as mentioned before, can be pasted into any class to allow the MemMalloc() macro to use more useful values of __FILE__ and __LINE__.

5.6 Extending to Other Resources

ResTrack could be extended to track other resources. In general, tracking them will be simpler than tracking memory, at the cost of lower functionality. While memory access can watch for overwrites/underwrites, etc., other resources typically are only tracked for leaks.

Tracking other resources is simple to implement, following the same steps as in ResTrack itself:

- Implement functions that allocate and release the resource, while simultaneously adding and removing an entry from a resource list.

If we were to add resource tracking for files, using fopen() and fclose(), we would want to keep tabs on the following information about each file: where it was opened (file and line number), which one it is (filename), and what mode it was opened in (read, write).

Typical resource tracking functions are:

```
FILE *SampFileOpen(char *pszFilename, char *pszMode, char *pszSourceFile,
                   unsigned long ulLine)
   {
    FILE *pResult=fopen(pszFilename, pszMode);

    if (pResult) /* only track if successful! */
    {
        SampAddEntry(pResult, pszFilename, pszMode, pszSourceFile, ulLine);
    }

    return(pResult);


void SampFileClose(FILE *pFile, char *pszSourceFile, unsigned long ulLine)
{
    SampRemoveEntry(pFile, pszSourceFile, ulLine);
    /* NOTE: SampRemoveEntry() warns inside if not found */
    fclose(pFile);

    return;
}
```

The SampAddEntry() function would add information about this file to a linked list. SampRemoveEntry() would try to find a matching entry and, if successful, remove it from the list. Otherwise, it would trigger an assertion to inform the developer that an illegal close operation was requested.

There would also need to be a function, akin to MemDumpUnfreed(), that would walk the list of open files upon application termination. For each entry found there, the function would describe which file was not closed and where it was opened.

- If desired and applicable, implement other functions that wrap around uses of the resource, to confirm that a valid one is being used.

One could create implementations of functions like fgets() that detect if an illegal FILE * is used. In this case, the application would probably crash if an illegal FILE * were provided. However, an assertion typically provides more information than a typical crash, so it is useful to implement something like:

```
char *SampFileGetString(char *pszLine, unsigned int uiSize, FILE *pFile)
{
    AssertValidFile(pFile); /* macro to complain if illegal */
    return(fgets(pszLine, uiSize, pFile));
}
```

- Create macros that wrap around the resource-tracking versions of the functions and have the same names as the untracked versions.

By defining macros like the ones shown below, resource tracking on files will be almost transparent:

```
#define fopen(a, b) SampFileOpen(a, b, __FILE__, __LINE__)
#define fclose(a) SampFileClose(a, __FILE__, __LINE__)
#define fgets(a,b,c) SampFileGetString(a, b, c)
```

Resource tracking might handle other situations that differ from the normal allocate-and-release cycle. For example, Windows NT provides a named pipe service; tracking could not only watch pipe openings and closings, but also note when the pipe is closed from the other side (and therefore might not need to be freed on this side).

5.7 Future Directions

While ResTrack offers basic functionality to track memory usage, more features could be added.

Unique Resource Handles

Although ResTrack tries to watch for duplicate releases, its logic will fail if the system reuses a resource handle (e.g., memory pointer).

Many implementations of malloc() and free() employ a "first-fit" algorithm. That is, the heap manager, when asked for a block of memory, will find the first available block of the proper size. Repeated allocations and releases of the same size block will thus use just one—if it was the "first fit" at the start and no other heap operations are done, it will always be the first fit.

The following sample code illustrates how two separate malloc() calls can wind up with the same pointer and how this can confuse ResTrack's duplicate-free detection scheme:

```
char *pszFirst, *pszSecond;

pszFirst=(char *)malloc(16);
// do something with pszFirst here
free(pszFirst); // the 16-byte block is now back on the heap

pszSecond=(char *)malloc(16); // possibly pszFirst==pszSecond
// do something with pszSecond here
free(pszFirst); // BUG: Should be free(pszSecond);
```

If pszFirst and pszSecond point to the same memory block, the second free() statement will free the appropriate one, even though it uses the wrong variable. This works because of a side effect of the fact that the heap manager returned the same block twice. If, later, other heap operations are added that make pszFirst and pszSecond point to different blocks, only then may ResTrack detect the duplicate release of pszFirst.

One solution would be for ResTrack to make sure, where possible, that a resource handle is never reused. For example, if a malloc() request would return an old pointer, ResTrack could re-request the allocation, asking for an extra four bytes and provide a different offset into the overall block. This would help ensure that duplicate releases (and some subset of using released resources) would be better detected.

Resource Management Functions

ResTrack could do the actions attributed to the resource manager described above. It could keep track of who asks for what and provide a "roll-back" capability to release all allocations for an operation.

AssertLib Integration

ResTrack could be more tightly integrated with AssertLib to provide canned assertion macros. For example, suppose a C++ object is given a pointer to some memory that it intends to hold on to for a while. Since memory allocated on the stack might become invalid during the lifetime of this object, the contract stipulates that the memory must have been allocated on the heap. ResTrack could provide an assertion macro (AssertMemoryOnHeap()) that would validate that the memory is heap-based, rather than stack-based. This would use the MemIsValidPointer() function together with assertions.

5.8 Summary

Managing resources is the trickiest aspect to writing quality software in C and C++. Mismanagement can cause errors both immediately and, in the case of leaks, long afterward. ResTrack is a library that can help detect common problems with utilizing heap memory. The techniques used by ResTrack could be extended to other resources as well.

CHAPTER 6

No Code Is an Island

"No man is an island, entire of itself; every man is a piece of the continent, a part of the main."

– John Donne
Devotions Upon Emergent Occasions

As in Donne's famous verse, especially in a team development environment, no code is an island—everybody's subsystem must interact with other subsystems and with the user interface. In many situations, the era of the "lone wolf" programmer creating quality applications by himself (or herself) is long gone. Instead, it takes a team of qualified developers to create large-scale applications.

This chapter discusses the testing phases one typically goes through on a large project. It focuses specifically on unit testing, the phase dealing with testing a single subsystem.

6.1 Testing Phases

Obviously, managing several people is typically more difficult than managing one person. One must devise a pattern or mechanism to coordinate multiple developers. With respect to testing, this pattern leads to three stages, called unit testing, integration testing, and system testing.

In the sole-programmer situation, the question of "who tests what" does not occur. In a team environment, programmers work on subsystems. The programmer might test the subsystem, but this is different than testing the application as a whole.

Hence, rather than having a homogenous testing phase, one sees a hierarchy, such as:

1. Unit testing, where developers test each subsystem by itself.
2. Integration or "string" testing, where chains of related subsystems are tested as a whole.
3. System testing, where the entire application is tested through the appropriate top-level interface, typically a user interface.

Unit Testing

Unit testing focuses on a single subsystem within the application. Its goal is to ensure that the subsystem works by itself, independently of outside components. Since most subsystems are connected via an API, unit testing is usually thought of as a programming exercise. Conversely, system testing is typically thought of as dealing with a user interface.

Unfortunately, as the title of this chapter notes, no subsystem exists independently, which makes testing one by itself difficult. What typically happens is that it is outfitted with drivers and stubs. Stubs are libraries with the same interface as partner subsystems that the one being tested calls. Linking the stubs with the subsystem, rather than the actual partners, will satisfy the compiler. Similarly, a driver simulates the callers of the subsystem being tested. As will be seen in Chapter 8 on UTCLang, there are several different ways one could build a driver, with various advantages and disadvantages.

Figure 6.1 illustrates replacing partner subsystems with drivers and stubs.

Figure 6.1 Replacing Subsystems with Drivers and Stubs

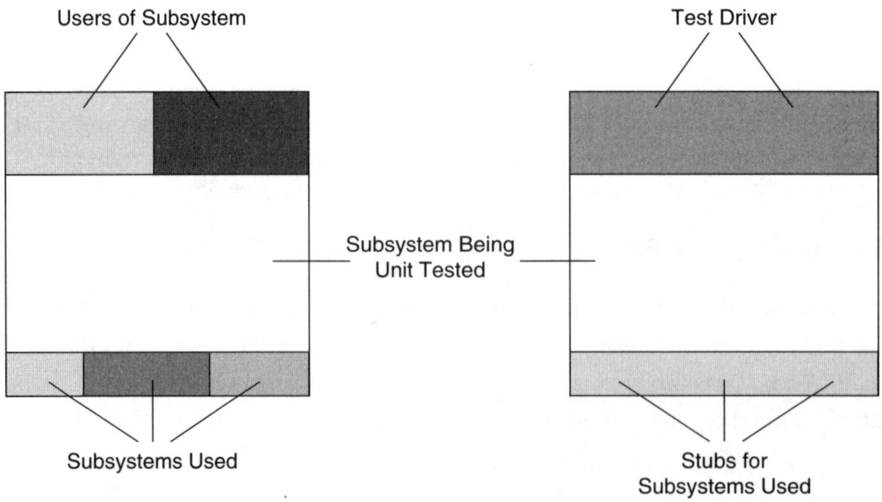

Integration Testing

Stubs and drivers are typically unsatisfactory for conducting substantial tests. For example, a stub for a database I/O library (such as the X-Base library supplied in this book), will allow users of that library to compile. However, it will not actually do the library's work. Hence, unit tests that require real database operations will be difficult to write.

What integration testing does is eliminate some stubs and drivers by linking subsystems directly. They are then tested as a whole, rather than as separate parts. This level of testing is also called string testing, since separate subsystems are "strung" together as part of the effort.

If there is a strict hierarchy of subsystems (e.g., subsystem A calls routines in subsystem B, but not the other way around), then the integration test will look like an enhanced unit test of the "higher-level" subsystem. Most, if not all, of the unit tests for the higher-level subsystem should still be valid and should still be exercised. This will show that the unit test code did not rely on "features" of the stub that the real subsystem does not provide. In addition, the integration test can exercise functionality that could not have been unit tested with only a stub in place. Figure 6.2 illustrates the procedure.

Most technologies used in unit testing still hold in integration testing. Typically, an integration test does not involve a subsystem embodying a user interface. Hence, the test will need a driver module. Similarly, for subsystems not yet merged into the integration test, stubs will be required.

System Testing

Eventually, one must combine all the subsystems, including any user interfaces, into the entire application. It, too, needs to be tested as a whole, typically in the final testing phase, called system testing. This is the final checkout performed by the project team before the software becomes available to others.

The philosophy and goals behind system testing are usually distinct from unit and integration testing. In those phases, the testers aim for narrow, technical functionality (e.g., "does this routine properly format the data for storage in the database?"). System testing, however, typically works more in the domain of the actual application. One tests whether application-level actions are properly conducted (e.g., "does the program save the address in the database, and can that address be retrieved properly?"). As later chapters will describe, this will affect considerations ranging from the tools one uses for testing to the staffing of the testing teams.

Figure 6.2 Integration Testing with Existing Drivers and Stubs

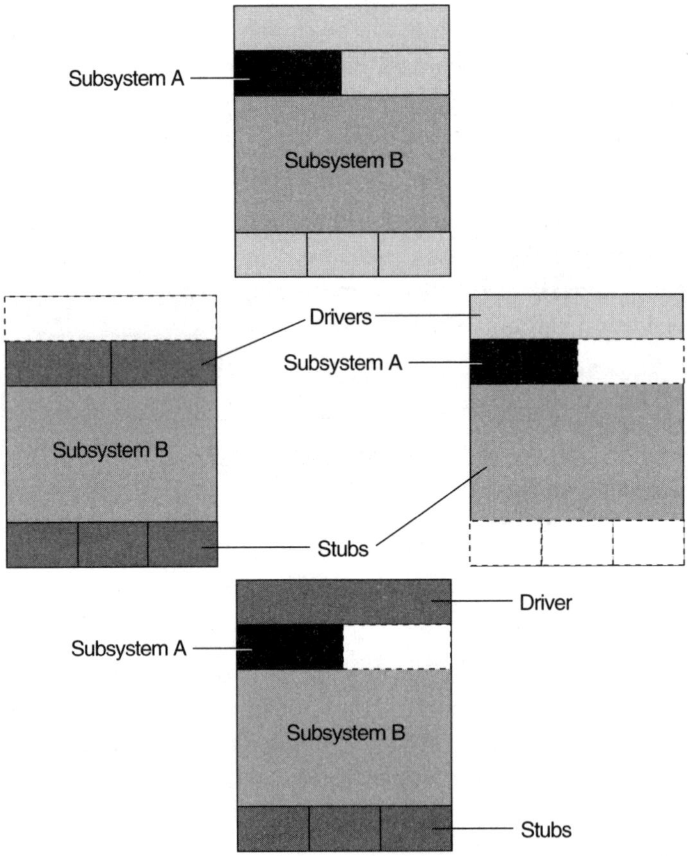

6.2 Why Not Just System Test?

One attitude that prevails in too many projects is that unit-level testing is unnecessary, that sufficient quality is possible by performing just a rigorous system test. There are many reasons why a project might want to skip unit testing:

- It takes too long.
- It is redundant given the system test; if the system test does not uncover a bug, then it does not exist.
- The developers are too busy on other tasks (such as fixing bugs) to test, and nobody else has the technical expertise.

These, of course, are in addition to the traditional reasons why not to bother with testing and quality assurance in general.

On one level, some arguments make sense, particularly redundancy. This is a variant on the "tree falling in the forest" phenomenon: If a bug cannot be triggered via the user interface, is it really a bug? Since unit tests might find bugs that system testing would not necessarily uncover, one can argue that this adds unnecessary work, both in testing and in fixing these "unreachable" bugs.

As one might expect, there are many other arguments in favor of a solid unit or integration testing phase. Some of them are outlined in the following sections.

Regression Testing

System testing involves more human interaction than does unit-level testing. At the user-interface level, system testing requires somebody to sit down at the application and put it through its paces, comparing the observed results with expected values. While session-capture tools can automate subsequent runs, it is still a human-intensive process to create the initial runs and to diagnose the changes detected by the tools.

Unit testing, on the other hand, is mostly a matter of writing code to try out the functionality of the subsystem. While this sounds time-consuming, recall that the developers are already familiar with their subsystems and have already used them in a "testing" mode (to prove that their code works at all). Techniques like using a script-based driver can further reduce the amount of complex code needed and may make it possible for nontechnical staff to assist in unit testing. Cutting down on new code provided and automating the testing process as much as possible will reduce the time required for a unit test.

Insufficient Coverage

A unit test has a well-defined domain, namely the API of the subsystem. It is almost a clerical process to determine what conditions a solid test suite should include. Coverage tools can confirm the thoroughness of the suite. Gaps can be quickly rectified by extending the suite.

In a system test, however, it is much more difficult to be certain that all areas of the program have been tested. Using coverage tools, while physically possible, is difficult. It is nearly impossible to determine what set of user interface actions are required to cause some logical branch to be taken false instead of true, for example. The combinations of subsystem interactions are just far too great by the time they reach the user interface.

Hence, one will be less certain that a system test has tried everything in the application, whereas an overlapping set of subsystem unit tests can be more certain. One cannot assume anything is unreachable just because a system test did not cause it to occur.

Reuse

Much ado has been made about reuse, especially in object-oriented environments. There is a much greater expectation that components of one application will be usable in other, future applications. This is certainly a laudable goal, especially with a well-managed central repository.

It is dangerous to assume, however, that a system test for an application will adequately test a subsystem that others would reuse. At best, the system test will adequately test the way the **application** uses the subsystem. There may be other options or combinations, however, that the application is not using; they cannot be tested at the system level. A separate unit test, however, can easily try them out.

Also, ideally, the unit tests themselves will be reusable along with the subsystem. Reused subsystems rarely remain static; the team will add extensions along the way to cover new territory and enhance existing functionality. The original unit test is a good starting point for adding tests to try this new functionality. In addition, regression testing the existing functionality is critical to ensure that the changes will not affect other users.

6.3 Who Should Unit Test?

One frequent controversy with testing is who should conduct it. As with most hotly contested issues, this one has compelling arguments for all major solutions. In the case of unit testing, the three most likely answers are the subsystem developer, another developer on the team, or a separate testing group.

Subsystem Developer

For a one-programmer project, there is no choice but to have the subsystem developer conduct the unit testing. However, even in larger projects, the author of a subsystem frequently does unit testing on it. The theory is that it will be done faster by somebody well-versed in the API.

While speed in testing is certainly an enviable goal, there is a conflict of interest in having the original developer do the unit test. Many organizations view testing as not only a product quality control exercise, but also a means of personnel quality control. Developers with high fault rates are viewed in a dimmer light than those with "better" code. In such situations, there is a strong disincentive to do a good unit test—developers will be blamed for bugs found in their work.

In projects where developers are measured by other criteria or solely on the quality of the final product, this conflict of interest may still exist from peer pressure. Nobody wants to look sloppy in front of one's colleagues; high fault rates from unit testing are embarrassing. Some groups therefore dispense with fault count collection during unit testing. The fact that a test was run and now (after fixes) executes correctly is the sole criterion for success. This eliminates the peer pressure but also loses information that unit testing might provide. Specifically, unless something is known about the actual faults uncovered, one cannot take steps to prevent them in the future via a continuous improvement program.

Peer Developers

Another approach has developers conducting the unit testing, but on each other's code. Nobody unit tests his or her own code, but instead each person works on other subsystems. This offers several advantages over having the original author do the unit test:

- Less conflict of interest, since nobody should be afraid to find faults in the code being tested.
- Cross-training in the application's inner workings, which may help later in solving problems, such as personnel leaving the project.
- If properly orchestrated, the team can think of itself as a group trying to improve the program's quality, rather than as individuals working to achieve the same end.

Of course, this approach has drawbacks. One is the opposite of the advantage to having the original developer do the testing: It will take time for peers to learn the API sufficiently to do the test. There is even the possibility that the lack of experience will result in a poorer test suite, since newcomers might miss certain aspects of the subsystem when designing it. One can overcome this problem by using appropriate tools, such as test condition generators (e.g., UTCGen) and coverage analysis tools (e.g., UTCCover).

The problem of the learning curve for peers picking up the API can be mitigated in some circumstances by a judicious selection of developer-subsystem unit test pairs. Some developers will already have experience in the API of a given subsystem, since they are the ones who use it in their own code. Having them do the unit testing will counter the experience problem. In addition, there may be a stronger desire to test well, lest some fault slip by that winds up reflecting badly on the person's own subsystem.

Another potential problem is the onset of "groupthink." Groupthink describes a situation in which the group prematurely comes to a decision solely to end the decision-making process. In testing, an attitude might still arise that "if you scratch my back, I'll scratch yours," with developers doing sketchy testing to avoid offending their peers. As with self-testing, this can be somewhat solved by using coverage analysis to ensure that unit tests are thorough.

Separate Testing Group

Outside staff could also do the unit testing. They could be developers on another project or a dedicated testing team. In this case, most conflicts of interest will be resolved, particularly if the testing team feels that it is being judged on the quality of the testing itself.

Here, however, there is a steep learning curve. At least with peer developers, even if they may not have experience in a given subsystem's API, they will at least be familiar with the application. Hence, they will know the terms, issues, and decisions that have brought the software where it is. Outsiders will lack such basic domain knowledge. While the independence of a separate testing group is quite useful, the time required to implement the tests may be more than projects can afford.

Another advantage of a dedicated testing team is that it may be better trained and better equipped (in terms of tools and techniques) than the average developer. It is often cheaper to outfit one group with a sizeable toolbox of quality-related applications than it is to provide each development team with the basic tools. The central team also will have more experience using the tools, aiding their effectiveness and productivity.

6.4 Unit Testing and Iterative Development

Iterative development is an up-and-coming methodology. It espouses a series of shorter design-development-testing phases, rather than the single-pass plan that the traditional "waterfall" development cycle employs. The work is the same: The application developed after all the iterative method's phases is the same as would have been done in a single pass under the waterfall method. The difference is mostly in organization.

Benefits of Iterative Development

Iterative development is replacing the waterfall methodology for several reasons, including the following ones.

Easier Scheduling

The waterfall methodology is marked by a series of major deadlines and concrete deliverables:

- High-level design document
- Detailed design document
- Developed system
- Tested/debugged/documented system

Everybody is working in lock-step, so one person's delay may cause the deadline to slip for everybody. Moreover, if the overall development period is long, the large blocks of time dedicated to each deliverable can lull people into a false sense of security, until they "hit the wall" as the deadline looms closer.

An iterative approach retains the first and last deliverables. The detailed design and application are developed in stages over the life of the project. The team designs parts of the system, builds and unit tests them, then goes back to designing other sections, using the knowledge obtained in previous iterations. These stages are typically more flexible. Some people can work ahead while others fall a bit behind schedule. The team can adjust the number of phases to match the length of the project, so no deadline is too near or too far away. The more frequent deadlines also help identify better where resources need to be redirected due to unforeseen difficulties.

Earlier Integration

In the waterfall approach, developers might work independently on their own subsystems for quite a while. Only toward the end of the project must they integrate their work. There invariably is trouble at integration time, as developers find discrepancies in each other's interpretation of the designs and interfaces. Waiting until near the end to integrate often means that these problems mushroom into a full-fledged crisis.

The iterative model leads to more frequent, and hence earlier, integration of components. The need to meet each phase's deadlines forces developers to work together more closely. The pain of the overall integration is therefore spread out across all the phases, rather than being concentrated at the end.

Earlier Fault Identification

When working independently, many developers try out their subsystems to prove that they work in general and in a few limited cases. Only when the subsystem is unit tested or integrated with another component are most bugs discovered. The testing or other users will exercise the subsystem in ways the author might not have expected; they will also use it more frequently and thoroughly than the quick-and-dirty tests the developer typically runs.

The waterfall method, once again, concentrates all this near the end of the development period. Neither unit testing nor integration occurs until late in the process. Faults then get discovered by the bushel in some cases, grinding everything to a halt as developers scramble to fix the problems.

In an iterative approach, the team performs unit and integration tests at every phase. This will uncover bugs over time, rather than all at once. Since the developers will be more familiar with the faulty code (as they will have written it not long ago), it should also be slightly faster to fix the bugs. As with the integration troubles, the pain is spread over a longer time, making a crisis less likely.

Parallel Work

With the waterfall method, if integration does not occur until late, the application itself does not really exist until the development period is nearly finished. This is fine from a technical sense, but does mean that nobody can get their hands on it until late. Especially if earlier deadlines slipped, this puts added pressure on those who must write the documentation or the packaging.

With the iterative method, documentors can gain access to the application earlier. Although they must leave some sections until the very end, they can do a reasonable amount of work in advance. Similarly, those responsible for packaging the application can start working on early releases to get a feeling for what will be required.

Unit Testing

In an iterative environment, unit testing is performed after every phase. This takes two forms:

- Adding tests to cover new functionality added during this phase.
- Regression testing the unit tests from previous phases to confirm that they still work, updating them as needed to reflect modifications in the subsystem.

As noted above, this will give more constant and earlier feedback to developers about the quality of their subsystems. Rather than waiting until the end and finding all the problems in one shot, the iterative cycle uncovers them piecemeal as development progresses. For problems that represent major design flaws, this allows the entire team to react in a planned fashion, rather than causing a crisis near the final deadline.

Frequently, unit-level testing done in iterative development would be more strictly defined as integration testing. Subsystems, rather than connecting to stubs, connect to their live partners. Stubs would be used only where a higher-level subsystem needs functionality to be implemented in a later phase at the lower level. This provides the benefits of earlier subsystem integration as noted above.

In this plan, rapid regression testing is crucial. Developers will get bogged down if running regression tests is a manual process. It is important to get the testing procedures in place in the first phase, to allow results to be captured and (where possible) automatically compared to master copies. Fortunately, unit testing infrequently involves user interface elements, so test drivers can more conveniently capture output as text files, binary data files, etc., for easier automated comparison.

6.5 Unit Test Phase Structure

As with any other aspect of application development, one cannot simply view unit testing as an ad hoc affair. A scattershot approach might be sufficient in some cases. The cost of a weak unit test phase is a more expensive system test phase, increasing overall project time and costs.

There are three traditional steps in unit testing: planning, test execution, and results analysis. A fourth one, applying the results for continuous improvement, is not part of the normal flow. However, it will help improve the overall quality control **process** to provide greater odds of better quality in future work.

Planning

Unit testing, as noted before, takes the form of additional code. Just as one must design an application, one must design a unit test to write this code.

One way of creating a test plan is to turn unit test conditions into test cases. Test conditions outline individual states or attributes to be tested (e.g., ensure that the function properly handles a zero-length string as input). Test cases combine conditions into implementable scenarios, similar to detailed designs. These cases are then written as unit tests, using the appropriate tools or frameworks.

Execution

Once tests have been written, they must be run to determine if the subsystem works properly. Hence, the unit test must not only try the test conditions but also report any unexpected results. Either the unit test itself can determine incorrect values, or it can simply output all data and allow the tester to determine what is right.

Important as executing unit tests is, even more important is being able to execute them repeatedly over time. This approach, called regression testing, takes the position that once one has code that determines program correctness, one might as well leverage it as much as possible. A regression test will compare the results from a known successful run against one using a modified subsystem, reporting all differences. The differences either indicate latent bugs in the subsystem code or a need to update the unit tests (either the test code or the master set of "correct" results).

Analysis

Analyzing the unit test results consists of two phases: success and coverage. The obvious analysis is to determine if the tests succeeded on all counts. Failures of specific test conditions indicate a fault in the code, the test plan (i.e., a wrong result expected for the condition), or the unit test. In any case, the team needs to determine the reason for the reported failure and correct the flawed component.

The other part of analysis is determining if the unit test suite really met its goal of covering all possible ways in which the subsystem could be used. It is likely that the initial version of the unit test will not try out some situations. Hence, one must somehow measure the coverage of a unit test suite to see if it really did exercise the subsystem thoroughly. This concept will be discussed in more detail in Chapter 9 on UTCCover.

Continuous Improvement

Most projects stop after the basic analysis. That will allow the team to determine what they need to do to complete the application being tested. Unfortunately, this limits the ability of the results from this unit test to assist in future development efforts.

A better approach is to use the results of the unit test not only to identify bugs, but also to identify how they were created. Perhaps coding-time quality steps can eliminate their source. For example, if several faults involve global variables, perhaps future projects can minimize their use or arrange for special code reviews to help find misuses earlier.

What such analysis will do is improve the development process. In an iterative methodology, this might even help the current project later. At the least, the knowledge obtained from the testing process, if properly retained by the organization as policies or plans, will make subsequent projects go more smoothly.

6.6 Summary

Testing is not a homogenous activity but, instead, a coordinated series of acts designed to detect problems at the micro level (unit testing) and macro level (integration and system testing). In particular, a strong unit testing program can isolate many faults earlier, especially if the project is using an iterative development methodology. Unit testing can not only improve the quality of the current application, but by analyzing the results to see how faults can be prevented during development, it can improve future projects as well.

CHAPTER 7

Test Conditions: UTCGen

Sam dropped by Randy's office. Randy was a newcomer to the TurboChem project and to Midearth Chemicals. He was just out of college, and TurboChem was his first professional programming job.

"I came by to see if your unit test plan is ready," Sam said.

"Uh, yeah. Here it is," replied Randy, handing over a piece of paper.

Sam looked somewhat dumbfounded at the single-sheet test plan. "Wait a minute, you only have eleven test cases here!"

"That's right," Randy said. "You were expecting more?"

"A lot more! You have more than eleven API functions; you should have significantly more test cases! Not everything could have possibly been covered in just these cases," exclaimed Sam.

"But I don't know what else to test," said Randy. "It's not like they teach testing at the university. Besides, you've got my word that this stuff works!"

Sam hesitated a moment. "Not that I doubt your programming ability, but we need proof that everything in TurboChem works as advertised."

"Ok. What else should I be testing?" Randy asked, a slightly surly tone entering into his voice.

Sam sighed. Since Randy had not gone through the first two releases of TurboChem, he was not familiar with its past quality problems.

"Well, I don't know. Just come up with more!" Sam said before exiting Randy's office.

As Sam returned to his own office, he wondered how one could determine what else to test in Randy's subsystem...

7.1 Introduction to Test Conditions

Software testing always involves organization. At the low end, a lone developer might just scratch out a list of things to test. At the high end, a large software product might have an entire set of deliverables for the quality process. They would include everything from an initial quality plan through formal unit, integration, and system test plans.

All test plans must answer two main questions:

- What is to be tested?
- How will the test be created and executed?

In many ways, a test plan resembles a detailed design—it indicates what code (or scripts, etc.) should be written to test specific functions. Both should be written to a similar level of detail. The test plan must specify enough to write the tests but not so much as to limit the ways in which they can be written.

Test plans and detailed designs typically share a common structure. A detailed design breaks down an application into subsystems, which are further divided into smaller units (functions, classes, roles, etc.). The design fully describes the underlying units, specifying their purpose, inputs, and outputs.

Similarly, test plans must provide a structure, both for implementing the tests themselves and for determining if they exercise the system adequately. One way to create this organization is by creating test conditions, followed by grouping them into test cases.

A test condition is a statement of a specific phenomenon to be tested. Well-written conditions must meet the following criteria:

- Conditions must be concrete statements of what is to be done and what is to happen. The condition must indicate both the input values and the expected result. Otherwise, how do you know if it has been met?

You may recall an API function in the X-Base library for XblOpen():

```
int XblOpen(XBL_HANDLE *phHandle, char *pszFilename);
```

One must have conditions that determine if this function works properly. One could state a condition as "Open a file," but that does not give a test code implementer any idea of how to do it. A more concrete form would be "Open a file by calling XblOpen() with a valid XBL_HANDLE and filename; the result should be zero."

- Conditions must specify a single action, not multiple (albeit possibly related) actions. Not only would multifaceted conditions be more difficult to test, but they also may mask hidden correlations between outcomes that might result in inefficient testing. Ideally, each condition should represent a single possible failure point—there should not be many ways to cause a condition to fail.

The X-Base library is record-based, in that it retrieves data one record at a time. One might decide that a condition should be "Read two records from an open file." This condition divides into several independent conditions: opening a valid file, reading the first record from an open file, and reading the second record. Each is an easily visible action using the API, and each can fail independently.

- Conditions can be positive (this situation **must** occur) or negative (this **must** be prevented from occurring). A single condition cannot be both. A negative condition is testing the subsystem's error handling.

For the XblOpen() function, one cannot have a single condition that demonstrates a valid filename and an invalid XBL_HANDLE (e.g., passing a NULL pointer). If the handle is invalid, the API function should return an error code, so this is a valid test condition ("Pass in an invalid XBL_HANDLE to XblOpen(), which should return an error code"). However, we cannot say anything about XblOpen()'s handling of the valid filename—we do not **know** if it even examined the filename before returning the error code.

After the test conditions have been created, the next step is to combine them into test cases. Cases are "detailed designs" for individual tests. There are guidelines for combining test conditions to create test cases (e.g., at most one negative condition per case). Some of these will be described later.

Choosing Unit Test Conditions

To have a solid testing plan, one must create a thorough set of test conditions. Poor conditions, or too few, will produce a weak plan. Hence, the process of identifying conditions is important. Some philosophies and techniques for finding conditions for unit testing are described below.

Valid and Invalid Values

When creating unit test conditions, one typically starts with the programming interface, either a C API or a set of C++ class definitions. Based on documentation, a software "contract," or a detailed design, one knows the expected values for each parameter to a given function. Obviously, the test conditions should include valid values for the functions to prove that they work as advertised.

One question that arises is whether a single valid value for each parameter is sufficient. For example, consider the ANSI C abs() absolute value function, which simply takes a number as a parameter. Can one safely use a single test case to prove it works?

Whether this approach works depends on what the function does and what the expected results are. If the results are the same for all valid values, then testing more than one value is technically superfluous. One would expect all values to either fail or succeed together. If, however, there are distinct types or values of results based on the input parameters, then one needs separate conditions for each type. This technique is called *equivalence partitioning*.

One must also recognize that there is an implicit partition in nearly every function's input space, that of invalid values. If defensive programming is used, every function should accept any physically possible input value (raising an exception if it is outside the contracted-for range). In this case, one needs test conditions to prove that such exceptions are raised. If, on the other hand, the contract assumes valid input parameters, then such conditions are not needed, since they will prove little. However, in this situation, the functions should use assertions to detect invalid parameters, so separate testing should not be needed.

The X-Base library contains an API function that returns the contents of a field in a string:

```
int XblGetFieldAsString(XBL_HANDLE hHandle, unsigned int uiFieldNum,
                        char *pszBuffer);
```

There are two partitions on the uiFieldNum parameter: a legal field number or an illegal one. An illegal number is one greater than the number of fields in the record. Two test conditions should be written to test each possibility. There should also be separate conditions for legal and illegal handles and buffers.

Boundary Conditions

An extension of the above technique recognizes that a frequent source of errors is in handling boundary conditions. A boundary is a place where the behavior of a function changes, based on an input value. Boundary conditions explicitly try those situations, since one frequently finds faults there.

One key boundary is the one between valid values and invalid ones. If a function requires a positive integer as an input value, testing 1 (being the smallest positive integer) might uncover a problem.

Below is a function with invalid defensive programming:

```
void TstPoorFunction(int iValue)
{
    // contract states that iValue must be positive
    if (iValue <= 1) return(ERR_INVALID_PARM);

    // rest of function goes here
}
```

Here, the comparison should be <= 0 (or < 1) to detect a non-positive integer. If the test suite does not try an input value of 1, it will not detect this fault.

Random or Iterated Values

Some people believe that mere equivalence partitioning is too weak—several values within a given partition should be tested. The argument goes that testers might not be able to identify precise partitions. Adding more tests might uncover new hidden partitions and, hence, more faults. Critics of this approach point out that tests and test conditions are typically time-consuming to create and so the minimum standard is appropriate.

The key criterion for determining if more than one test should be run is how cheaply multiple conditions can be met. There are three common approaches:

- Using a random set of valid values; the number of conditions is determined by how many can be executed by a test program in a reasonable period of time.
- Iterating over all possible values, when the range is finite and countable (e.g., numbers from 1 to 10).
- Manually creating a manageable number of additional tests, just as the ones for the different partitions and boundary conditions were produced.

The number of conditions provided by the first two techniques is large or unknown in advance. Two ways to determine the correctness of the output of these tests are:

- Have the tester manually validate all results. This is a time-consuming process and therefore expensive.
- Have an independent implementation of the same operation. The tests can be applied to the two implementations; if they produce different results, this can be reported to the tester for manual validation. The difficulty with this approach is that it assumes the implementations have distinct faults, since the same fault in both may cause both to report the same erroneous result.

Test Condition Catalog

All the above techniques imply that the developer knows how to create test conditions from an API or class interface specification. Testers will have varying levels of ability in this area; even the best are likely to miss conditions occasionally. This is merely an indication of human fallibility—if people were infallible, there would be no faults to test for, anyway.

One way of augmenting the manual approach to finding conditions is to use a test condition catalog. Such a catalog lists likely types of conditions, grouped by parameter types or common programming data structures (e.g., linked lists). When a testers examine a given function, they can use the catalog to help find likely conditions to include.

The following are conditions one would find in a test condition catalog for dealing with a queue:

- Retrieve from an empty queue.
- Retrieve from a queue with exactly one element.
- Retrieve from a queue with several elements.
- Retrieve an element from the middle of a queue with several elements.
- Retrieve from a queue at the same time as an element is being added to it.

Not all conditions will be valid in all situations. Retrieving from the middle, for example, is useful only if the API supports random queue access. The developer using the catalog must make a reasoned judgement as to which conditions are appropriate.

The last example is a *race condition*, something that might happen in a multithreaded environment if two threads try to manipulate the queue at the same time. If the application is single-threaded, the problem cannot occur.

Any test condition catalog will not be all-inclusive: There may be other conditions (particularly boundary ones) specific to a given implementation that will not appear. On the flip side, there may be suggested conditions that are irrelevant to the particular function.

Black Box versus White Box

Each condition-generating mechanism described above works only with a published specification, either in text form (e.g., a detailed design) or in a programming language (e.g., a C/C++ header file). This is called "black box" testing, in that each unit is treated as a black box—only the external interface is known.

The theory here is that if we try valid inputs and get valid outputs, the exact implementation is arbitrary. While this is technically true, it relies on perfect equivalence partitioning (i.e., every input that yields a significantly different output is tried). Since, as noted, nobody is perfect, this theory can fail in practice.

The alternative approach, "white box" testing, says that one should generate conditions not only from the specification, but also from the implementation itself. Testers should peruse the source for the subsystem and add conditions based on it.

Suppose we have the following function from UTCCover:

```
long UtcLogEvent(UTC_EVENTCODE iEvent, long lValue,
                     char *pszFile, unsigned long ulLine)
{
    if (!pLogFile && !bAtExitDone)
    {
        pLogFile=fopen("utccov.log", "a");
        atexit(UtcCloseLogFile);
    }

// other work done here

    return(lValue);
}
```

Black-box conditions will only look at the prototype for UtcLogEvent(). However, there are two significant white-box conditions: testing the function when bAtExitDone is both true and false. This global controls the opening of the log file and registration of the atexit() function. The function might fail on one of those conditions.

This technique, in turn, assumes that the testers are literate in the application's programming language. If a tester cannot read C, he or she will not be able to figure out what appropriate white-box cases are. Since the unit testers are often the programmers themselves, this is an infrequent concern.

Also, this technique will balloon the number of conditions generated, which will require more test cases to implement, thereby increasing the cost (in time) of testing. However, it is more likely to find bugs than a black-box search alone.

Appendix C contains a list of test conditions generated for the X-Base database access library.

Developing Cases from Conditions

Given a list of conditions (like the one shown above for the sample X-Base library), the next step is to combine them into test cases. Such cases are real-world descriptions of how to exercise test conditions and determine if they are truly met by the subsystem. They are then turned into code that physically implements the test.

One could argue that each condition should be its own case. Conditions might interact with the code that implements them. Allowing multiple conditions in a case might cloud the testing. On the other hand, such interactions might disclose a bug that would not have been found if each were tried independently. The goal is to uncover the most software faults possible.

One rule of thumb is that there should be at most one negative condition per test case. Moreover, a case should not try any conditions following a negative condition. The reasoning behind this is that a negative condition, which triggers error handling, is a de facto violation of the software contract. Anything that happens after it, beyond the error handling itself, is typically uncertain. Results from conditions tried after a negative condition are suspect because of breaking the agreement. The exception to this rule is if the state of the system after a negative condition is itself contracted for—then test cases **should** attempt to prove that the application upholds this part of the contract.

The other rule of thumb is that fewer is better, when it comes to test cases. Obviously, the cases need to try all the conditions. Depending on how one combines conditions, there might be more or fewer test cases than in another combination. It is better to have fewer cases overall. One reason is that the more complex test cases tend to uncover more hidden bugs, as noted above. The other reason is much more pragmatic: Fewer test cases typically reduces testing costs.

Appendix C also lists the test cases for the X-Base library.

7.2 Using UTCGen

Unlike AssertLib and ResTrack, UTCGen is a tool, not a library. An application need not be modified to use it. Hence, the steps to using UTCGen are to build its executable, prepare the input files for it to examine, run it, then peruse the results. Instructions on building UTCGen are in Appendix A. The remaining steps appear in the following sections.

Preparing Input Files

UTCGen expects an ASCII text file as input, containing only ANSI-style function prototypes for the subsystem's API. These prototypes can be obtained in two ways:

- If they are already used in a header file or source file, they can be extracted from there.
- One can use a tool designed to create them from C source.

Note that UTCGen cannot parse C++ class definitions to reach member functions. Hence, one needs MKPROTO or a similar tool to create ANSI C-style function prototypes for C++ member functions from the source file.

Prototype Extractor: MKPROTO

On the enclosed diskette is the source code and DOS executable for MKPROTO, a tool for taking C source and creating ANSI-style function prototypes. It scans through the input file, identifies all C functions it contains, and emits prototypes for them. UTCGen can use MKPROTO's output as input.

The original version of this program was written by Eric R. Smith. It was modified to create prototypes for C++ member functions.

To use MKPROTO, simply provide the name of the source file. It will send the resulting prototypes to C standard output, which can be redirected to a file. For example, to take LIST.CPP and generate function prototypes for it, simply execute the following at a command prompt:

```
MKPROTO LIST.CPP > LIST.PRO
```

LIST.PRO will contain the prototypes.

The only other constraint on the prototypes is that a space must precede the variable name for each parameter.

Frequently, one might have the '*' denoting a pointer directly touching the name of the function parameter, as shown below:

```
int EXPORT XblOpen ( XBL_HANDLE *phHandle, char *pszFilename);
```

Unfortunately, UTCGen presently cannot handle this input and properly recognize the type. One must have function prototypes with at least one space between the entire type and the parameter name:

```
int EXPORT XblOpen ( XBL_HANDLE * phHandle, char * pszFilename);
```

MKPROTO properly embeds this space.

Running UTCGen

Given the prototype file, running UTCGen is simply a matter of providing the file name. Since UTCGen sends its results to standard output, one can redirect them to a file or the *more* command.

The only restriction on UTCGen is that it must be able to find the CATALOG.TXT test condition catalog. If the catalog appears in the current working directory UTCGen will use it. Otherwise, it will look in the paths set in the UTCGEN environment variable for this file. If it cannot find CATALOG.TXT, UTCGen will run without generating any test conditions.

To generate the unit test conditions for the X-Base library, execute a command like:

```
UTCGEN XBASE.PRO > XBASE.CND
```

This will create a test conditions file, XBASE.CND. The command shown above assumes three things:

- UTCGen's executable is in the execution path (e.g., in the PATH environment variable on DOS and OS/2) or in the current working directory.
- UTCGen's catalog is in the current working directory or in one indicated by the UTCGEN environment variable.
- XBASE.PRO, a file containing the function prototypes for the whole library, exists. To create it, either modify DBFAPI.H to include only prototypes or apply MKPROTO to the library source files and concatenate the results.

Using UTCGen's Output

The output file generated by UTCGen lists all function prototypes found in the prototype file. For each parameter, the suggested test conditions, based on CATALOG.TXT, are listed.

The following is a fragment of the test conditions generated by UTCGen for the X-Base library, specifically for the XblOpen() function:

```
Function: int EXPORT XblOpen ( XBL_HANDLE * phHandle , char * pszFilename )
    Parameter: phHandle
        Try a NULL pointer
        Try a non-NULL pointer
        If used as an array, provide one-element array
        If used as an array, provide multi-element array
    Parameter: pszFilename
        Try a NULL pointer
        Try a non-NULL pointer
        If used as an array, provide one-element array
        If used as an array, provide multi-element array
        Try a zero-length string
        Try a one-character-long string
        Try a string longer than 1 character
```

Not all conditions UTCGen reports will make sense. The person implementing the unit test must use only the appropriate conditions. On the flip side, UTCGen will not suggest all conditions that should be applied. The tester will still need to examine the code and add more conditions before creating test cases.

Since the pszFilename parameter in XblOpen() is used as a string, not an array (per se), the "if used as an array" suggested conditions do not make sense. In fact, they are effectively superseded by conditions for various string lengths.

Also, UTCGen will report at most 32 recommended conditions per parameter. This is enough for most purposes.

7.3 UTCGen's Test Condition Catalog

UTCGen expects to find a file, CATALOG.TXT, in the current working directory or in the one pointed to by the UTCGEN environment variable. It is the test condition catalog: a listing of data types and the conditions associated with them. It is a simple ASCII file and can be edited with any text editor.

The file consists of lines of the form: regular expression, condition text.

Regular Expressions

A regular expression is a string that serves as a pattern against which to match strings. For example, in MS-DOS, one frequently uses "wild cards" when managing files. Here, a string like "*.*" means "match any number of characters, then a period, then any number of characters." This is a simple regular expression.

Regular expressions are, in effect, a compact language identifying the means by which to match strings conforming to a certain pattern. Due to their terseness, they are difficult to read for those who do not use them regularly. However, several tools use them, such as the popular Unix utility *grep*, which takes a regular expression and hunts for strings in files matching it.

The regular expression indicates the types that should have this condition. The text of the condition can be any ASCII string, including whitespace and punctuation. Its length, however, cannot exceed 224 characters. There can be at most one regular expression/condition pair per line. Blank lines are supported, however, to divide catalogs into logical sections. Also, lines beginning with a semicolon are treated as comment lines and are ignored.

Here is a sample listing from a fragment of a UTCGen CATALOG.TXT file:

```
; Strings
*char~\*, Try a zero-length string
*char~\*, Try a one-character-long string
*char~\*, Try a string longer than 1 character
; Files
FILE~*, Try a file in the current working directory
FILE~*, Try a file in a different directory
FILE~*, If reading, try a file that is too short
FILE~*, If writing, try a drive that is too full
; Variable arguments
..., Try no parameters
..., Try one parameter
..., Try several parameters
va_list, Try no parameters
va_list, Try one parameter
va_list, Try several parameters
```

Since UTCGen looks in the current working directory for CATALOG.TXT first, a team can maintain separate catalogs for separate subsystems, if desired.

Regular Expression Syntax

The regular expressions employed by UTCGen may contain any character except a comma, which is used to delineate the expression and separate it from the test condition. Since C data types cannot have commas in them anyway, this should not pose any difficulty.

Table 7.1 outlines the regular expression pattern-matching characters available in UTCGen's parser.

Table 7.1 Regular Expression Character Interpretations

Character	Meaning
*	Match 0–n characters of any type
?	Match any single character of any type
[a-b]	Match any single character in the range a–b
~	Match 0–n whitespace characters
~~	Match a tilde (~)
\	Treat the next character as a literal, not a regular expression character

Adding Entries

Adding custom entries to CATALOG.TXT is fairly simple. The biggest challenge is determining what test conditions to try. This knowledge mostly will come from experience in using the data type, or ones like it. An existing test condition catalog, like the one found in Spuler [14], can serve as a source of ideas.

Here are test conditions one might add if one uses the List class provided in this book:

- Test with an empty list.
- Test with a list with one element.
- Test with a list with several elements.
- Test with different types of List subclasses.

The next step is to determine the regular expression pattern that will recognize the desired type. UTCGen will handle keywords such as const and far. The pattern must therefore simply match the base type name, plus any other valid characters (such as asterisks denoting pointers). It may take a few patterns to cover all cases, since the parser has no mechanism for handling "this OR that" cases.

For the List class, one could pass a list by value (using a copy constructor), by reference, or by pointer. The regular expressions would look like:

```
List~\* "for list pointers"
List~& "for list references"
List "for lists directly"
```

Depending on naming conventions, one can make this simpler. If all subclasses of List end in "List", and if no conditions differ among the three types shown above, one could have a single expression:

```
*List~* "covers all three"
```

The asterisk preceding the "List" token supports subclasses that use "List" as a suffix.

The final step is purely clerical: adding entries to CATALOG.TXT for each test condition for each regular expression.

Note that there is a crude form of "inheritance" in CATALOG.TXT. Every pattern is checked against every type, so multiple patterns might match a given data type. For example, all pointers match the supplied pointer regular expression, so they will get the conditions attached to it.

7.4 UTCGen and the Sample Code

UTCGen is designed for testing subsystems, not user interfaces. Hence, it is applicable to the X-Base library but not to Address Lite. Many test conditions were identified by UTCGen for the X-Base library; these are outlined in Appendix C. Those conditions were then incorporated into the unit test suite for the library, to help ensure that it worked properly. In many cases, the test outlined failures, typically due to improper defensive programming. Some invalid values were not checked in the API functions, causing crashes or other failures. These, of course, have been corrected for the version on the disk.

7.5 How UTCGen Works

UTCGen consists of three components:

- A command-line interface
- A library that processes function prototypes and determines the appropriate test conditions
- A regular expression parser, used by the UTCGen library

This division allows flexibility in constructing test case generation tools. For example, one can replace the command-line interface with a graphical interface without needing to change the rest of the code. This distinction between the model and the view is an increasingly popular metaphor for application development.

Interface

The command-line interface (UTCGEN\UTCGEN.C) provides a means for specifying the function prototypes and displaying the results. It obtains the prototypes from files specified when invoking UTCGen. In the main() function, each file is read into memory and processed in turn.

Each prototype is extracted from the file, using the semicolon following it as a delimiter. The prototypes are then given to the UtcProcessFunction() library API, which determines the appropriate test conditions. This information is represented by a handle (UTC_HANDLE). The interface knows nothing of its contents; only the library can manipulate them.

After letting the library process the prototype, the interface displays the results on standard output. This can be redirected by using the operating system's command processor to a file, by piping to another program, etc. A graphical interface would send the results to a text pane, perhaps with an option for saving as a text file or printing.

Library

The bulk of the work is done in the function prototype processing library (UTCGEN\UTCGENL.C). It includes several API functions available for interfaces to use:

- UtcProcessFunction(): Given a function prototype as a string, creates a handle that contains the results of the processing. All other API functions take this handle as input.
- UtcFreeHandle(): Releases the storage held by the handle created by UtcProcessFunction().
- UtcGetFunctionName(): Returns the function name from the handle.

- UtcGetParmCount(): Returns the number of parameters in the function prototype, represented by the handle.
- UtcGetParmName(): Returns the name of a parameter, given a handle and the index.
- UtcGetConditionCount(): Returns the number of conditions associated with a handle/parameter pair.
- UtcGetCondition(): Returns the text of a particular condition, given a handle, parameter number, and condition number.

A C++ implementation of this library would have a UtcFunction object that contained a collection of UtcParameter objects, each holding a collection of UtcCondition objects. Member functions would replace the API functions shown above. The handle would be the UtcFunction object itself. C was chosen over C++ here for greater portability, since C++ compilers are not yet available on all platforms.

The library assumes prototypes of the form:

```
<return type> name(<type> <name>, <type> <name>, ...);
```

The library uses various fixed points (opening and closing parentheses, commas) to extract the function names, data types, and parameter names. A more robust implementation might use *lex* and *yacc* or other tools designed for parsing strings. However, for the limited purpose of this tool, an ad hoc system is sufficient.

Regular Expression Parser

The regular expression parser is separated into its own source module (REGEX\REGEX.C), since it is usable outside UTCGen. There is a single API function, RegMatch(), which takes four parameters:

- The string to match against a pattern
- The pattern, containing literals and regular expression "wildcards"
- Two pointers to strings (char **), which hold the start and end of the last part of the string to be matched with a 0–n (*) wildcard

RegMatch() returns a boolean (1=success) indicating whether the string matches the supplied pattern.

While many regular expression parsers involve a finite-state machine or other complex implementation, this one (modified from a public domain routine written by J. Kercheval) takes a simpler, albeit slower, approach. RegMatch() simply "walks" through the pattern and string. It advances the string pointer 0–n bytes based on how the string matches the current character in the pattern.

Most of the time, only one character at most will be "consumed" by RegMatch() from the string for matching a pattern character. The ?, ~, [], and \ constructs all try to match against a single character. If there is a match, the string pointer is incremented by one; if not, RegMatch() returns a failure.

Matching * against the string is handled by recursion. RegMatch() calls itself, trying to find a match of the trailing portion of the string (with 0–n characters "consumed" by the *) against the rest of the pattern. RegMatch() returns the result of this recursive call to itself. Note that a complex pattern, with dozens of * characters, could overflow the stack through the recursion.

7.6 Future Directions

There are several ways in which UTCGen could be improved.

Expanded Catalog

One could increase the number of conditions identified by the catalog, via more entries. The catalog supplied with UTCGen is far from complete. Once more conditions are determined (not easy), they can be simply added to the file, as described above.

One way to expand the range of possible conditions would be for the catalog to include ones related to application-specific types and C++ classes. The supplied catalog only knows about base C types—everything else is unknown (except for generic pointer conditions). If developers have a class library or types they use frequently, they can add conditions specific to those types to their custom copy of the catalog.

Conditional Compilation

Also, UTCGen could handle conditional compilation. Right now, it processes all functions in the supplied header files, regardless of whether they are truly accessible. Some might be "untouchable" via an #ifdef construct. This leads to spurious conditions that are unusable in practice.

Typedefs

UTCGen could also interpret typedefs to serve as "synonyms" to existing types. Many APIs, particular the Windows API, use typedefs for nearly every parameter as a means of maintaining platform independence. UTCGen could read typedefs from a C header file and recognize them when examining function parameters. This, on occasion, may yield strange test conditions (e.g., an HGLOBAL < 0) but may still prove useful.

Remove Limitations

UTCGen has three noteworthy limitations:

- An upper limit of 32 conditions per parameter, which could be removed.
- Inability to handle C++ class definitions, forcing C++ programmers to use MKPROTO or a similar tool to pick up ANSI C function prototypes for member functions. UTCGen could be updated to directly parse C++ class definitions.
- Inability to handle pointer-indicating asterisks that are immediately adjacent to the parameter name. UTCGen forces the two to be separated by a space. This could be fixed so one would not need to manually modify prototypes.

7.7 Summary

The creation of test conditions is a first step toward building a unit test plan for a subsystem. While testers will always have to do some work to select conditions, one can apply a test condition catalog to the function prototypes. UTCGen does this in an automated fashion, emitting a list of candidate conditions that testers can incorporate into their lists. The UTCGen conditions, along with others determined by testers, can then be combined into unit test cases and, eventually, a test suite.

CHAPTER 8

Test Framework: UTCLang

"Oh you must be kidding me!"

Sam, now used to random loud statements echoing down the halls, wandered into the office that was the source of this outburst. Michelle, the TurboChem testing coordinator, had her head cradled in her hands, staring at a report.

"What seems to be the trouble?" Sam asked gingerly.

"I just got George's unit tests. This is now the fifth different way somebody has implemented a suite of unit tests. He has one test program per test case—that's 78 separate programs! It's enough to drive me out of my mind!"

Sam winced. This sort of problem had plagued TurboChem 2.0 as well. Release 1.0 was spared largely because nobody had done much testing at all.

"Well, so everybody has their own taste in testing. I don't see why this is much of a problem," Sam said, although he really did not believe what he was saying.

"Not a problem?" exclaimed Michelle. "How on earth do you expect me to be able to efficiently run regression tests if I have to root through the documentation to figure out how to make each test suite work? They don't even report their results in the same way. One even says, 'If the test program does not crash during execution, all tests succeeded.' What kind of test suite is that? Why couldn't they all use one system for conducting the unit testing?"

"Why, indeed," Sam mused. Surely there must be a way to get all the developers' unit tests to look and work similarly.

"Hey, why not get the developers together for a meeting, where we can...," offered Sam, shortly before ducking yet another flying wad of paper.

8.1 Ad Hoc Unit Testing

Unit testing is recognized as an important phase of the overall software quality process because it catches faults early in the game. Catching faults earlier means quicker repairs and higher overall quality and productivity. Unfortunately, unit testing can also be implemented in a slipshod manner, which will not yield the long-term benefits of a well-orchestrated test program.

A number of reasons why unit testing, if given limited attention, can lead to problems are outlined in the following sections.

Focus on Production Code

One issue is that both developers and managers focus on the code that "does things" (i.e., the system being produced) rather than on test code. Since unit tests are seldom included in the shipped application, well-intentioned individuals can still spend inadequate time on unit testing. This can even be formalized in a staffing plan or production schedule that assigns inadequate time and resources to testing.

Tedious Test Process

Testing is not always an easy phase of development. In an interpreted language like Basic or Smalltalk, writing unit test cases can be done easily in the application itself. Version control software can remove this testing code at shipment time for the production system.

In C or C++, on the other hand, it is not that simple. For languages that are compiled, rather than interpreted, there must be associated files (makefiles, etc.) created for the implemented tests. In addition, the tests become a part of the "compile-link-run-debug" cycle that is the nature of compiled languages. A significant productivity loss is incurred by the continual wait for the compiler and linker to do their work. While this situation is readily dealt with in production systems, it can easily be a physical and psychological barrier to the "less-important" phase of unit testing.

Test Maintenance

Another problem is in the maintenance of the batteries of tests that developers create during unit testing. Without a common framework and coordination, five programmers are likely to create five different testing mechanisms. The differences will be in areas ranging from command-line interface syntax through required supporting files. This makes regression testing more difficult, especially as team membership changes. Each mechanism will have to be separately documented, so others can execute or modify the tests over time. Large, long-lived systems will wind up with a veritable potpourri of unit test systems. This may cause the tests to be discarded after being first run.

The maintenance problem is exacerbated by changes in the application itself over time, particularly if the project is using an iterative development methodology. As the subsystems expand over time, new API functions will be added and older ones changed or dropped. Developers must update earlier unit tests to reflect the changes. The more difficult this test code upgrade becomes, the less likely that it will be done, particularly if schedules are tight. And, of course, changes made in this iteration could well cause a bug in the modified code, which would not be found if not tested.

In summary, several forces combine to make unit test implementations fragile and their development and maintenance tedious. To combat these problems, one needs to take proactive steps to organize test code suitably. This typically takes the form of a unit testing framework, standard code from which all unit tests are derived.

8.2 Test Frameworks for C/C++

A test framework is similar to any framework one uses in C/C++ coding, such as Microsoft's Foundation Classes (MFC) for Windows development. It provides the basis for the test programs and allows separate subsystems to have similar test results. Those using the framework "flesh it out" to perform the subsystem-specific behavior. With a framework, this should lead to consistent unit tests.

Given the above problems, a testing framework for any language should have two primary goals:

- Make testing as easy as possible, by eliminating or encapsulating "overhead" beyond the actual test logic itself. The less work involved in unit testing, the more likely it will be done well, or done at all.
- Make tests created by separate individuals or teams compatible, in terms of setup, implementation, execution, and results. This will make longer-term reuse of the tests much more likely.

The following sections describe several ways to create a unit testing framework for C or C++.

Template Executable

One simple and popular approach is to create a standardized "template" program for unit test executables. It defines the command-line interface as well as input and output standards. For example, the template could provide the C main() function and route interaction to C standard input and output.

A standard makefile must accompany the template. It contains slots for developers to add their subsystem information. They only have to write functions to execute tests, plus provide a controlling function (with a standard name to hook into the template).

A template executable would typically come with main() already coded, perhaps resembling:

```
int main(int argc, char **argv)
{
    int i;

    TstParseCommandLine(argc, argv);

    for (i=0;i<TstTestCount();i++) // TstTestCount() is custom
    {
        (TstGetTestFunction(i))(); // custom function
    }

    return(0);
}
```

All command-line switches are parsed by TstParseCommandLine(); their settings are accessible by a public API. For example, it might define /q as being a "quiet" flag to restrict output to error messages. All one must do is implement and link the following two functions:

1. TstTestCount(), returning the number of tests to execute
2. TstGetTestFunction(), which returns a pointer-to-function to a unit test function, given the test number

---

This provides execution-time standardization, which will simplify regression testing. It may not help much in the way tests are structured, beyond the influence of the template itself (along with team coding standards). It is unlikely that it will help much in writing the unit test functions.

C++ Unit Testing Class

Another approach is to create C++ unit testing classes that provide the same features. Each unit test is a subclass of a unit test base class; only a virtual function that executes the test itself is absolutely necessary. A test manager class has a function for actually executing the individual tests in order. The rest of the framework is provided by member functions in the base classes. This has the same benefits and costs as the first approach, with an added bonus of greater structure imposed upon the tests themselves.

One approach is to have a TstUnitTest class, instances of which implement a particular unit test. Each instance registers itself with the class via a static member function:

```
TstUnitTest::TstUnitTest()
{
    TstUnitTest::AddInstance(this);
// other initialization here
}
```

One creates subclasses for each unit test, overriding ExecuteTest() in each. Then, to run the test suite, one executes TstUnitTest::RunAllTests(). This member function loops through the list of instances of TstUnitTest and invokes ExecuteTest() for each.

C/C++ Interpreter

Both approaches still are tied to the "compile-link-run-debug" cycle. An alternative is to employ a C or C++ interpreter. Under this scenario, the unit tests are written using the interpreted environment and executed from there. A framework like the above two examples is still needed for a mechanism for common usage of the tests themselves. What the interpreter provides is a faster means of getting the tests written and working—faster development means better testing.

Interpreted Language Front End

The above techniques are still tied to the C/C++ language. For many subsystems, if the programmers themselves are writing the unit tests, this is acceptable. It does preclude, however, the use of anyone not literate in C/C++ from writing or modifying test cases. Many people who are knowledgeable about computers could implement a unit test from a plan if the language were more approachable. C and C++ are simply too complex to be worth training someone solely for unit testing.

Many languages can access C libraries, particularly in dynamic-linking environments such as Windows and OS/2. These languages let one mix native code with calls to C functions contained in dynamic-link libraries (DLLs). One can implement the unit tests in the native language, calling out to the libraries as needed. One then gains the advantage of the interpretive environment.

Custom Script Language Front End

Another solution, similar to using a third-party interpreted language, is to create an interpreted language on top of the subsystem itself. The "little language" would execute scripts that describe test cases. The scripting language should have much simpler syntax than C or C++, making it easier for non-C programmers to write test scripts. The interpreted environment results in faster script development. The language interpreter and available commands/classes help in providing structure both for the test scripts themselves and for their interaction with outside resources (e.g., input files).

One advantage of this approach is insulation against API modifications. If separate test programs in C/C++ code are written for each unit test case, each will need to be modified to reflect changes in API functions. Depending on how frequently such updates occur, a tester may find a mountain of modifications needs to be implemented at one time. Since each API function is typically used only once within the script language, there will be fewer C/C++ code modifications to make. With a strategic approach to creating the language, many scripts may not even require modifications. Obviously, new scripts would still need to be written to exercise new and changed features.

Also, the interpreter would enforce a common execution mechanism. Typically, one executes a script by simply invoking the interpreter from the command line, perhaps with some switches to control its behavior.

The difficulty with this approach is the need to create the language itself. One must be able to justify the expense. One option is to use it for purposes beyond testing (e.g., installation scripts). Another is to use an existing framework for creating such a language. UTCLang, the focus of this chapter, provides such a framework.

Thus, there are several ways in which one can create test frameworks that will provide consistency between unit test suites, while making it easier to build them. This chapter focuses on the last option, the custom script language, by showing how to use UTCLang. Table 8.1 outlines the pros and cons for each approach.

8.3 UTCLang's Test Framework

The key to a script language is for it to be easy to build. General-purpose language creation tools, such as the Unix *lex* and *yacc* compiler generators, are definitely more than is needed. On the other hand, a cumbersome language will make testing more difficult. UTCLang addresses these concerns by providing a simple, flexible way to create a scripting language for subsystems. The resulting language is easy to program, so it can be used by those who are not ready to tackle the intricacies of C or C++.

Table 8.1 Test Framework Pros and Cons

Approach	Pros	Cons
Template Executable	Easy to set up, easy to execute from batch file/shell script	Not much leverage, so does not make unit testing much easier
C++ Unit Testing Class	Same as template executable	Same as template executable
C/C++ Interpreter	Interpreted environment for fast testing turnaround	Tough to find in all environments, difficulty in linking subsystem into interpreter, frequently forced into using their development environment
Interpreted Language Front End	Interpreted environment for fast testing turnaround, simpler language for test writing	Frequently forced into using their development environment
Custom Script Language Front End	Interpreted environment for fast testing turnaround, simpler language for test writing	Difficulty in creating custom language

UTCLang was used to create a test driver for the X-Base library that provides the data storage for the Address Lite application. The driver allows one to exercise the full X-Base library API from within scripts. One can compare output from run to run to confirm that the results have not changed. As new functions are added to the library, the driver can be quickly extended to add matching functionality.

UTCLang's script language is object-oriented, making it excellent for testing C++ classes. A script class can match one-to-one with a C++ class. However, UTCLang uses a syntax similar to Smalltalk, an easier language to learn than C++.

UTCLang provides the full script language interpreter. All that custom drivers must do is indicate what classes and functions the script requires and how they map to the subsystem being tested.

UTCLang is a library, although it comes with a standard command-line interface "shell" program. The shell runs script files indicated on the command line and sends the results to standard output, suitable for redirection to a file. However, the library allows other shells to be written, perhaps using a GUI or other user interface. This also allows UTCLang to serve as an embedded language. It makes no assumptions about the input and output devices available.

Figure 8.1 outlines how the pieces of UTCLang couple with a subsystem to create the test environment.

Figure 8.1 UTCLang Custom Driver Structure

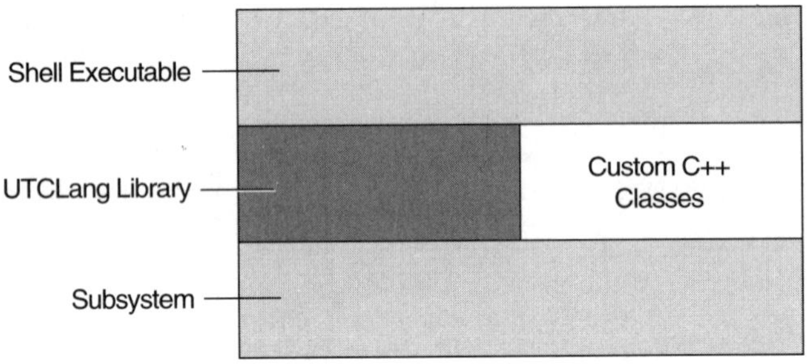

8.4 Components of UTCLang's Language

One creates a UTCLang driver by combining a "shell" executable with the UTCLang library, the subsystem being tested, and custom C++ classes to connect them. The library, however, is in many ways the most important piece, as it interprets script files, which are ASCII files containing language statements. It provides the base language; the custom classes extend the language to test the subsystem.

Objects and Classes

UTCLang deals with all pieces of data in the language as objects. Numbers and strings are objects on a par with ones created for testing a subsystem. Even blocks of code can be treated as objects and passed around.

UTCLang comes with several classes for common objects, including numbers and strings. One can extend the raw language by adding new classes in one of two ways. Interpreted classes are ones written in the script language. They are simply classes whose behaviors are interpreted by the UTCLang interpreter. One can also create UTCLang classes by using a C++ class. Instead of writing the code in the script language, these compiled classes are linked directly into the test executable.

The X-Base test driver contains two compiled classes, one representing database files and one for records within a file. The driver does not use any interpreted classes, although sample scripts for UTCLang demonstrate their use.

The result is that script writers will have a library of classes at their disposal, a combination of ones provided in UTCLang and ones added to support testing the subsystem.

Messages and Methods

In C++, when one invokes a behavior in an object, it is termed "calling a member function." UTCLang terms it "sending a message" to the object. This message is processed by a method (akin to a member function) of the same name. The net result is the same: One specifies in the source what to do and who does it. The distinction is mostly a matter of terminology.

Variables

C++ has four main types of variables:

- Global variables, visible to anything in the system (or, if marked static, only to this file)
- Local variables, used in functions to allocate temporary storage
- Function parameters, providing custom data to manipulate
- Data members of classes, the data associated with C++ objects

UTCLang also offers all four variable categories, with the following caveats:

- UTCLang offers global variables. Since UTCLang processes only one script file at a time, a global variable is visible only within one script.
- Temporaries are equivalent to local variables. They are used within a method for short-term data storage.
- Method parameters are the objects provided to indicate what specifically to do in this message. They work like member function parameters.
- Instance variables are the data associated with objects. One can have them in interpreted classes (the ones added in a script file).

8.5 Using a UTCLang Driver

The first step to using UTCLang to implement a subsystem driver is to become comfortable with UTCLang drivers in general. UTCLang has its own syntax. Hence, while it is easier to learn than C++, it still takes practice. This section outlines the features of languages derived from UTCLang.

As an illustration, this section will look at the driver for the X-Base library used by Address Lite. This example is included with the source code on the diskette. In addition to the base language implementation that all UTCLang drivers share, it adds a mapping to most API functions provided in the X-Base library.

The examples shown here will work with the X-Base library driver. Those that do not refer to database files or records will also work with any UTCLang driver.

Simple Scripts

UTCLang drivers are message-based object systems. Here, "message-based" means that the terminology revolves around sending messages to objects, rather than calling member functions, as in C++.

To send a message to an object, simply join the two with a period. Hence, to send the Print message to the Log object, use Log.Print. This is similar to calling a member function in C++.

The following single-line script logs a string to standard output:

```
Log.Print "Hello, world!"
```

The result of executing this script is:

```
Hello, world!
```

Many methods, like Log's Print method, require parameters. Rather than being comma-delimited within parentheses, like C++, they are whitespace-delimited directly following the message, like parameters on a command line.

UTCLang has several global objects, such as Log, which is used for logging output to be displayed to the user. Table 8.2 lists the globals and their purposes.

Table 8.2 Globals in UTCLang

Global Name	Purpose
Log	Means of sending output of script
System	Used to create classes and manage other global actions
true	Boolean true (1) value
false	Boolean false (0) value
nil	Represents no other object, logically equivalent to C NULL pointer

One can create global variables by sending the AddGlobal message to the System global object. The value is initially set to nil, but one can initialize it with the assignment message, Assign.

The following script creates a global instance of an X-Base database object:

```
System.AddGlobal "MasterDB"
MasterDB.Assign DbfFile.New
```

One can also create temporary variables. At the top of the script, simply list them (delimited by whitespace) within vertical bars. They will be initialized to nil. Like any variable, they understand the Assign message to change their value.

The following script creates a temporary variable, assigned an X-Base database file object:

```
| TempDB |
TempDB.Assign DbfFile.New
```

Here, the New message sent to DbfFile creates the database file object. Classes added to UTCLang typically respond to New to create instances. The base UTCLang classes either support literals (such as strings) or have only a single instance, created by the driver itself. Hence, the base classes do not respond to New.

Each message has a result, an object returned by the method. To assign the result to a temporary, simply enclose the message in braces.

This script prints the number of records in a database file. Note that we must put the file.Size message inside braces, since it represents an expression.

```
| file |
file.Assign DbfFile.New
file.Name "..\on_hand.dbf"
file.Open
Log.Print "Records=" {file.Size}
file.Close
```

Only the Assign message will take an expression as a parameter without braces. As an example, note that when we assign a new DbfFile to the file temporary, the DbfFile.New message is not enclosed in braces.

Numbers and strings can be embedded as literals within a script. Numbers can be either integers or floating-point values. Numbers also understand the basic arithmetic operators (+, -, *, /, %) and logical operators (AND, OR, NOT). To use an arithmetic expression in a script, enclose it in parentheses.

The following script shows some basic arithmetic:

```
Log.Print (5 + 7)
Log.Print (5.25 * 7.5)
Log.Print (1 AND 0)
Log.Print (1 OR 0)
```

The results are:

```
12
39.375
0
1
```

Like most object languages, UTCLang deals with both objects and classes. It has a few built-in classes (see Table 8.3). Developers can add others, either as C++ classes or in the script language itself.

Table 8.3 Classes Provided in UTCLang

Class	Description
Object	Base class for all classes in UTCLang
CodeBlock	Represents blocks of UTCLang source code, can be evaluated, and used in branches and loops
_Log	Class implementing Log object, used for capturing output to script
Message	Represents a message that was sent, used for DoesNotUnderstand
Number	Represents integer and floating-point values
String	Represents character strings of arbitrary length
_System	Class implementing System object, for controlling UTCLang environment

Table 8.4 lists the classes provided in the X-Base library driver, above and beyond those in UTCLang itself.

Table 8.4 Classes Provided in X-Base Library Driver

Class	Description
DbfFile	Represents a database file
DbfRecord	Represents a single record within a file

As noted above, literals and predefined globals can be addressed directly. To create a new instance of a class, simply send New to it.

The script that prints the number of records in a database, shown above, also illustrates how to create new instances. In that case, an instance of DbfFile is created and used to get the number of records in the database file.

A single statement can be enclosed in brackets, creating a code block. This is more than simply a statement—it is an object that can be passed around like any other. A block will understand the Value message to evaluate its statement.

The true and false objects understand conditional messages of IfTrue and IfFalse. Hence, an expression (in braces) that returns true or false can also receive the IfTrue and IfTrueElse messages, providing a simple form of logical branch. The parameters are code blocks that will be evaluated if the logical expression and the desired branch match.

The following script, used with the X-Base test driver, creates a new file object, opened on a particular database, and prints a message if the file is empty:

```
| file |
file.Assign DbfFile.New
file.Name "on_hand.dbf"
file.Open
({file.Size}>0).IfTrueElse [Log.Print "Not Empty!"] [Log.Print "Empty!"]
file.Close
```

In the second-to-last line, {file.Size} evaluates to a number, representing the size of the file. The result of the parenthetical expression (used because > is a arithmetic operation) will be either true or false. This is then sent IfTrueElse to print an appropriate message. The result might be:

```
Not Empty!
```

Similarly, code blocks themselves respond to WhileTrue and WhileFalse messages. As long as the block evaluates to true or false (matching the message), the one provided as a message parameter will be evaluated as well. This provides the foundation for more complex loops.

Interpreted Classes and Methods

One can also add interpreted classes, ones whose definition is entirely defined within interpreted code. Their primary function is as utility classes one uses in test scripts. For example, one might create a class that knows the details of a database layout, for use in testing the X-Base library driver. It would use the compiled DbfFile and DbfRecord classes to access and modify the database.

Since one can create fully functional drivers without interpreted classes, they are not discussed further here. Appendix F contains more details on how to create interpreted classes and methods.

8.6 Creating a UTCLang Driver

While UTCLang comes with a handful of simple classes "out of the box," it is really designed to be extended. This is done by adding classes and behaviors related to a C/C++ subsystem, such as was done for the X-Base library driver. The process is straightforward, involving designing the custom driver, setting up the basic driver, adding new classes, and giving them behaviors to attach to the subsystem. This section outlines the steps of creating a custom driver, using the X-Base library driver as an example.

Designing a Custom Driver

Before embarking on creating a new driver, one should determine what the new classes and behaviors should look like. Moreover, there should be some idea of how they will map to the subsystem's data structures and APIs.

C Subsystem

For a C subsystem such as the X-Base library, one typically maps classes to its exported data structures. In the X-Base case, there is one key structure: the database file handle, filled in when a database is opened and passed into all other API functions. Hence, there should be a class (DbfFile) added to the driver to map to this handle. All behaviors related to files as a whole, at minimum, should belong to it.

The X-Base API also deals with records and fields. One could create classes for them as well. In this implementation, a class (DbfRecord) provides a mapping to a database record. It uses its record number within the database file to access and update its data. Fields, however, are simply implemented as instances of the built-in String and Number classes. Accessing a LastName field, for example, returns a String.

Table 8.5 outlines these two classes (DbfFile and DbfRecord) and how the API functions are mapped between them.

Given this design, one can construct the desired driver extensions.

C++ Subsystem

Frequently, one can simply have the UTCLang classes match the C++ classes in the subsystem one-to-one. Sometimes there will be C++ classes that are "too small" to worry about directly in a script; their functionality can be tested by behaviors on other UTCLang classes.

Member functions may not match one-to-one to UTCLang methods on these classes, however. First, typically only public member functions, the ones that serve as the "API" of the class, would need to be surfaced in a script. Next, some functions may have no real purpose for a driver. Examples include the following:

- Member functions designed solely to flesh out a framework being inherited from (e.g., overriding a pure virtual method) and not being directly called by any other subsystem
- Functions that serve as callbacks or are otherwise provided to agents outside the program being built

Table 8.5 X-Base Driver Classes and Related API Functions

DbfFile	DbfRecord
XblOpen()	XblUpdate()
XblClose()	XblGetFieldAsString()
XblFlush()	XblPutFieldAsString()
XblAppend()	XblFieldNameFromNum()
XblBlank()	XblFieldNumFromName()
XblSeek()	XblFieldType()
XblRecordCount()	XblFieldLength()
	XblFieldDecimals()
	XblDelete()
	XblUndelete()
	XblIsDeleted()
	XblFieldCount()
	XblGetFieldAsInt()
	XblGetFieldAsFloat()
	XblPutFieldAsInt()
	XblPutFieldAsFloat()

- Member functions solely used as accessors for private data that should not be manipulated directly by a script

Creating the Base Shell Executable

The next step is to set up the working copy of the driver. UTCLang drivers consist of three parts:

- A library containing the bulk of the UTCLang code
- A stub executable that loads scripts into memory and requests their execution
- "Glue" C++ classes that link the driver to the subsystem and add compiled UTCLang classes

The UTCLang library will remain constant, even given the additional classes required by the custom driver. The custom classes will inherit from UTCLang-provided classes and will use other functions provided by the library. However, great pains have been taken to allow them to be written without modifying any UTCLang source code. Hence, most UTCLang C++ source can be left in its own master directory; custom drivers will work in their own directory and reference UTCLang files from there. One can copy the entire UTCLang distribution, especially when making substantial modifications to the base code.

To merely make a new driver, one must create a shell executable and makefile suitable for compiling it. To use the standard UTCLang command-line shell interface, simply copy DRIVER.C from the UTCLang distribution. Similarly, the makefile is already set up to compile the plain driver, so it can serve as a good starting point. This makefile can compile the copied shell stub and create another UTCLang-only driver after it has been updated to reflect its new location in the directory structure. Note that there are makefiles for each compiler. Consult Appendix A or the README.TXT file in the UTCLANG directory for assistance in identifying the proper one to use.

Since DRIVER.C is too long to represent here, the following is the pseudocode for it. Note that the behavior described here is typically implemented in the C main() function, to be executed at driver startup.

```
Initialize the driver via UtcInitDriver()
For each file listed on the command line
    Open the file and read into a memory buffer
    Execute the script (UtcExecuteStatements), returning Log text
    If there is Log text, display it and free the buffer
    Free the buffer used to hold the script itself
EndFor
Release the driver via UtcFreeDriver()
```

Adding Compiled Classes

The next step is to add the new classes outlined during the design step. They are implemented as C++ classes in files tied solely to the custom driver. One does not need to modify base UTCLang code to create a custom driver. Since the new classes are compiled into the driver, rather than defined in a script, they are called compiled classes.

Creating a Compiled Class

All compiled classes must have UtcObject as a superclass, either directly or indirectly (if subclassing from another custom compiled class). Hence, one must create a header file declaring the custom class that references OBJECT.H (where UtcObject is declared) and a source file for any member functions.

Here is the declaration for the DbfFile class from the X-Base driver:

```
class DbfFile : public UtcObject
{
public:
    DbfFile(GcSpace *pSpace);
    ~DbfFile();
    virtual UtcObject *PerformMethod(char *pszName,
                                     UtcObjectList &Parms,
                                     UtcHandle *pHandle);
    virtual char *GetClassName();
    virtual char *PrintString(char *pszBuffer);
    static UtcObject *New(void *pSpace);
// these member function support API calls/script commands
    UtcObject *Open(UtcHandle *pHandle);
    UtcObject *Close(UtcHandle *pHandle);
    UtcObject *Flush(UtcHandle *pHandle);
    UtcObject *Size(UtcHandle *pHandle);
    UtcObject *Fields(UtcHandle *pHandle);
    UtcObject *NewRecord(UtcHandle *pHandle);
// other member functions go here -- too long to list!
    virtual void SweepChildren(GC_SWEEP_FN pfnSweep, void *pData);

private:
    UtcObject *pName;
    XBL_HANDLE hHandle;
};
```

As shown above, compiled classes can hold on to whatever data they choose. Here, DbfFile holds on to an XBL_HANDLE, provided by the X-Base library.

Five member functions are mandatory for all compiled classes:

- A constructor, to perform standard initialization for instances. At a minimum, it must also call the UtcObject constructor. Compiled class constructors take a single parameter, a GcSpace pointer, which represents the object space in which the instance belongs. This is provided by UTCLang when instances are created; object spaces are described in the section on garbage collection in Appendix F.

Here is the source for DbfFile's constructor:

```
/*
    DbfFile(): Set buffer to NULL
*/
DbfFile::DbfFile(GcSpace *pSpace)
    : UtcObject(pSpace)
{
    pName=(UtcObject *)0;
}
```

All it does is call the UtcObject constructor and set the name of the file (as a UtcObject) to be NULL. The constructor could also do anything other normal C++ constructors do, such as initialize other data members.

- PerformMethod(), which gets control whenever a script sends a message to an instance of the compiled class. It takes three parameters: the name of the method, a list of parameters, and a UtcHandle pointer. UtcHandle is a class that provides access to globals and exception handling. PerformMethod() should examine the method name and execute if this class defines it. If no name matches, the function should return the result of the superclass's implementation of PerformMethod(), to support inheritance. Typically, the PerformMethod() function simply calls other member functions to actually implement the method, as shown above. Initially, the PerformMethod() function can simply chain to the superclass—one can add new methods at any point.

Here is the source for a do-nothing implementation of PerformMethod():

```
/*
    PerformMethod(): Respond to messages
*/
UtcObject *SampleClass::PerformMethod(char *pszName,
                                      UtcObjectList &Parms,
                                      UtcHandle *pHandle)
{
    return(UtcObject::PerformMethod(pszName, Parms, pHandle));
}
```

Here, PerformMethod() simply chains upward to SampleClass's superclass, in this case UtcObject. Any methods defined in UtcObject (such as PrintString) will be invoked, or else UtcObject will raise an exception.

Here is part of the source for DbfFile's implementation of PerformMethod():

```
UtcObject *DbfFile::PerformMethod(char *pszName,
                                   UtcObjectList &Parms,
                                   UtcHandle *pHandle)
{
    UtcObject *pParm=Parms.GetFirstEntry();
    UtcNumber *pNumber=(UtcNumber *)pParm;

    if (strcmp(pszName, "Name")==0)
    {
        pName=pParm;
        return(this);
    }
    else if (strcmp(pszName, "Open")==0)
    {
        return(Open(pHandle));
    }

// rest of function goes here

    return(UtcObject::PerformMethod(pszName, Parms, pHandle));
}
```

Since DbfFile provides script-level methods, PerformMethod() does some work before control passes to UtcObject. The pszName parameter to the function provides the name of the method being invoked. PerformMethod() compares it to the methods to which DbfFile responds (such as "Name"). If there is a match, PerformMethod() executes whatever is to happen. For the Name method, the DbfFile will now hold on to the first parameter as the name of the file to be later opened. In the case of the Open method, DbfFile implements the behavior in a separate member function, called Open().

Note that all methods must return an object. Here, the Name method returns the DbfFile object (this), while Open returns the result of the Open() member function.

The full implementation of PerformMethod() for DbfFile contains checks for many other methods.

- New(), a *static* function that creates a new instance. It typically turns around and just calls the constructor for the class.

All that DbfFile's implementation of New() does is create and return an instance of itself:

```
/*
    New(): Return a new instance
*/
UtcObject *DbfFile::New(void *pSpace)
{
    return(new DbfFile((GcSpace *)pSpace));
}
```

- GetClassName(), which returns the name of this class as it should be referred to in a script. Frequently, this is the same as the C++ class name, although any single-token string will work.

All that DbfFile's implementation of GetClassName() does is return the static string "DbfFile":

```
/*
    GetClassName(): Name for class
*/
char *DbfFile::GetClassName()
{
    return("DbfFile");
}
```

- SweepChildren(), which is passed a function pointer to be executed for each UTCLang object this instance holds on to. If this class only holds on to C/C++ data, not instances of UtcObject (or subclasses), the function can simply do nothing. However, if instances hold on to other UTCLang objects, they must be "swept" by the function. The garbage collection subsystem uses Sweep-Children(), to see what objects are reachable from where. Appendix F contains more details.

Below is the source for DbfFile's version of SweepChildren():

```
/*
    SweepChildren(): Execute a function with child as argument
*/
void DbfFile::SweepChildren(GC_SWEEP_FN pfnSweep, void *pData)
{
    if (pName)
    {
        pfnSweep(pName, pData);
    }

    return;
}
```

DbfFile holds on to a single UtcObject in a data member: the name of the file to be opened. This child, therefore, must be "swept"—the provided function is called with the name and the provided data pointer as parameters. If there were more children in DbfFile, the sweep function would have been called multiple times, once for each child. If there are no children in a given class, one could simply return without doing anything.

There is an optional function one can implement, PrintString(). It should return a string representation of the object suitable for showing on the Log. The default implementation is "a ...", where the ellipsis is replaced by the class name. By overriding PrintString(), one can provide any desired text. A character buffer is provided, if needed; static strings can be returned directly, if desired.

All that DbfFile's version of PrintString() does is return the static string "Database file":

```
/*
    PrintString(): Indicate what this object is
*/
char *DbfFile::PrintString(char *pszBuffer)
{
    return("Database file");
}
```

Linking Classes to the Driver

One other required step is to inform UTCLang that the new compiled class exists. UTCLang has no way of automatically finding this out. Failure to inform the driver of the new class simply means that a script will not be able to access it.

The UtcAddCompiledClass() function (prototyped in UTCLANG.H) allows one to tell the driver about a new compiled class. It takes three parameters: the driver handle (returned by UtcInitDriver()), the name of the class as it should be referred to in a script, and the New static class function.

In XDRIVER.CPP, the "shell" for the X-Base driver, the main() function makes two calls to UtcAddCompiledClass() to register the two compiled classes. The calls are:

```
UtcAddCompiledClass(hHandle, "DbfFile", DbfFile::New);
UtcAddCompiledClass(hHandle, "DbfRecord", DbfRecord::New);
```

Besides the driver handle, the calls provide the name of the class as a string, plus the function pointer to the static New() member function. It is used by the internal New method to create instances of the class when requested in a script.

Given that the driver calls UtcAddCompiledClass() for all compiled classes, they will be available to script writers just like the built-in classes. Instances can respond to the standard Object messages (e.g., PrintString), even with no other methods implemented in PerformMethod().

Even with just a bare-bones implementation, containing the above member functions with a do-nothing PerformMethod(), the following script:

```
| file |
file.Assign DbfFile.New
Log.Print "The file temporary now holds a " file
```

yields the following output:

```
test2.scr
The file temporary now holds a Database file
```

One also needs to modify the makefile to include the stub executable source, UTCLang library, and C++ source files for the compiled classes.

Adding New Behaviors

Adding new methods to a compiled class is simple. The first step is to create a member function that maps to the desired method, typically having the same name. The model the X-Base driver uses is that the member function receives just the parameters it needs to implement the method, plus the UtcHandle object (pointer) for globals access and exception handling.

Below is the implementation of the Open() member function on DbfFile, implementing the behavior behind the Open method:

```
/*
    Open(): Opens a database file
*/
UtcObject *DbfFile::Open(UtcHandle *pHandle)
{
    char *pszName, szName[64];
    int iResult;

    if (pName)
    {
        pszName=pName->PrintString(szName);
        iResult=XblOpen(&hHandle, pszName);
        if (iResult)
        {
            return(pHandle->RaiseException("LIBERROR"));
        }
        return(this);
    }
    return(pHandle->RaiseException("NONAME"));
}
```

If the name is not set, Open() raises a “NONAME” exception in the final statement. If Open() cannot open a file with the name, it raises a “LIBERROR” exception. Otherwise, the DbFile object will hold on to the X-Base library handle for the database file, in addition to the filename.

Note that the filename is not a C string, but rather a UTCLang object. Hence, Open() uses the PrintString function of the parameter to get the name of the file to open.

If the member function detects an exception condition (such as being unable to open the database file), it should call RaiseException(), a member function of UtcHandle. The object returned from RaiseException() should be returned by the method, in case an exception handler was provided. Appendix F covers exception handling in more detail.

Once a suitable member function is set up to implement the method, all one must do is add it to PerformMethod(). PerformMethod() must watch for whatever method name is to be used in a script, then call the member function for it.

Here is part of the source for DbfFile's implementation of PerformMethod(), which was examined earlier in this chapter:

```
UtcObject *DbfFile::PerformMethod(char *pszName,
                                  UtcObjectList &Parms,
                                  UtcHandle *pHandle)
{
    UtcObject *pParm=Parms.GetFirstEntry();
    UtcNumber *pNumber=(UtcNumber *)pParm;

    if (strcmp(pszName, "Name")==0)
    {
        pName=pParm;
        return(this);
    }
    else if (strcmp(pszName, "Open")==0)
    {
        return(Open(pHandle));
    }

// rest of method checks goes here

    return(UtcObject::PerformMethod(pszName, Parms, pHandle));
}
```

Since the Open method does not take a parameter, the Open() member function needs only the interpreter handle (pHandle). Otherwise, some objects in the Parms list would have been extracted and passed into Open().

8.7 Implementing a Unit Test with UTCLang

Given a driver that surfaces all the API functions from the subsystem to be tested, a unit test is merely a series of scripts. They can be organized in any way: one test case per script, or several. Since scripts cannot easily share information, it would be unusual to have a single test case span multiple script files.

The default shell sends script output from Log.Print to C standard output. One can use redirection to send it to a file. Even a series of scripts can all be redirected to one output file, with each script chaining its output on the end. The result will be a single file that can be compared, during regression test, to a master copy to detect changes. For this to work best, a script should not write information known to change from run to run, such as the current date or time.

To chain multiple output files, using normal shell redirection, use >> rather than >. The >> means "append," whereas > means "overwrite." For example, here are the first two lines from the batch file (UNITTEST.BAT) that tests UTCLang itself:

```
..\utclang test1.scr > unittest.out
..\utclang test2.scr >> unittest.out
```

UNITTEST.OUT will now contain the concatenated results of both test scripts. One can compare it against a master copy to identify differences.

One could also build an automatic comparison mechanism into a modified shell, if desired. This may be difficult to write and may make adding new test cases somewhat tedious if the shell must be modified each time.

Scripts should be version controlled just like C/C++ source files. After all, scripts are just another form of program source, albeit one that may not be shipped with the product. Somebody might modify a script, thinking that it reflects an update to the subsystem, when in reality it masks a fault. Without version control, there will be no way to restore the original script to diagnose the problem properly.

8.8 UTCLang and the Sample Code

The UTCLang driver used to test the X-Base library has been described throughout this chapter. It was used to implement the unit test cases, outlined in Appendix C, to ensure that the library works. The test scripts for the driver are included on the disk (see Appendix A for details).

Since Address Lite lacks an API, UTCLang could not be used to test it. In theory, one could create a driver for the user interface classes and directly manipulate them. This is impractical for MFC-derived classes; moreover, user interfaces are designed for a different style of testing, described in Chapter 11 on WinCapT.

8.9 How UTCLang Works

UTCLang is the most complex tool in this book. Whereas the other chapters describe the inner workings of their tools, UTCLang's description appears in Appendix F. Readers who intend to use UTCLang are encouraged to read that appendix for more details on creating interpreted classes and how the interpreter works in general.

8.10 Built-in Classes and Globals

A full-fledged object-oriented language would come with a whole library of data types (classes), each providing useful functions. UTCLang is much smaller in scope, providing only the most basic classes and globals required for simple script development. Users should augment it with classes designed specifically for the driver being developed.

The following sections describe the classes and other globals available to all UTCLang script programmers.

nil

nil is a "magic" object representing solely the lack of any other object. All temporaries and instance variables are initialized to nil at the outset. As new globals are added by name, they too are given nil as a starting value.

If one were to execute the following script:

```
System.AddGlobal "NewGlobal"
Log.Print "NewGlobal value = " NewGlobal
```

one would get the following result:

```
NewGlobal value = nil
```

The nil object responds to all basic object messages, plus IsNil, which reports if the receiver is the nil object.

String

UTCLang represents strings as instances of the String class, created as literals (e.g., "This is a string"). The String class provides no protocol beyond the standard object methods, although it could easily be extended to add size, concatenation, copying, and other behaviors. The C++ class UtcStrClass implements the UTCLang String script class.

Number

Numbers, like strings, are represented by a UTCLang class, Number. A Number can be either an integer or a floating-point value, using the C long and double base data types to hold the value. Numbers are created as literals (e.g., 5 or 3.14). The literals can contain a sign, but not an exponent. Hence, 5.3e14 is not a legal number, as it is in some languages.

Numbers understand the basic arithmetic (+, -, *, /, %) and logical (AND, OR, NOT) operators, besides the standard object messages.

Numbers are represented in the C++ code as instances of the UtcNumClass class.

true and false

Two special numbers are true and false, stored as globals. They are the special values returned as the result of logical operators and various Is* methods (e.g., IsNil). The true and false globals also properly respond to the IfTrue and IfFalse messages to implement logical branching. The IfTrue and IfFalse messages take a code block (described below) as a parameter, returning its value if the receiver matches the desired value.

System

The System global provides a script-level interface to some behaviors of the driver handle (UtcHandle). They include:

- Exception handling via the AddExceptionHandler, RaiseException, Abort, and GetExceptionMessage methods
- System manipulation via the AddClass and AddGlobal methods

One cannot create new instances of the _System class, of which System is the sole instance. For details on the System global, examine the UtcSystem C++ class.

Log

The Log global is a repository for text to be given back to the user. Log understands the Print message, which takes the PrintString of all parameters and enters it onto a line of text in the Log's output. When the script completes, the contents of the Log are returned by the UTCLang API to indicate the results. The standard UTC-Lang shell sends this text to C's standard output.

Although there is a _Log class (backed by the UtcLog C++ class), one should not try to create new instances of it.

Message

Message objects are created only by the DoesNotUnderstand processing described above; one cannot create a message by any other means. Messages can return the name, receiver, and parameters of the message that triggered DoesNotUnderstand. It might be used for proxy implementation, where messages are relayed to other objects. Unfortunately, there is no way to execute a message again given a Message object.

CodeBlock

Code blocks, instances of a UtcCodeBlock C++ class, can be created only as literals, not via a New message to any UTCLang script-level class. Code blocks are used to determine what is done on a logical branch or exception. They also understand the WhileTrue and WhileFalse messages. These messages repeatedly evaluate the receiving block and, while the result matches the desired value, evaluate another block passed as a parameter.

8.11 Other Uses for UTCLang

UTCLang, as described in this chapter, is used solely as a means of implementing a unit test at a higher level than raw C/C++ stubs. However, there are other uses for UTCLang-based script languages.

Install Utility

Some programs need to do domain-specific tasks at install time, such as creating or populating database tables. Most commercial install programs are good at copying files from disks. Only a few have an interface to external C routines, typically in the form of DLLs. Instead, a UTCLang script can be run during the installation to accomplish the same end. If the driver exists from unit testing, creating the script is likely to be faster than creating a custom program from scratch. Also, the script will be far easier to modify as install-time needs change.

Embedded Language

Many commercial applications come with a macro language for automating complex activities. An example is the Visual Basic for Applications (VBA) that connects the components of the Microsoft Office suite. Since UTCLang is constructed as a library, one can easily integrate it into a host application to provide runtime execution. Macros could be written by users in text panes and sent to the UTCLang kernel for execution.

8.12 Future Directions

UTCLang, as it stands today, offers a fair amount of power in a small package. It certainly can be extended, however, to provide more features and functionality.

Larger Class Library

Classes that provide support typically found in programming languages could be added. They would include methods bound into the kernel, plus interpreted methods as needed. Examples include file I/O, string management, and type conversion (strings<->numbers).

Preprocessor Directives

The C preprocessor provides features that would be useful for any language, UTCLang-based ones included. The #include directive to merge two script files and the #ifdef directive for conditional execution are two likely extensions. The #include directive in particular would be useful for longer-term maintenance of a class library.

Operating System Shell

Some unit tests may require an external application. While external libraries can be accessed via UTCLang programs (by creating compiled classes to link to them), external executables are not directly supported. This shell would resemble the C system() function, with a single command line being sent to the host OS for execution. Given some file I/O capability, the script could even read and parse redirected output.

Debugger

It is not easy to debug a UTCLang script without a debugger to step through it, examining variables, etc. Debugging a script presently involves using print statements to send output at various points. A debugger could even use the GUI capabilities of various host operating systems; it would interact with the script through the UTCLang library like anything else. The challenge would be in merging the debugger with the custom extensions written by the driver's authors.

8.13 Summary

Implementing unit tests on C or C++ subsystems can be a nuisance, if everyone has to devise his or her own way of writing a test framework. Employing a common framework will help in regression testing through standardization. One such framework could be a scripting driver, which creates an interpreted language to invoke a C API or C++ public member functions. UTCLang provides such a framework, in the form of a library implementing a Smalltalk-like language. One can extend the language via classes in C++ or in the script language itself. After connecting UTCLang to the subsystem, unit tests take the form of scripts and their output.

CHAPTER 9

Test Quality Measurement: UTCCover

"On to problem report #16," said Michelle. With unit testing behind them, she had moved on to being the receiver of all problem reports from the Midearth Chemicals team that was system testing TurboChem 3.0.

George groaned. "How many of these did you say there were?"

"Twenty-nine. And this is just the first week's batch. Get used to it!" replied Michelle.

Sam, nursing his second cup of coffee, had to agree with George. Reviewing all these problem reports was quite tiresome.

"Before we go on, do we have any real idea how we missed these in unit testing?" Sam inquired. "After all, we did write up and implement decent test plans."

Linda replied, "All the ones we've investigated so far just fell through the cracks of the test plans. The unit test reviews managed to catch the glaring gaps in the tests, but there are still things we missed."

"Cracks? With all these problems, our test plans must look like Swiss cheese!" grumbled George.

"Well, it's not like you were immune to bugs!" Linda retorted, eyes glinting.

"Wait, hold on, relax!" cried Sam. "We really need to figure out how to prevent this from happening again!"

George said, "But if we made a conscientious effort to write a good test plan, how can we catch places we've missed? By definition, we won't have thought of those cases."

George was right. How could they find out what they had forgotten to test? Sam thought about this problem while Michelle described problem report #16.

9.1 Introduction

It is bad enough that unit test code, like any other code, might contain bugs. What is in some ways worse is that it is difficult to determine if a given test suite adequately tests its subsystem. It is easy to tell that a single case for a 10,000-line subsystem is probably inadequate. However, for larger suites, it becomes difficult to tell by manual inspection. This chapter focuses on one solution, test coverage, that can help determine the quality of the test suite, just as the suite helps determine the quality of a subsystem.

Approaches to Test Suite QA

A test suite must be large and deep enough to thoroughly test its subsystem. Failure to accomplish this will result in little benefit from unit testing. After all, the goal of testing is to identify the faults in the subsystem. Any faults missed due to incomplete unit testing will be found and dealt with during system testing or, worse, will be shipped with the product. Conversely, the more faults found during unit testing, the fewer will slip into the shipped application.

One approach to assuring the quality of a test suite is by using a condition catalog (e.g., UTCGen) or other heuristics for case selection. These give testers ideas of what a suite should include. Even here, though, humans make mistakes, forgetting possible conditions by missing sections of the catalog, etc. White-box test case generation is particularly susceptible to this. It is difficult to identify all possible situations by manually examining the C/C++ source code.

Another approach is to perform structured walkthroughs of the test code, in addition to the subsystem itself. People reviewing the tests will track what has been tried and what should be tested that is not being tested. However, again one runs into the problem of people making mistakes. Also, the bookkeeping for the reviewers, to determine what yet needs to be tested, is nontrivial. Finally, this is a labor-intensive process, involving a few team members for hours per subsystem.

Test Coverage

To determine the quality of a test suite, one must answer two questions:

- What is an objective measurement that can suggest, if not prove, that a unit test suite thoroughly tests its subsystem?
- What is a practical means for making this measurement?

One approach is to use the concept of **test coverage**. It can be defined loosely as "a measurement of what fraction of the possible states a program can be in that are tried by a test suite." Just as one worries about putting down an even, full coat of paint when painting a wall, one must write a test suite that leaves no gaps. Test coverage, in effect, does the same thing the structured walkthrough group does when reviewing test code for completeness. The difference is that test coverage is automated, with tools that handle the bookkeeping.

The easiest way to depict coverage is by showing **incomplete** coverage. Suppose we have a for() loop and fail to try the case where it is never executed (i.e., the test condition fails immediately). Perhaps there is something set inside the for() loop that will not get set if it is never executed. If, however, the test suite never tries this condition, it will never find the fault. Even if it tries every other likely combination for this for() loop (i.e., going through it once and several times), the coverage on the block is incomplete.

Suppose we have the following function:

```
int TstMustLoop(int iPasses)
{
    int iResult; // note: not initialized to a value
    int i; // loop index

    for (i=0;i<iPasses;i++)
    {
        iResult=TstChecksum(pszGlobalString, iResult);
    }

    return(iResult);
}
```

If iPasses is set to zero when this function is called, iResult will never be set to a value, since it is not initialized and the loop will never execute. The return value is undefined. If a test suite only tries iPasses greater than zero, this case will never be detected.

If the specification calls for iPasses to be positive, there should either be an assertion or a defensive programming test to ensure this is true for each call. Hence, one might wind up with the following function:

```
int TstMustLoop(int iPasses)
{
    int iResult; // note: not initialized to a value
    int i; // loop index

    Assert(i>0); // confirm contract being upheld

    for (i=0;i<iPasses;i++)
    {
        iResult=TstChecksum(pszGlobalString, iResult);
    }

    return(iResult);
}
```

What measuring coverage can do is ensure that your test suite tries all combinations stipulated by that coverage type. For example, complete branch coverage states that all logical branches (if() statements) have been tried in both the true and false directions. Coverage analysis tools can measure these metrics, giving varied views as to how well the test suite exercises the subsystem.

Goal: Complete Coverage

As with any new process, coverage analysis must have goals. Primarily, it must objectively determine how well a unit test suite is exercising its subsystem. Uncovered gaps indicate areas that need further testing.

One might expect, therefore, that the goal is to achieve 100% coverage. While this might be true in an ideal world, from a practical standpoint, it is impossible. Coverage measurement tools do not know everything about an application. What is desired from this analysis is 100% coverage of the **practical** conditions, not necessarily of the conceivable ones. Therefore, less than 100% coverage may be acceptable.

Software Contracts

Especially when software contracts are used, some branches (or other conditions) are simply physically impossible. Values that the contract prohibits may cause a missed-coverage notice if they are not tried. The coverage tool, of course, knows nothing about the contract, so it will point out these gaps even in impossible situations.

A common case is in defensive programming, one approach to embedding information about the software contract into the program itself. It leads to statements that check for illegal input values, returning error codes as needed. Of course, in a properly implemented application, there will be no illegal values. However, failing to try them may trigger a coverage warning. There are three ways to deal with this:

- Ignore the extraneous warnings.
- Switch from defensive programming to assertions and disable the assertions during coverage testing, thus preventing the coverage warnings.
- Add unit tests on subsystem API functions that specifically try the illegal values. This will eliminate the warnings for API functions, but if one uses defensive programming in private functions, warnings on those checks may still be raised.

Exception Handling

Other warnings may arise from exception handling procedures that are not normally part of a test suite. Some exceptions are difficult or impossible to create in a controlled testing environment, or at least in an automatic regression test mechanism. Hence, coverage analysis will report that these sections have not been tried. Obviously, one must still test them, perhaps in a manner that will not involve the coverage analysis tool (e.g., strict code walkthrough only).

Suppose one is creating a subsystem that interacts with a database server. There is surely an error code indicating that the server is down. The application's response is to retry the operation at 10-second intervals for 40 seconds, then shut down the application after informing the user.

Testing this error code may be difficult. One can use a custom stub that returns the error value. Typically, though, one would not unit test or regression test such a low-level subsystem with a stubbed-out database library. The error handler may have to be tested separately, using such a stub. This would not be a part of the "normal" unit test suite that can be regression tested. Coverage warnings about missing that logic can be ignored. However, the team must ensure that if changes might affect the error handler, it must be manually re-tested.

Faults in Coverage Tools

Coverage tools are not perfect, by any stretch of the imagination. Some may report gaps that, in reality, are simply impossible due to language constraints.

UTCCover will report incomplete coverage on do...while() loops. It cannot tell the difference between a do...while() and a while() loop and so always reports that do...while() loops are never tried where the loop is never executed (i.e., when the test fails the first time).

Limits of Coverage Analysis

Even if one could achieve 100% coverage of every type, this is **still** not a guarantee that the application is free from faults. The ultimate type of coverage, path coverage, states that each potential way an application could be executed has been tried. For most applications (which could run forever), there are an infinite number of paths. Even for finite-duration programs, the number of paths is typically ridiculously large. So 100% path coverage is usually impossible to achieve, yet it is the only type that has a chance of guaranteeing that all faults have been executed.

9.2 Why Use Coverage?

As noted above, coverage analysis cannot guarantee anything. One might wonder what use it is, given this limitation. There is the argument, of course, that quality assurance does not guarantee anything, either. Yet we still are concerned about it, so it must have some benefit. However, there are several more direct reasons why coverage analysis is useful.

Quality Reassurance

While coverage analysis does not provide a rock-solid guarantee that the tested subsystem works, it does help reassure project teams that their testing is robust. 100% practical coverage is a strong statement regarding the depth and breadth of the unit testing. Conversely, low coverage levels indicate that the team should conduct more testing.

Having coverage metrics to cite to end users or clients may also be useful, to reassure them that the application will work without failures.

Continuous Improvement

Continuous improvement has been discussed frequently in this book. It is the process by which quality assurance activities improve both the current product and the process by which future products are made. Feedback from unit testing, for example, can affect the development and unit testing of the next generation of products, hopefully preventing whole categories of faults.

When coverage analysis indicates that something was not tested enough, one must determine how to complete the coverage. In addition, one should determine the reasons for the gap—what can the team do during test design to prevent such gaps from occurring? This will help testing for future products, perhaps even eliminating the need for multiple passes to achieve 100% coverage.

Staff Education

Not only should the process “learn” from coverage gaps, using continuous improvement plans, but the staff should also learn from mistakes. No one is born a perfect tester! Hence, there should be no shame in failing to reach 100% practical coverage, so long as one gets a better understanding of how to implement more effective tests the next time around. Even with tools like coverage analyzers, it is still better to enable people to implement better tests, because that training may well pay dividends in areas where tools cannot help.

9.3 Types of Coverage

As described above, there are several ways to measure the abstract notion of "code coverage." Each uses a different programming construct (e.g., branches, loops) as its measure. They also differ in ease of implementation. The following sections describe the most common coverage types.

Function Call Coverage

The simplest type of coverage is the answer to the question: "Have we tried every function at least once?" This seems trivial—if a function has not been tried, nobody knows if there are bugs lurking within it. Hence, even without the strict concept of coverage, calling every function at least once is a common goal.

Missing Function Calls

Obviously, one misses on function call coverage by failing to call functions. This can occur for many reasons, including the following:

- Junior testers failing to try each API function, based on assumptions about their related implementation
- Failing to select proper API input values to cause certain internal functions to be evaluated
- Ignoring certain subsystems (e.g., a linked list manager used by several application-specific subsystems)

Impractical Coverage

Some functions may defy function call coverage. Special error-handling functions may be difficult to test and therefore might be excluded from the normal test suite. An example would be an error-handling function that takes control when a database server reports a critical error (e.g., data indexes corrupted). It may not be easy or effective to force such an error on the server manually. If possible, such functions should be tested in isolation; they may depend on other parts of the program, however, and be untestable this way.

Available Coverage Tools

Depending on how the unit test suite is set up, a source code profiler can measure function call coverage. For example, if a UTCLang driver is used for unit testing, one can have a single script that invokes all unit test cases. In this case, running the driver under a profiler can capture which functions were called. Although usually only thought of as a performance analysis tool, source profilers can also be important testing tools.

UTCCover, the tool profiled in this chapter, can track function call coverage for both C functions and C++ member functions.

Branch Coverage

Branch coverage asks "Have all logical branches been taken in both the true and the false directions?" As with function call coverage, large chunks of code can be left untested if branches are not tried in both directions.

Missed Coverage

Branches are missed because an inadequate set of input values is provided, either as parameters or as data obtained from external sources (e.g., databases). Even though the function may be called (and, hence, call coverage satisfied), if one does not try certain logical branches in both directions, one might miss faults..

One can see this in a variant on the TstMustLoop() function shown previously:

```
int TstMustBranch(int iBool)
{
    int iResult; // note: not initialized to a value

    if (iBool)
    {
        iResult=TstSomeOtherFunction();
    }

    return(iResult);
}
```

Again, iResult is never set if the boolean parameter is false; if the unit test suite never tries false, nobody will catch this bug.

Impractical Coverage

Certain branches may be unreachable from one direction. Error handling, as described in the function call coverage section above, is a classic example. Another example is when defensive programming has been used instead of assertions to validate input parameters. If the function being called is not directly tested by the unit test suite, the parameters may never be invalid, so the validation test will never fail. As with all coverage mechanisms, these conditions will simply have to be recognized as unreachable.

Suppose we have a function that employs defensive programming to check parameters for validity:

```
void TstDefendedFunction(char *pszBuffer)
{
    if (!pszBuffer) return(TST_NULL_BUFFER);

// rest of function here
}
```

A well-written program will never pass a NULL buffer to this function, so the defensive programming test will never be true. Hence, coverage analysis tools might complain unnecessarily about "unfulfilled" coverage. There are three ways to deal with this:

- Modify the tool to stop it from reporting these cases.
- Ignore the messages when they appear.
- Switch from defensive programming to an assertion-based system (with the assertions turned off during coverage analysis runs).

UTCCover, in addition to function call coverage, measures branch coverage.

Loop Coverage

Loop coverage is similar to branch coverage. The question here is "Have we tried all loops in all three ways they can be executed: zero times, exactly once, and several times?"

This type of coverage is more difficult to understand than the previous two. Executing a loop zero times means that the loop body is never executed. The distinction between this and going through the loop at least once is fairly easy to see. This is exactly the same as the branch true/false option, just coded with a loop construct (for(), while(), or do...while() in C/C++).

This was demonstrated earlier, with the TstMustLoop() function. In that function, one would miss a bug if it were not tested in a zero-pass loop situation.

This does not explain the distinction between exactly one pass through the loop and more than one. There is no strong underlying logical distinction between the two. It is merely a common heuristic: Executing a loop exactly once might have a bug, whereas executing it several times might not. This is similar to some of the rules in a test condition catalog, recommending that one try arrays with zero, one, or several elements. Strictly speaking, this extra level of coverage is not necessary, but it has been demonstrated to point out additional faults and so is worth the effort.

Suppose we have a function like the one below, which iterates over a linked list and returns the entry before the one containing a specified value:

```
LIST_ENTRY TstFindEntryBefore(LIST_ENTRY *pHead, char *pszValue)
{
    LIST_ENTRY *pPrev
    LIST_ENTRY *pCur=pHead;

    while (pCur)
    {
        if (strcmp(pCur->pszValue, pszValue)==0)
        {
            return(pPrev);
        }
        pPrev=pCur;
        pCur=pCur->pNext;
    }

    return(pCur);
}
```

One might use this function to maintain a sorted, singly linked list.

If this loop is executed zero times, meaning that pHead is NULL, it will return a NULL value (the final value of pCur). If the loop is executed one or more times, it will return either the element before a match (the value of pPrev) or, if there is no match, NULL.

Suppose there is a match on the first list entry (pHead->pszValue matches pszValue). In this case, the loop will be entered once, and, since there is a match, it will return the value of pPrev. However, pPrev has not been initialized. The actual value returned will not necessarily be NULL, which is the logical return value in this case, since there is no link "before" the match. If there is a match on the second or later entry, pPrev will have been set to a value, so it will return the proper result.

Hence, this is an example of a loop that displays a bug only when executed exactly once.

UTCCover, in addition to function call and branch coverage, can measure loop coverage.

Multiple Condition Coverage

Multiple condition coverage is a specialization of the branch and loop coverages described above. The question here is "Have we tried all permutations of loop condition parameters based on the logical operands being used?"

Suppose we have an if() statement that looks like:

```
if (A | B) {...}
```

According to the ANSI C "short circuit" rule, if A is true, B will not be evaluated. This leads to three ways in which the statement can be executed, as illustrated in Table 9.1.

Table 9.1 Short-Circuit Evaluation of A | B

A Value	B Value	Result
False	False	False
False	True	False
True	Not evaluated	True

Branch coverage may be satisfied, meaning the if() statement as a whole is taken both true and false, without B ever evaluating to true. Branch coverage would be met by both A and B being false, plus one pass with A being true. These conditions are met by scenarios 1 and 3. If those two were selected, there will be no case where B evaluates to true (second scenario). It is entirely possible, though, that B might have a bug when it evaluates to true, or it might never evaluate to true (although it should).

Suppose we have the following function, which returns a pointer to the first occurrence of a newline ('\n') or NULL in the character string:

```
char *TstLastCharInLine(char *pszLine)
{
    char *pszCur=pszLine;

    while (*pszCur && *(pszCur++)!='\n');

    return(pszCur-1); // back up one to offset postincrement
}
```

This function will behave inconsistently, depending on which condition is met, because the second one uses the postincrement operator to change pszCur. If *pszCur is NULL, the first condition will fail, so pszCur will be pointing to the NULL on return. If, however, *pszCur is the newline character, pszCur will point to the character after it when the function returns. This change is courtesy of the postincrement (++) operator. Since the return statement subtracts 1 from pszCur, the proper value will be returned for newlines but not for NULLs.

A unit test might test various locations for a newline character (first, second, or later position in the string) and meet loop coverage. However, if it fails to try a string without newlines, it will not uncover this bug.

What multiple condition coverage does is indicate whether each *term* in the logical expression has been taken both true and false, whereas branch coverage examines the entire statement's outcome.

As with branch coverage, multiple condition coverage can turn up spurious failures due to defensive programming. In fact, defensive programming often takes advantage of the short-circuit facility by putting "sanity check" terms in branches before the real condition is tried.

The most frequent use of short-circuit behavior is in checking string parameters for validity. Suppose a function takes a string (pszInput) as input, and the contract calls for it to be non-NULL and non-zero in length. This check could be coded in two statements:

```
if (!pszInput) return(TST_NULL_BUFFER);
if (*pszInput=='\0') return(TST_BUFFER_TOO_SHORT);
```

If the same error code were to be returned for both failures, one can take advantage of the short-circuit rule, using the following code:

```
if (!pszInput || *pszInput=='\0') return(TST_ILLEGAL_STRING);
```

One might worry about this code, because if pszInput is NULL and the second test were executed, one would be dereferencing a NULL pointer, probably causing a protected memory exception. However, the ANSI C short-circuit rule guarantees that this will never happen. If pszInput were NULL, the left-hand test would fail and the right-hand one would never be evaluated.

Statement Coverage

Statement coverage's question is "Have we executed each line of code at least once?" This is a frequently thought-of coverage metric, especially for teams that use lines of code as a productivity measure. Like function-call coverage, it makes perfect sense: If the test suite did not execute the line of code, the testers have no idea if it contains a bug.

In many ways, however, statement coverage is weaker than loop and branch coverages (with or without multiple condition coverage). Both these types might cover the same lines of code in different ways, but the differences can point out bugs of their own.

Earlier, we described a function TstMustBranch() that shows how missed branch coverage might not catch a bug. In this case, one could have 100% statement coverage without catching that bug. Complete coverage requires that the branch be tried in the true direction only, so the test executes all statements in the function. A test in the false direction, which would have shown the bug, is not required to achieve full statement coverage, since it adds no statements.

As with function-call coverage, a source code profiler can usually measure statement coverage. Most profilers, such as Borland's Turbo Profiler, can track the time or execution counts for each line of code in a function, source module, or application. C statements that have zero execution counts were not tried during the period being profiled. When the entire unit test suite is run under the profiler, the profiler can report on statement coverage for the entire subsystem under test.

Path Coverage

Path coverage is an extremely powerful coverage measure. It asks "Have we executed the function/subsystem/application in all logically distinct manners?"

Suppose we have the following C function:

```
void TstFourPaths(int iFirst, int iSecond)
{
    if (iFirst>1)
    {
        // some logic here
    }
    else
    {
        // more logic here
    }

    if (iSecond > 10)
    {
        // and more logic here
    }
    else
    {
        // yet more logic here
    }

    return;
}
```

The two branches can have branch coverage satisfied by selecting iFirst=0, iSecond=0 and iFirst=2, iSecond=11. In this case, each branch will be taken both true and false.

However, there are four paths through the function altogether:

- First branch true, second branch true
- First branch true, second branch false
- First branch false, second branch true
- First branch false, second branch false

It is possible that by only achieving branch coverage on a function, a test will not try a particular path that contains a fault. In general, if there is more than one decision point (branch or loop) in a function, there are more paths than branch/loop coverage will cover.

As one might imagine, path coverage is difficult to measure. To measure coverage, one must know all possible outcomes and whether they were tried. This is simple for coverage measures such as branch coverage (was a given if() statement taken true and false?). However, path coverage assumes we can determine, by static analysis, every possible logical path. Usually, this is difficult to achieve. Furthermore, creating a tool that could determine path coverage automatically would be difficult as well. This is especially true when data outside the program itself (e.g., database records) determines program paths. It may be impossible for a static analyzer to determine which paths that data might trigger.

Mutation Coverage

One would think that path coverage is the ultimate solution. After all, if we execute every logical path in the system, every software fault must have been executed. While this might be true, it misses one key element to testing: Not only must the fault be executed, it must be detected.

Suppose we have a function like:

```
void TstSubstring(char *pszDest, char *pszSource, int iStart, int iCount)
{
    int i;

    for (i=0;i<iCount;i++)
    {
        *(pszDest++)=pszSource[iStart-i];
    }

    return;
}
```

There is a typo here: iStart - i should be iStart + i. If this function were tested with iCount=0, the test would not catch the bug. Moreover, both our version and the proper one would behave the same. Loop coverage would report incomplete coverage on the for() loop, but if it is not available, one might miss this bug.

Mutation coverage takes an entirely different approach. One might say that it tries to prove that every possible typographical error has been proven not to have occurred. Mutation coverage takes a piece of code being tested and tries the unit test on the original version, as well as on every possible semantically correct version with one (or more) tokens altered.

There are several ways in which TstSubstring() could be mutated, including the following:

- Replace the 0 in the for() loop initialization with 1, or another likely constant (constant mutation).
- Replace the iCount in the for() loop comparison with iStart (variable mutation).
- Replace the - with + in the array index (operation mutation).

Note that this last mutation actually yields the "correct" version.

If a unit test suite cannot differentiate the original source and copies of the mutated source, then it is inadequate. There is no way to tell by the unit test alone which version is correct. One might assume that the original is right, but the developer might have made a typo and the "proper" edition is one of the mutations. The unit test should be augmented to prove that one version is correct.

Suppose we implemented a test suite that only tried TstSubstring() with iCount=0. If we apply mutation coverage, generating the three mutations shown above, the second one would result in a different copied string than the original, assuming that iStart is not zero. However, the first one would have the same results, since the for() loop would never be executed, as will the third mutation. The fact that our test suite cannot distinguish the original function from two mutations indicates that it needs to be augmented. To force a difference between the original and the third mutation, we would have to try making iCount greater than zero, which will point out the bug.

Path coverage may be difficult to determine, but mutation coverage is nearly impossible. For a given piece of source, the number of possible mutations is extremely large. All of them would have to be generated, compiled, and tested with the test suite. A hefty percentage will fail to run at all, because the mutation will cause the program to crash. One can discard them immediately—valid programs are assumed not to crash. However, the remaining ones must have their test results compared to the original source. Any that have identical outputs are failures in the unit test suite. All of this would take an enormous amount of time and computing power for even small units of code.

Sometime in the future, mutation testing may be a viable option for mission-critical sections of code. Until then, simpler metrics will be the only ones available.

Summary

There are many possible coverage metrics, assuming one can find a tool to capture them. Table 9.2 outlines the different metrics and identifies which are available in UTCCover, this book's coverage analysis package.

Table 9.2 Summary of Coverage Metrics

Metric	Description	In Profiler?	In UTCCover?
Function Call	Have we tried every function at least once?	Y	Y
Branch	Have all logical branches been taken in both the true and the false directions?	N	Y
Loop	Have we tried all loops in all three ways they can be executed?	N	Y
Multiple Condition	Have we tried all permutations of loop condition parameters based on the logical operands being used?	N	N
Statement	Have we executed each line of code at least once?	Y	N
Path	Have we executed the function/ subsystem/application in all logically distinct manners?	N	N
Mutation	Has every possible typographical error been proven not to have occurred?	N	N

9.4 What Is UTCCover?

Coverage analyzers, based on the previous discussion, are a worthy addition to the toolbox of projects. This book contains one, called UTCCover. It provides a simple means of measuring function call, loop, and branch coverage. Furthermore, one can use it with any ANSI C compiler, regardless of platform.

UTCCover, like ResTrack, takes the approach of "instrumenting" code. The term "instrumenting" basically means that one adds behaviors to existing actions, such as indicating when functions return, without altering them. ResTrack instruments the memory allocation/release functions (e.g., malloc()) to track what blocks have been allocated and freed.

UTCCover instruments C operations to handle its coverage metrics. Specifically, it alters the following:

- The return statement (both void returns and returns with arguments), to indicate that a specific function has ended
- The if() statement, to identify branch coverage
- The while() statement (both as while() { ... } and as do { ... } while();) for loop coverage
- The for() statement, also for loop coverage

Some coverage analysis tools have their own preprocessor, which "filters" normal C code and adds in the instrumentation. The resulting file is then compiled with the normal compiler. This not only requires the ability to parse C and C++ files correctly but also changes the makefile.

UTCCover takes a simpler route by using C macros to add the instrumentation, as ResTrack did. This has the advantage of eliminating the need for a separate preprocessor. It does, however, restrict the capabilities of the coverage metrics, since some (e.g., path coverage) cannot be measured this way.

Using UTCCover, given this instrumentation approach, is fairly simple. One includes a special C header file containing the instrumentation macros. One then links the program as usual, including an extra file with logging functions used by the instrumentation code. Running the instrumented program will collect statistics on what happened in the program. These statistics, coupled with the source, allow a separate reporting tool to identify what has been adequately covered and what needs more work.

9.5 Using UTCCover

UTCCover has ease of use as one goal. Without it, few developers will take the time to measure coverage, and the value of the tool is diminished. One can generate coverage statistics with simple modifications to the source code and makefiles; results are available via a separate reporting tool.

The following sections describe how to use UTCCover for C/C++ programs.

Instrumenting Code

As mentioned above, UTCCover uses a special header file, UTCLOG.H, which provides macros to instrument source code. They augment the return, if, for, and while operations to log these events in addition to their normal operation. The log is then used to determine what needs to be tried for complete coverage.

To set up a subsystem to track coverage using UTCCover, only two steps are required:

- Include UTCLOG.H in every source file to be instrumented.
- Add UTCLOG.C to the source files.

If coverage statistics are to be repeatedly yet infrequently collected, using the #ifdef directive can make it easy to selectively compile the program with coverage analysis enabled.

In the following example, if a macro named COVERAGE_ON is defined, coverage will be enabled for the source file:

```
#ifdef COVERAGE_ON
#include "utclog.h"
#endif
// rest of file here
```

One can then enable coverage simply by defining COVERAGE_ON, which most compilers allow from the command line. For example, in the Borland compiler, -DCOVERAGE_ON as part of the compilation command would enable coverage.

Note that one still must include UTCLOG.C in the overall library or executable. Many makefile interpreters allow a conditional expression, akin to an #ifdef, that can allow a single makefile to work in coverage and normal modes.

Capturing Test Information

A program instrumented with UTCCover will automatically create a file named UTCCOV.LOG in the current working directory to hold coverage statistics generated by the instrumented code. This file is automatically opened by the coverage functions in UTCLOG.C and closed when the application is stopped.

Running several tests in a row in the same directory will cause all coverage information to be stored in UTCCOV.LOG, since it is opened in append mode. This makes it easy to collect statistics from a whole unit test suite. If the tests must be run from different directories, for whatever reason, simply concatenate the log files manually.

Since UTCCover adds multiple test runs to UTCCOV.LOG, one must delete it at the **beginning** of each overall test suite run. Otherwise, the results over many versions of the source would be combined. Moreover, the file names and line numbers in the old data may be inaccurate. Also, the reporting tool (described below) can read results from multiple log files. Hence, one can arrange for a test suite to generate a single coverage file or multiple ones, as desired.

Obtaining Results

Given coverage results for an application or subsystem, one must generate a report outlining what was missed. This book provides such a tool, called UTC-COVER, that generates the report. It uses a command-line interface, similar to the UTCGen test condition generator. Hence, one can use it in any environment offering a command shell.

To generate a report, simply run the tool with the coverage files to be parsed on the command line. Since the results are written to standard output, one can redirect them to an ASCII file by using the shell's normal redirection facility.

If all results go into UTCCOV.LOG, then, under most shells, the command line simply would look like the following:

```
UTCCOVER UTCCOV.LOG > RESULTS.OUT
```

Here are some results from an early version of the UTCLang unit test:

```
handle.cpp:84 Try making expression false

        pRef=new UtcObjectReference(1, pszName, pClass, (UtcObject *)0);
-->     if (pRef)
        {
            Globals.AddEntry(pRef); /* add the global with given name */
-------------------------------------------------------
parser.cpp:32 Try following loops: once
        szEndQuote[1]='\0';
        cChar=*pszInput;
-->     while (cChar!='\0') /* while not end of input string    */
        {
            if (bStopOnSpace && isspace(cChar))
-------------------------------------------------------
```

Interpreting Results

The final step is to examine the report UTCCover generates and determine what needs to be done to gain complete practical coverage. Each spot in the code that fails a coverage metric generates an entry in the output file. Each entry provides three pieces of information:

- The location (file and line number) of the code that did not meet the coverage standard
- A description of what needs to be done to complete the coverage
- A snippet of the code around the failed location, with the failing line highlighted

---

The first entry in the above example was from line 84 of HANDLE.CPP, one of the UTCLang source files. It listed five lines of source, including the offending branch. The recommendation is to "try making expression false," meaning that the branch was only taken in the true direction during the test.

The goal, of course, is to modify the unit test plan to gain 100% coverage on all metrics. If a function was never called, for example, one should add test cases that ensure that it gets called. For loop and branch coverages, one must examine the loop itself and see what happened. One knows that 100% practical coverage has been met when all items reported by UTCCover are known, expected misses of coverage (e.g., exception handlers not regression tested).

9.6 How UTCCover Works

UTCCover consists of four main pieces:

- A header file providing macro redefinitions of C language elements that provide information relative to coverage
- A C library for recording the coverage information provided by the macros
- A C library for providing coverage statistics based on the coverage logs
- A shell executable that provides these statistics to users

The following sections describe each area in greater detail.

Macros

Like ResTrack, UTCCover uses C preprocessor macros to add behavior above and beyond normal actions taken by C keywords. Here, the goal is to get the instrumented C code to provide information regarding what paths through the code have been taken so the tools can measure coverage.

Four such macros are defined in UTCLOG.H.

while

On a while() loop, one needs to know what happens on each pass. To do this, while() is instrumented as shown below.

Here is the macro in UTCLOG.H that instruments the while() operation:

```
#define while(a) while(UtcLogEvent(UTC_WHILE, (long) (a), __FILE__, \
__LINE__))
```

The UtcLogEvent() function, described in greater detail below, will return the value provided to it. The result of the while loop will not change; the sole difference is that the events are logged.

If one had a while() operation like:

```
while (i < 5)
{
// some work here
}
```

it would look like this with the UTCCover macro expanded:

```
while (UtcLogEvent(UTC_WHILE, (long) (i<5), __FILE__, __LINE__))
{
// some work here
}
```

Table 9.3 outlines which events get generated for different ways of using a while() loop.

Table 9.3 Events Generated by UTCCover for While() Loops

Condition	Description	Events
Zero passes	Condition is false on first invocation	UTC_WHILE:0
Exactly one pass	Condition is true first time, false second time	UTC_WHILE:1, UTC_WHILE: 0
More than one pass	Condition is true several times, then false	UTC_WHILE:1 (several times), UTC_WHILE: 0

if

An if() statement is simpler than a while()—it is only executed once per pass (rather than in a loop). Its macro is largely the same as for while(), in that the boolean expression is "wrapped" in a call that returns the same value while simultaneously logging it.

Below is the macro used by UTCCover to instrument an if():

```
#define if(a) if(UtcLogEvent(UTC_IF, (long) (a), __FILE__, __LINE__))
```

If we had an if() that looked like:

```
if (i < 5)
{
// some work here
}
```

it would look like this with the macro expanded:

```
if (UtcLogEvent(UTC_IF, (long) (i<5), __FILE__, __LINE__))
{
// some work here
}
```

---

for

The for() construct, in theory, would work like the while() loop. Unfortunately, there is a problem, caused by a limitation of the C preprocessor. A for statement has three parts delimited by semicolons: the initialization, the comparison, and the index change section. Ideally, the event-logging function call would be in the comparison section, as in while(). The problem is that the preprocessor does not recognize semicolons as delimiters. Hence, the entire contents of the for() statement can be replaced, but not a single section, and certainly not the middle one.

In a perfect world, the following would be UTCCover's macro for tracking for() loops:

```
#define for(a;b;c) for(UtcLogEvent(UTC_FORSTART, 0, __FILE__, __LINE__); \
                       UtcLogEvent(UTC_FORPASS, 0, __FILE__, __LINE);c)
```

Since semicolons cannot be used for parameter delimiters in the C preprocessor (as in for(a;b;c)), this will not work.

The solution is to tag the event log at the end of the for(), which gets fired on every completed loop. If the for() comparison fails the first time, the event log will not be called, but it will otherwise be executed once per pass through the loop. To handle the zero-iteration case, the macro also logs an event before the for() gets executed. If the loop fails on the first comparison, the pre-for event is the only one logged.

Here is what UTCCover actually uses for for() loops:

```
#define for(a) UtcLogEvent(UTC_FORSTART, 0L, __FILE__, __LINE__); \
               for(a, UtcLogEvent(UTC_FORLOOP, 0L, __FILE__, __LINE__))
```

If we had a for() loop like this:

```
for (i=0;i<5;i++)
{
// some work here
}
```

it would look like the code shown below with the macro expanded, except that the first two lines below would physically be one line in the source file:

```
UtcLogEvent(UTC_FORSTART, 0L, __FILE__, __LINE);
for (i=0;i<5;i++, UtcLogEvent(UTC_FORLOOP, 0L, __FILE__, __LINE__)
{
// some work here
}
```

The reason for keeping the entire macro on one line is so the value returned by the __LINE__ manifest constant is the same for both UtcLogEvent() calls. This makes it easy to match up loop starts with loop passes—the file and line numbers are the same.

Table 9.4 outlines which events get generated for different ways of using a for() loop.

Table 9.4 Events Generated by UTCCover for For() Loops

Condition	Description	Events
Zero passes	Condition is false on first invocation	UTC_FORSTART
Exactly one pass	Condition is true first time, false second time	UTC_FORSTART UTC_FORLOOP
More than one pass	Condition is true several times, then false	UTC_FORSTART, UTC_FORLOOP (several times)

return

To measure function call coverage, one needs to know which functions were executed. There is no good way to instrument a function call itself. However, it is easy to instrument returns by adding a macro redefinition of return.

Here is the macro used by UTCCover for tracking function returns:

```
#define return UtcLogEvent(UTC_RETURN, 0L, __FILE__, __LINE__); return
```

If we had a function like:

```
int TstReturnCoverage()
{
// some work here
    return(1);
}
```

it would look like this with the return macro expanded:

```
int TstReturnCoverage()
{
// some work here
    UtcLogEvent(UTC_RETURN, 0L, __FILE__, __LINE__); return(1);
}
```

This redefinition works for both void returns and ones with a value. With return statements logging events, the uncovered functions are those that have no return log event. Admittedly, there are other ways to leave a function which this approach will miss. Also note that the instrumentation will not measure whether constructors or destructors are executed, since they do not contain return statements.

One type of function that would not encounter the macro would be one that uses longjmp(). It is used for non-local "goto's" and is sometimes used in error handling or coroutine packages. The longjmp() call returns control to a prior setjmp() by unwinding the stack rather than by executing return. This could be overcome by instrumenting longjmp() as well.

Another example would be the use of C++ structured exceptions, which cause non-local jumps when an exception occurs. They, too, might be covered via another macro.

Event Logging

All the above macros use UtcLogEvent() for the physical act of logging the event. It takes four parameters:

- A number indicating the type of event
- A number indicating the boolean value of the event (used for if() and while())
- The filename where the event occurred (provided by the __FILE__ manifest constant)
- The line number where the event occurred (provided by the __LINE__ manifest constant)

The function returns the value passed to it. Thus, a UtcLogEvent() call can be simply "wrapped" around the original expression without any effect on it.

The following is the source for UtcLogEvent():

```
long UtcLogEvent(UTC_EVENTCODE iEvent, long lValue,
                     char *pszFile, unsigned long ulLine)
{
    if (!pLogFile && !bAtExitDone)
    {
        pLogFile=fopen("utccov.log", "a");
        atexit(UtcCloseLogFile);
    }
    if (pLogFile)
    {
        fprintf(pLogFile, "%d,%ld,%s,%lu\n", iEvent, lValue,
                pszFile, ulLine);
    }
    return(lValue);
}
```

If the log file has not been opened yet, UtcLogEvent() opens it by using a global file handle. It also registers an atexit() function to close the file when the application terminates. Then, the values provided to the function are written to the log.

Note that the global file handle means that UtcLogEvent() is not thread-safe. If UTCCover is used for Windows 3.1 DLLs, do not try to run two programs using that DLL at the same time while coverage is enabled. Similarly, do not use UTCCover in multithreaded programs.

This function opens the UTCCOV.LOG file on the first event, registering an atexit() function to close the file when the program terminates. This, of course, means that abnormal terminations might not close the file, resulting in lost statistics.

The UtcLogEvent() function is in UTCLOG.C. One must add it to all applications adding coverage analysis with UTCCover. It can be removed when the application is recompiled for production use, of course.

Reporting

Given that one has obtained coverage statistics from sessions running instrumented code, one needs a way to generate metrics that are usable for improving the test suite. As with many tools provided in this book, UTCCover has been split into an interface shell and a library performing the bulk of the work. This allows new user interfaces to be built (perhaps using a windowing GUI) without having to touch the actual application logic.

Shell

The command-line-based shell for UTCCover is in UTCSHELL.C. It simply parses the log files provided on the command line, then uses the library to obtain and display the results. The defined value UTC_LINES (in UTCSHELL.C) indicates how many lines to show when displaying code fragments. Here, 5 means that two lines around the one with the missed coverage should be shown. All output goes to standard output, so one may redirect it to a file if needed.

There are three main phases to the shell's operation. It first initializes a handle to the UTCCover library and asks the library to parse the files shown on the command line.

Here is a piece of the UTCSHELL.C main() function that performs the initialization and parsing:

```
if (UtcInitHandle(&hHandle))
{
    printf("Error initializing coverage API!\n");
    return(0);
}

for (i=1;i<argc;i++)
{
    if (UtcParseLogFile(hHandle, argv[i]))
    {
        printf("Error parsing file %s\n", argv[i]);
        UtcFreeHandle(hHandle);
        return(0);
    }
}
```

The second phase prepares the output lines, then iterates through the library's missed coverage entries and displays each on the output file. The library can supply the location (filename/line number), source code, and description of the missed coverage. The entries can be iterated by use of UtcGetFirstEntry() and UtcGetNextEntry(). They return a structure with the coverage information. One can obtain the source for a given entry via UtcGetSourceForCurrentEntry().

The final phase simply cleans up all resources—the allocated space for the lines and the data held by the UTCCover library behind the requested handle.

Library

The UTCCover library works like many of the libraries in this book. It exports a handle (COV_HANDLE), which is an opaque data handle that references information it needs. It also exports API functions that use the handle to perform various coverage-related functions. A C++ implementation would probably create a UtcCoverageAnalyzer class to perform the same operations.

There are three function categories in this API:

- The handle initialization and termination functions, UtcInitHandle() and UtcFreeHandle(), respectively. One must call UtcInitHandle() to create a library handle before using any other API functions. Similarly, one must call UtcFreeHandle() at the end to release resources held by the handle.
- The parsing function, UtcParseLogFile(). This function, given a library handle and filename, will read the coverage results listed in the file and generate a list of misses.
- Functions for returning results, which allow shells to obtain information about where coverage was missed. Table 9.5 outlines the four functions related to this operation.

Table 9.5 Coverage Reporting API Functions

API Function	Purpose
UtcGetFirstEntry()	Returns a coverage information structure (UTC_COVERINFO) about the first entry in the list of missed coverage
UtcGetNextEntry()	Iterates through the list of entries and returns a coverage information structure on the next entry; fails when end of list is reached
UtcNameForType()	Given an enumerated value for a type, returns the string for that type
UtcGetSourceForCurrentEntry()	Returns the source code surrounding a given missed coverage entry, using a provided set of buffers

Below is the structure definition for the coverage information returned by UtcGetFirstEntry() and UtcGetNextEntry():

```
typedef struct { int iType;
                 char szFilename[UTC_MAXFILENAME];
                 unsigned long ulLine;
                 int bPassed;
                 char szDescription[UTC_MAXDESCRIPTION];
               } UTC_COVERINFO;
```

The type (iType) is an enumeration, as shown below:

```
typedef enum {  UTC_IF_ENTRY          = 0,
                UTC_WHILE_ENTRY       = 1,
                UTC_FOR_ENTRY         = 2,
                UTC_FN_CALL_ENTRY     = 3,
             } UTC_COVERAGETYPES;
```

The filename (szFilename) and line number (ulLine) are provided by the __FILE__ and __LINE__ manifest constants. The passed flag (bPassed) will be true if the test suite properly covered this construct, false otherwise. The description (szDescription) will only be filled in if coverage failed, and it will describe precisely what was missed.

9.7 Future Directions

UTCCover by itself offers a simple means of generating coverage statistics. However, it is unsophisticated in its instrumentation mechanism. Hence, it is limited in what it can measure and how it can interpret the results. Below are ways in which it could be enhanced to produce better results.

New Coverage Types

Other coverage types could be added to UTCCover's repertoire. While path and mutation coverage are currently beyond the scope of any tool at the present time, UTCCover could add support for multiple condition and statement coverage. This would require a more powerful C preprocessor than the ones provided with C/C++ compilers. It would instrument the source before passing it to the normal compiler, rather than using macros.

Generic Coverage Tool

Brian Marick of Testing Foundations has made publicly available his Generic Coverage Tool (GCT). This Unix package is more powerful than UTCCover, in large part because it uses a custom preprocessor to more fully instrument code. From the GCT documentation:

"The Generic Coverage Tool (GCT) is a freeware coverage tool that measures how thoroughly tests exercise C programs...GCT can measure the following:

1. how often branches have been taken in either direction (branch coverage)
2. how often cases in switches have been taken
3. how often nested logical conditions have evaluated to true and false (multiple condition coverage)
4. how often loops have iterated zero, one, and more than one time (loop coverage)
5. how often the boundaries of relational operators have been probed (relational coverage)
6. how often routines have been entered
7. how often call sites have been exercised
8. how often routines have had multiple threads of execution in them
9. weak mutation coverage (a research technique)"

Chapter 12 describes how to obtain a copy of GCT.

Linking Function Call and Loop/Branch Coverage

Presently, if 100% function call coverage is not achieved, the loop and branch coverage measures are inaccurate. If a given branch or loop is **never** executed (because the function or nested branch that contains it is never called), UTCCover does not know about the statement's existence and therefore does not report that it was never reached. This could be fixed by examining the source as a part of reporting the results and scanning for not-reached if(), while(), for(), or do...while() constructs.

Noting Impossible Situations

Presently, there is no way to tell UTCCover that a particular branch or loop is known never to be used in one particular fashion. Hence, UTCCover always reports that the affected branch/loop is incompletely covered. It would be useful to build a list or flag in the source to indicate to UTCCover that this situation is known. UTCCover would then strike references to it from the report. This would help in interpreting the test results.

Preventing Spurious Failures

There are places where UTCCover will give an obviously incorrect result, regardless of what the application is doing. The case where it fails to detect do...while() constructs was outlined earlier. The incorrect result occurs because the macro instrumenting while() cannot distinguish the two forms. Ideally, UTCCover would overcome this in the future.

Missed Function Call Coverage

There is one situation where function call coverage can fail quietly in UTCCover. If no functions in a source file are ever executed, UTCCover, in effect, does not "know" about it. Hence, it will never scan for functions in it and will not report that they were never called.

This is seldom a problem for subsystems that have several functions per source file, because typically at least one will be executed within a unit test suite. However, it becomes more acute when subsystems opt for a single function per source file. Here, function call coverage fails completely because the definition of missed coverage guarantees that UTCCover cannot report the miss. UTCCover needs to handle this better in the future, since many developers use the single-function approach.

9.8 Summary

Coverage analysis is a powerful tool for measuring the quality of a test suite. It helps managers and developers know how well the test suite measures the quality of a subsystem or application. Coverage analysis comes in many forms, from simple metrics measurable by a profiler (such as statement or function call coverage) to ones that are effectively impossible to measure. UTCCover handles several simpler coverage metrics, providing an easy means for measuring coverage on a C or C++ subsystem.

CHAPTER 10

The Final Stand

Given everything said so far, it should be clear that system testing is the final stand in the battle to avoid shipping faults. Ideally, unit/integration testing, coupled with sound designs and steps to ensure quality during development, would catch all software faults. In practice, this is unrealistic, even when using tools such as the ones provided here. Hence, system testing is necessary.

This chapter examines system testing, what it involves, and how to organize it effectively. It also discusses how to integrate system test into a continuous improvement program.

10.1 Form of a System Test

The "system" determines what a "system test" looks like. If the product is a library, such as a commercial-quality X-Base file access library, then a system test is effectively the same as the unit/integration test of the public API. In this case, the "system" is programmatic, and the "system test" will reflect that.

If the system is a noninteractive program, such as a C compiler, then a system test will entail trying out a wide variety of input files and ensuring that the results are correct. In the case of a C compiler, the test would try a number of C programs. It would ensure that the compiler behaves as expected (e.g., gives the proper warnings). In addition, it would confirm that the compiled output is the same as that produced by other compilers. In this case, the "system" is noninteractive, so one tests via file-based inputs and outputs.

Most systems, however, involve user interaction, either through a simple command-driven interface or a complex GUI. In this case, a system test will involve a user exercising the options available through the user interface, ensuring that the program behaves as expected. This is the traditional view of a true "system test."

10.2 Who Performs System Test?

One point upon which projects differ greatly is in who implements the system test. There are many possibilities; a full system test for some applications may include some or all as testers. Chapter 6 on unit testing looked at this issue and concluded that having the subsystem authors do the job is the best approach. The following sections outline the candidates for conducting system testing and the pros and cons of using them.

Project Team Members

The most likely people to work on system testing are the project team members themselves. This includes not only the application developers but also other members, including project managers or "quality czars." It may also include other people brought into the team solely for system testing.

The main advantage of using project team members is that they are already familiar with the application. One does not need to teach them how it works or what it means. This saves significant time.

Other advantages include the following:

- System testing can begin on a more flexible schedule, perhaps together with final unit/integration testing. If outsiders are doing the testing, they will require fixed dates for starting and stopping the test process.
- Project team members are, by and large, guaranteed to be available—outsiders might have other commitments.

Myopia is one problem team members may have as system testers. Since the team built the application, members will be less likely to find errors of omission (required features not implemented), in large part because they do not realize the features are really required. Overall, they are less likely to criticize their own work than are separate reviewers, who are presumably more objective.

Other potential problems include the following:

- Team dynamics, such as the formation of "cliques," will carry over into system testing, affecting how it is conducted.
- Testing will typically be done on the same machines used for development, which may taint the results if different installations behave differently.

Separate QA Group

Many larger organizations have a separate quality assurance group that is available on a rotating basis to perform system tests and other quality checks. Such a team is likely to have significant experience and training in system testing, as well as a full set of test-related tools. This is not the same as merely designating people on the project team as being the system testers—this group is a permanent entity that exists solely for testing.

The advantages and disadvantages here are similar to those cited for unit testing. On the plus side, a separate testing group has fault-finding as its mission, so it will not have any built-in bias to hide bugs. It also is likely to be better trained and better equipped than the development team.

The biggest problem is that this group is unfamiliar with the application. Hence, there will be a learning curve that will limit their effectiveness. Also, there is a cost issue: A full-time testing team, if not working on testing close to 100% of the time, is an overhead expense. This approach is really only effective with large organizations that are able to keep the team busy most of the time.

Client or Users

Another candidate set of system testers would be the actual end users. In the case of a small-volume application, they may be members of a team within a company or a small outside firm. Other applications could have a user base ranging from hundreds to millions. In either case, one could ask users to join in the quality assurance process via system testing.

This approach should not be confused with beta testing. Beta testing refers to pre-released versions of an application shipped to a few users, who try out the application and report their experiences. Ideally, a beta test should not find any faults, beyond ones indicating hardware or software configurations not tried and not compatible with the application. Using clients or users for system testing makes it very plain that the team is still working on the application. Moreover, users are expected to find faults and report on them. Sometimes the testing may even be done in the developers' offices, rather than where the users normally work.

This testing also should be distinguished from an acceptance test. An acceptance test involves having the application evaluated by clients or users for suitability. The stated intent is that if it is not up to par, the team must fix it before it can be deployed to all users. This is a formal evaluation of the application in its final form. The users conducting the acceptance test should not encounter any faults.

An acceptance test is typically found in custom development, whereas a beta test is used for packaged software to be widely distributed. Neither represents a system test by the users.

The biggest advantage of this approach is that the application will be tested in the way users will actually employ it, rather than how developers think they will use it. The most frequent fault found this way is an error of omission—a feature that should be there but is not. Such problems are unlikely to be found by anyone but the users, since the others all have a faulty view of what the application is to do.

This approach is not common, for several reasons:

- System testing is often a drawn-out process, and clients may be unwilling to make staff members available for so long.
- The users' computer experience may be limited, making it difficult for them to explain and recreate problems.
- If users encounter many bugs, it may affect their attitude toward the application even after the faults have been corrected. The bad impression may cause them to use the application less frequently or less effectively.

10.3 Organizing System Testing

Proper organization has been one of this book's guiding themes, and with good reason. One can almost consider organization to be one of the metrics of a quality assurance program. While ad hoc work may occasionally achieve the same results as well-orchestrated work, the odds are in favor of the more organized effort.

As with unit testing, several steps can help ensure a quality system test program:

- Build a plan that will "leak" the fewest bugs while taking the least effort.
- Implement the test program and capture results.
- Make sure the test was as thorough as desired.

A fourth step, using test results in a continuous improvement program, will be discussed later.

Selecting and Outlining Test Cases

Determining system test cases can be a daunting task. With a unit test, there typically is a small, easily described domain in which testing is conducted. In a system test, however, the entire application is being tested. Beginners often wonder where to even begin testing, let alone end it.

The goal of the system test is to ensure that the application performs system functions (e.g., business operations) properly. Hence, one obviously winds up selecting most test cases from the functions the application is supposed to provide. One way to do this is to return to the original designs and requirements and see what they called for. Given these, one can determine how the application is supposed to provide its functions, turning them into test cases. Not everything in a design is necessarily current or accurate, given the inevitable "moving target" syndrome. However, it is a starting point. Note how well-written requirements and design documents can help a project continuously over its lifetime.

One can also derive test cases from other approaches from other directions, such as:

- Data-driven testing, such as ensuring that the data model can handle all required situations (e.g., a zero-to-many relationship between two types of data works in the 0, 1, and many cases)
- Interface-driven testing, making sure that all user interface components provide the correct information and respond in the proscribed way
- Behavior-driven testing, examining the major objects in the system and ensuring that their critical behaviors have been exercised as needed

The individual test cases must be organized into a consistent whole. This is particularly true when external resources, such as a database, are involved. Ideally, each system test case would be self-contained, so it does not require much setup (e.g., seed data in a database) yet still tests the desired functionality. Unfortunately, this is difficult in general, requiring each test to create its initial data and dispose of it afterward. Otherwise, databases would grow to ridiculous sizes, making further testing difficult. At least, the system test cases should be ordered into a contiguous set in which they work together (e.g., test A creates data for test B to use). This adds documentation requirements, since some tests cannot be run if earlier ones failed.

The result should be a system test plan that can lead to an implementation. Therefore, it must be specific in terms of what testers should do and what the expected results are. The documentation requirements will be controlled by the mechanisms used for implementing the system test, described below.

This topic will also be discussed in Chapter 11 on session capture tools, WinCapT in particular.

Ensuring Completeness

One key question in any testing phase is "How much is enough?" One must be sure that everything is tested, hopefully to prevent any faults from being shipped. On the other hand, one cannot spend inordinate amounts of time doing testing, lest future users become restless.

In unit testing, the answer was to use coverage analysis. When a unit test suite has achieved 100% practical coverage, the subsystem is deemed to be tested. Note that the goal is not 100% physical coverage, as there may be legitimate reasons why certain conditions are not tried.

Coverage Analysis

One approach, therefore, for system testing is to use coverage analysis yet again. When it indicates that everything has been tried in an application, the system test is complete. While this would be a good goal, achieving 100% practical coverage is extraordinarily difficult at the system test level. Determining what user actions will cause a branch nested four layers deep in the application to go false is quite a challenge. Given the number of decision points in the average application, it is easy to see that coverage analysis cannot be the metric defining completion.

Bug Rate

Another metric sometimes used in this case is the "bug rate," the number of faults detected per unit time. When it falls below a certain value, for a consistent testing level of effort, testing is considered complete. The idea is that the bug rate is monotonically decreasing, and one can project how many faults the team might find from a certain point forward. When that number is small, it may be worthwhile to go ahead and deploy the application.

The assumption that the team will find faults at a predictable pace may be reasonable for huge systems, but not for smaller projects. It also rewards sloppy testing, as the sooner the testers get to a low rate of fault-finding, the sooner testing ends.

A variant on this approach, outlined by Glass [5], involves projecting the number of faults that an application contains. The projection is done by intentionally putting faults into the program. This is akin to how scientists count deer (or other wildlife) in a given area. A number of deer are caught, tagged, and released. After a reasonable time, enough to allow the deer to randomly scatter, they are caught again. Some will have been tagged, whereas others will not. The estimated number of deer is directly related to the fraction of tagged ones found. In the same way, the total number of faults in an application is related to the number of intentional ones found, compared to the number of unexpected ones. While this is more scientific than the bug rate approach, intentionally fouling up an application is unpopular.

Test Matrixes

Yet another approach returns to the notion of coverage but does not use programmatic means of measuring what has been done. Instead, the QA staff creates test matrixes for the application. A matrix outlines a set of tasks that testers should try in the course of a test suite. The matrix also notes which particular scripts try those tasks. Matrixes can be developed by use of any of the following types of tasks:

- User interface elements, to ensure that all elements are tried at least once
- Requirements or design criteria, if available
- Use cases or other identified scenarios

This puts the emphasis on system test design, the act of determining what to do in various test scripts. The application is considered to be tested when the following criteria are met:

- The scripts try all tasks denoted in the matrix.
- The application works as all scripts indicate.

This is nice in that it has a measure of determinism. Given the matrixes and test scripts, one can create a reasonable estimate of the time required to perform system testing. It relies on solid matrixes, however; gaps will represent areas not tested. Here, low-level coverage analysis may be useful, not as a metric to achieve but to identify operations that might have been missed entirely. The programming staff can help identify what missing a particular function might mean overall and how one can force it to be tried from the user interface.

Example: Address Lite

Since Address Lite is very small, there was little to be done in the way of a system test. However, it does illustrate the use of system test matrixes and scripts, samples of which appear in Appendix F.

Two matrixes were created for Address Lite. One contains a cross-reference between test cases and user interface elements. This ensures that every control on the application has been tried at least once. The other matrix lists the major data operations that Address Lite should support. In effect, this matrix ensures that it uses the X-Base library effectively.

In most situations, there would be a matrix listing the application's requirements. It would help make certain that every requirement works as expected. Since there were no formal requirements for Address Lite, this matrix was skipped.

10.4 Maximizing Benefit for Effort

To put it bluntly, system testing is hard. In many ways, it is more difficult than unit testing. Automation is hampered by the user interface, so the work is more likely to be manual. Given the broader scope of the tests, it is harder to identify what caused certain failures. Also, there is the work required to set up a test environment separate from the development environment. Furthermore, one typically must allow several testers to work in parallel on the same application and the same data, adding to the challenges. Finally, as noted above, there is less certainty that everything has been tried from the user interface, as a strict coverage is difficult to measure.

One thing should be clear: Emphasizing system test too much can be harmful to overall project quality. If system testing is so difficult, the effort required to achieve a certain level of quality will be high. Unfortunately, too many projects wait until the end of development to thoroughly test their application, then run into the above problems.

A better approach is to put more SQA effort into preventive measures, like those taken during development itself. Greater effort should also go into unit testing, as its higher automation and smaller scope make for easier fault detection and diagnosis. Given those steps, the system test should be more of a final checkout than an important stage for removing bugs. It can focus on usage scenarios, usability, and the correctness of documentation.

The biggest challenge of this approach is that it requires earlier allocation of SQA resources, plus earlier planning. Resources, of course, are always an issue. The combination of these requirements may slow down a project's early phases, whereas many groups prefer to get more "visible" work done earlier for political or marketing reasons. Everything must be balanced. Project management must make a determination as to where priorities lie.

10.5 Continuous Improvement

System test, like every other SQA phase, needs to tie into a continuous improvement program. In many ways, the system test will be the judge of the process to date. If the team finds many faults here, the earlier phases did not do their job. Hence, this phase involves two main continuous improvement activities: reflecting on prior phases and augmenting system testing itself.

Auditing Prior Phases

In theory, if the unit test were done correctly, there would be no faults in the application come system test. In reality, this is rarely the case. What is key is for every fault that is found, one must determine how it survived this long. Some faults will be due to last-minute changes that were not adequately tested. Some will be the result of complex interactions between subsystems that were not modelled in unit testing. Still others will be due to failure to handle boundary conditions, exceptions, or high levels of resource utilization.

Each fault should be "dissected," if you will, to determine its root cause. The development team, schooled in the procedures outlined in the quality plan, should be able to identify when the fault should have been detected. There will be two general types of causes:

- The developer in charge of the faulty subsystem will have inadequately applied the quality plan. Hence, its procedures and processes are fine, but the organization needs a better educational system. In addition, perhaps earlier audits might have caught the poor usage sooner.

- There is nothing in the quality plan that necessarily would have detected such faults. This suggests that the quality plan must be amended.

In some cases, the fault represents something that cannot be effectively tested earlier. Perhaps some techniques for catching such bugs were tried, but they were deemed to be not worth the effort. That is fine and will be inevitable—not all faults can be found economically. However, the quality plan should contain a "hints" section that points out categories of faults that are known but not covered elsewhere in the plan. If nothing else, this will serve as a means of knowledge transfer. Future designs might try to prevent such situations, or developers might keep their eyes (rather than some tool's) open for this fault.

System Test Improvement

System testing itself should also be analyzed for effectiveness. As noted above, there are many techniques for designing test suites and determining completion. Some may be more useful than others for certain groups. Projects may experiment with other techniques, beyond those in the quality plan, to see how well they work. Those experiences should be reflected in the quality plan, either as "hints" or revised procedures. Similarly, if procedures seem to be too much work for the faults they find, they should be modified or removed.

Of course, the final arbiter of the success of system test will be what happens when users start employing the application. If they find lots of problems, system test procedures (and those of prior test phases) must be examined and augmented. This book's final chapter covers how quality after deployment fits into continuous improvement programs as well.

10.6 Summary

System test is one of the most frequently employed of the common SQA phases. In many ways, though, it is among the most difficult to implement. Common sense and sound procedures are essential to make sure that the system test adequately tries the application's functionality yet does not take too much time or effort. Automation, while more difficult to use in system testing, is available. The next chapter will describe a tool, WinCapT, for automating Windows system testing.

CHAPTER 11

User Interface Testing: WinCapT

"Of course the bug is there! We reported it, right?"

Sam was meeting with Michelle, George, and the TurboChem system testing team. George was explaining that he could not recreate a problem the testers had reported. Leroy, head of the testing group, was equally emphatic that the bug existed.

"Look, I'll show it to you" growled Leroy, using a tone generally reserved for small children. He rapidly clicked and typed his way through a myriad of screens, then suddenly stopped.

"Wait a minute, that was supposed to fail!" he said, surprised.

*"Hmmph. I **told** you it worked," replied George.*

Leroy was about to begin a nasty retort when Michelle stepped in. "No, Leroy's right. I saw that problem once, too."

*"Can **you** recreate it?" George sneered.*

"Probably not. I watched Leroy try it now—I thought what he did would cause the crash."

Sam sighed inwardly. This was not the first time testers had reported bugs that just could not be found again. It was as if someone was playing the old "shell game" with the program's failures. He really wanted a way to record a testing session, so his team could replay it to exactly recreate the steps needed to cause the crash. Sam wondered what he could find that would do that effectively.

11.1 User Interface Testing and Tools

The above scenario occurs frequently in real-world testing situations, let alone fictional stories. A team is performing a system test on an application. Invariably, the development staff cannot duplicate some failures, even in similar environments. Sometimes not even the testers themselves can remember the steps necessary to trigger the bug. This and other similar problems have led to efforts to formalize testing.

Goals and Options

The goals of user interface system testing are:

- Find all remaining faults in the application before it is handed over to users.
- Ensure that the user interface is usable and friendly.
- Be able to repeat the test over time with minimal effort, so one can see if faults were repaired or new ones added.

The challenge is to find a mechanism to meet the goals. Inevitably, all such mechanisms will involve human testers to a large degree. The second goal, after all, is largely an aesthetic opinion, which is not easily automated. Similarly, determining what is right and wrong with a user interface's output requires the assistance of the designers and developers.

This leaves the final goal: easy repeatability. It is the key to regression testing, as one must be able to rerun the original test to make sure that everything is still working correctly. Any system test can be repeated. It is the ease of doing so that determines if regression testing is conducted.

Some teams use a formal human-language "script" for the tests. They literally write down every step (e.g, "Click the Resume button, then double-click on the printer icon."). This is sometimes useful in its own right, as it provides a means of recreating the situation exactly. However, the scripts are tedious to write. In addition, rerunning the tests and seeing if any results changed over time is a totally manual process. As a result, regression testing is unlikely to be performed frequently, if at all.

Session Capture Tools

When one thinks about it, it is obvious that the computer itself should record the steps necessary to recreate a situation. The computer was the one that performed the processing, anyway. If the system could record the events in addition to carrying them out, then that information could be used to rerun the scenario.

Unfortunately, it typically is not that simple. Most user interface systems lack a built-in means of recording application events. This is true for both graphical systems and their character-based counterparts. Neither the operating system nor the application development toolkits has this capability. One winds up using another tool, external to both, that "intercepts" events and records them before passing them along to the application.

In Figure 11.1, the operating system captures user keystrokes, passing them along to the application for processing. The arrows represent user events.

Figure 11.1 Normal User Interface Event Flow

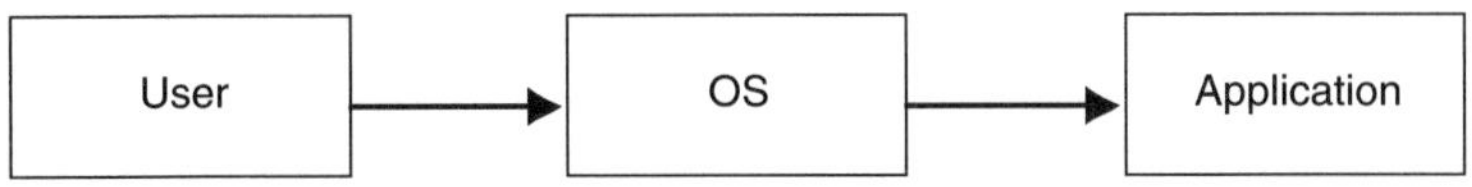

Figure 11.2 shows user events behaving in the same way, except that they are rerouted through the session capture tool. It records them for later replay. There is no effect on the application at all.

Figure 11.2 Event Flow with Session Capture Tool

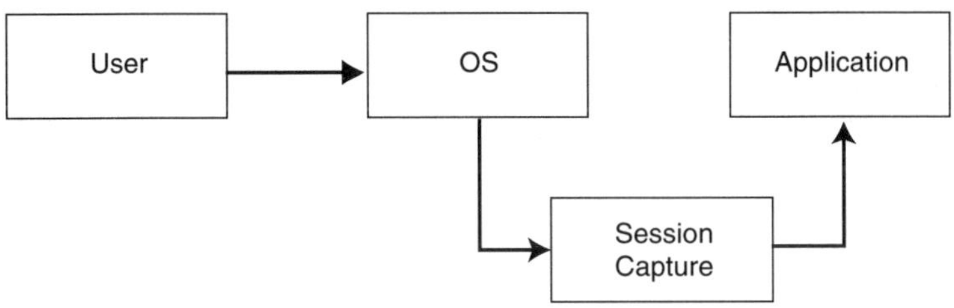

This is not a great solution by any means. Any external tool, no matter how well written, is limited in what it can see: the messages between the I/O subsystem and the application. The application knows much more about what is going on than does the operating system, let alone the recording tool. There tends to be significant information loss.

For example, the application may know that the user just changed the text in a field from "Hello" to "World". The recording tool, on the other hand, merely knows about two button actions sandwiched around a mouse movement (highlighting "Hello") and five keystrokes (<W>, <o>, <r>, <l>, and <d>). These events are outlined in Table 11.1. Many such tools do not even recognize that there is a field involved. They just know that after each event, the bitmapped image changed in one area.

Table 11.1 Sample User Interaction and Resulting OS Events

User Interaction	OS Events
Click at start of field	Left mouse button down
Highlight "Hello" text in field	Mouse movement and left mouse button up
Overtype "Hello" with "World"	Five keystroke events

Suppose we use a session capture tool to record a system test case for Address Lite where a user adds a record to the address list. First, one would run the tool, which typically starts in an "off" state (meaning it is not recording or playing anything back). Then, the user would open Address Lite. Next, he or she would tell the tool to begin recording. Now, all mouse and keyboard events are filtered through the tool.

If the user then walked through the steps to add a record (open a file, ask to add a record, provide the name, etc.), the session capture tool would record each event (<Alt>-<F>, <O>, etc.). When the case is done, the user would turn off the session capture tool, which would save the recording.

To replay the test case, the user would proceed as follows:

- Run the session capture tool and Address Lite.
- Put Address Lite in the same general state as it was when the test was recorded.
- Ask the tool to replay the events.

Address Lite should respond as if the user were manually repeating the actions and should go through the same steps to add a record. When the recording is done, the session capture tool would automatically shut off.

What Session Capture Tools Do

Session capture tools, therefore, have two major functions: capturing user interactions and capturing application state information.

Capturing User Interactions

A session capture tool must capture user interactions as operating system events. Typical examples are keystrokes, mouse button clicks, and mouse movements. Other types of input, such as pen gestures, would be recorded as applicable. Basically, anything the user does to the application must be recorded so that the same events can be replayed to see if anything has changed.

In addition to the events themselves and, for button/mouse events, where they happened, the tool must also record the interval between them. In some situations, timing is critical. For example, a button might not become enabled until a few seconds after another action. If the playback does not honor this time, a disabled button will be clicked, deviating from the original scenario.

Capturing Application State Information

The tool must capture information about what is happening, as reflected on the screen. Typically this involves capturing a screen or window. The information is stored, along with its relative position in the event stream. When the recording is played back, the same screen areas can be captured at the same places to see if the results changed.

Uses of Session Capture Tools

Session capture tools have several uses:

- Recording system test activities, to determine the exact steps leading up to a software failure. This is useful for demonstrating the fault and for recreating the failure under debugging conditions to try to diagnose the problem.
- Regression testing successful system test cases. As new releases of the application become available, it is useful to be able to automatically rerun the system test and identify changes. Teams can use this both to find bugs and to document all changes.
- Ancillary activities, such as product demonstrations and training materials.

Graphical versus Character Mode

One can divide session capture tools, and development environments in general, into two main categories: character-based and graphical. A character-based tool would be used in "terminal I/O" programs, such as DOS, Unix terminal sessions, and OS/2 and Windows NT command-line windows. Graphical session capture tools are for environments like Windows, OS/2, and X Windows.

Character-based session capture tools are frequently less sophisticated than their graphical counterparts because of their operating environment. Most graphical systems are event- and message-driven, meaning that on user interaction events they send messages to applications. There usually is a "hook" for determining when messages are sent. It can serve as the recording mechanism.

Such message-based systems are rare in character-mode interfaces. Under DOS, for example, a testing tool could capture raw mouse and keyboard interrupts but is limited to crude "screen scraping" means for determining output. "Screen scraping" refers to capturing the screen text in a file, perhaps with manual indication of where critical data resides.

This chapter, therefore, focuses on graphical session capture tools. Many points, however, apply to character-based tools as well.

Critical Features

Session capture tools offer many features above and beyond the physical basics of recording and playing back user interactions. The important ones are described in the following sections.

Window Location Independence

Depending on the application, windows may not appear in the same place twice. For example, many systems will record the last position of a window when it closes and will reopen it there. Hence, if the test involved moving a window, when it is replayed, the window will already appear in the "destination" location.

If the session capture tool relies on fixed window locations in its recording of an event, those locations may be invalid on playback. Suppose the operating system informs the tool of a mouse click. The tool must record where the click occurred, so it can simulate one in the same spot during replay. Further suppose that the tool uses absolute screen positions. Now, during playback, the window has moved, because the user opened it in a different place. When the tool replays the button click, it will not occur in the original spot, since the window has moved. The mouse click might be applied to nothing at all, rather than to the button that was clicked during the original recording.

If, on the other hand, the tool can identify a window by another means (e.g., its title) and use that to record the window's position, it can overcome slight changes. Using the above scenario, the mouse click would have its position recorded relative to the window being clicked on. During replay, the click would be simulated in the same position relative to the window. If the window significantly changed geometry (i.e., the button was moved), the mouse click still will not hit it, but this now indicates a test that failed. If the window geometry is the same, even if the position on the screen is different, the mouse click will hit the button as in the original.

Support Multiple Types of Output

Most session capture tools can capture the entire state of a window/screen, simply by recording its image as a text file or bitmap. Particularly in the case of bitmaps, a slight noncritical change (e.g., font) will trigger a comparison difference between two otherwise identical bitmaps. This can lead to spurious test "failures."

Better session capture tools can capture the key states of windows or screens, typically by recording information about controls (e.g., buttons, fields). This information can be recorded in text mode. It would take a more substantive change (e.g., text in a field) to denote an error.

Unfortunately, such recording is insufficient for many applications, such as drawing packages. In system testing a painting program, one would need to ensure that the drawn image has not changed—this is not on a control, so the state-information system would not work. Tools that provide both means of capturing output are the best, because they can handle nearly any situation.

Ease of Use

Like anything else in the quality assurance area, if the tool is difficult to use, it will not be used as frequently or as effectively as desired. Testers will not want to fuss with it while testing, and the quality team will not want to bother rerunning the tests in regression test mode later. Hence, it must be simple to start and stop a recording, as well as to mark the screen areas to track. Also, the means of determining what changes occurred should be as simple as possible.

11.2 Comparing Tools

Many session capture tools are available, but most cost extra money. This section will compare two that are easily available: the Microsoft Recorder (which comes as an "applet" with Microsoft Windows) and WinCapT.

Microsoft Recorder

Microsoft Windows (not NT) comes bundled with a program called the Recorder. It is designed to create macros for Windows applications by recording keystrokes and mouse movements and playing them back on demand. One can also use it for system testing.

To use the Recorder, one specifies a macro name in its window and then records user actions until stopped via the window or the <Ctrl>-<Break> hotkey. This set of actions can then be played back at will, using either an assigned hotkey or via the Recorder window.

The Recorder allows one to specify whether the actions are recorded relative to the screen or to the window the events are directed against. By selecting window-based recording (the default), one obtains the location-independence feature mentioned earlier.

The biggest problem with using the Recorder for system testing is that it has no built-in mechanism for capturing state information. While it can replay user events faithfully, it has no way of helping testers determine if anything changed from run to run. One should, in principle, be able to combine the Recorder with other tools designed for information capture, such as ones that grab portions of the screen and record them as bitmaps. This, however, will be cumbersome, since neither tool knows about the other's existence or purpose.

WinCapT

WinCapT performs the same operations as the Recorder, in terms of capturing and replaying user events. In addition, it has built-in state capture capability, so it provides a more complete solution.

Running WinCapT is, in many ways, the same as running the Recorder. After starting the tool, a tester can start recording a session, denoting where the event information is to be stored (here a filename, rather than a macro name as in the Recorder). Similarly, the tester can replay a script, with events going against the same windows as when it was recorded.

The big difference is that, during recording, the user can press <PrintScreen> to capture the state of the window under the cursor, in terms of control states (e.g., checkbox settings, field text). This same information is captured at the same points during playback, and logged to a separate state file. One can then compare the two files to identify changes from run to run. WinCapT thus meets two of the major criteria outlined above: window location independence and ease of use.

11.3 Using WinCapT

WinCapT is easy to use. The interactions with a user are recorded while working through a test scenario. The test can be replayed at any point, either to demonstrate a problem or to compare window states against the original run.

Planning Tests

Perhaps the most difficult part of using WinCapT is determining what test cases should use it. Just as in creating test case scripts for UTCLang, one cannot simply start recording the application. One must figure out what has to be tested, and how. One needs a plan to test effectively, a point described in greater detail in the previous chapter.

Running WinCapT

WinCapT requires no special installation; it can be used right from the diskette (see Appendix A for details). Running the WINCAPT.EXE program will bring up the WinCapT window, shown in Figure 11.3.

Figure 11.3 WinCapT Main Window

This window contains three buttons:

- Record, which starts a recording of a user session
- Stop, which stops a recording of a user session
- Playback, which starts a playback of a user session (stopping automatically when the session is complete)

The window can be closed at any time from the system menu (e.g., double-clicking on the button in the upper-left corner). Do not do this while a script is being recorded or played back!

Recording Sessions

To record a session with WinCapT, simply click the Record button. A pair of "Save As" dialogs will be displayed (shown in Figure 11.4), asking for two files:

- The session data file, containing information about all mouse movements and keystrokes done during the session
- The window state file, containing information about all window states captured at user request (described below)

Figure 11.4 "Save As" Dialog for WinCapT

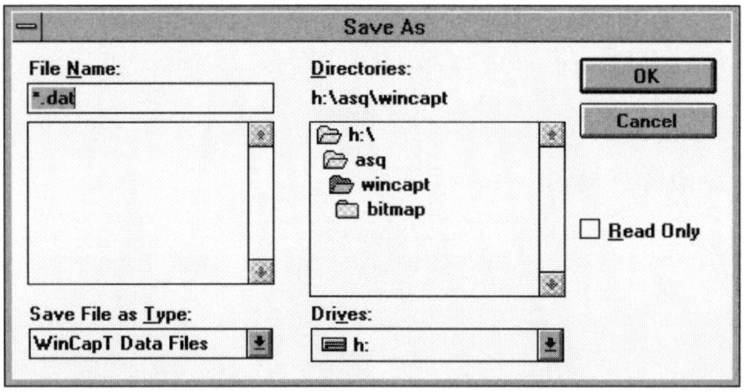

After providing appropriate file paths, WinCapT will begin recording each mouse and keyboard action taken. By exercising the application, WinCapT will capture the steps to execute a test case. When done, simply click the Stop button to halt recording.

Playing Back Sessions

To play back a session, set up the environment to be the same as it was during recording. For example, if the application's main window was open, it should be open for playback. Then, click the Playback button on the WinCapT window. Another pair of dialogs are displayed:

- One to select the session data file to replay.
- One to name the file used to store window state information from the playback (**not** the same as the original recording file). Window state capture is described in the next section.

At this point, WinCapT will take over the mouse and keyboard, going through the same steps as originally recorded. There is no way to stop the playback once started. When the session is complete, WinCapT will return control of the mouse and keyboard to the user.

Capturing Window States

The idea behind WinCapT is to capture and compare window states from run to run. To capture a window state during a recording, simply press the <Print-Screen> key. This will capture information about each control on the window under the mouse cursor, plus its parent windows. The information will be written in ASCII form to the window state file after the recording is complete.

Below is the output from capturing the state of a Windows File Open dialog:

```
Window: Select a File
Class: Static
    [Edit/Static] ID=-1, text=&Directories:
Class: Button
    [Button] ID=1, checked state=0, text=OK
Class: Button
    [Button] ID=2, checked state=0, text=Cancel
Class: Button
    [Button] ID=1038, checked state=0, text=&Help
Class: Button
    [Button] ID=1040, checked state=0, text=&Read Only
Class: Static
    [Edit/Static] ID=1088, text=e:\taipei
Class: Static
    [Edit/Static] ID=1089, text=List Files of &Type:
Class: Static
    [Edit/Static] ID=1090, text=File &Name:
Class: Static
    [Edit/Static] ID=1091, text=Dri&ves:
Class: ListBox
    [ListBox] ID=1120
      TP.EXE
Class: ListBox
    [ListBox] ID=1121
      E:\
    * TAIPEI
Class: ComboBox
    [ComboBox] ID=1136, dropped state=0
    * Executables (*.EXE)
      Batch Files (*.BAT)
      PIF Files (*.PIF)
      DOS .COM Files (*.COM)
Class: ComboBox
    [ComboBox] ID=1137, dropped state=0
      a:
      c:
      d: ms-dos_6
    * e:
      g:
      h:
Class: Edit
    [Edit/Static] ID=1152, text=e:\taipei\tp.exe
```

The asterisks next to the listbox and combobox entries indicate the one that is presently selected.

When a session is replayed, the same windows' states will be captured at the same point in the script. The states will be saved in the file named for the playback. One can compare the two files to identify changes.

If there are no changes in the window states, then the test presumably succeeded. If there are changes, the tester must determine which results (original or new) are correct. For example, if the original test recorded a bug and the new one's results show it was fixed, the new file is the correct one. The tester should hold on to the correct ones for later comparison against other runs in order to detect bugs that creep into the system.

11.4 WinCapT and the Sample Code

WinCapT can be applied easily to Address Lite. It will faithfully record and replay test sessions without difficulty. WinCapT and Address Lite were used to try out several scenarios outlined in the system test matrices in Appendix C.

Since the X-Base library lacks a user interface, WinCapT cannot test it except through Address Lite. This is appropriate, as X-Base is really a subsystem and should be tested accordingly.

11.5 How WinCapT Works

WinCapT is purely a Windows application—it is not innately portable to other GUIs, such as X Windows. It uses Windows-specific abilities, such as journaling hooks. Therefore, this discussion centers around how it uses Windows to perform session capture and playback. However, the techniques apply to other environments.

WinCapT, like most tools provided here, has two components: a library (DLL) and an executable. The DLL provides an API for requesting capture and playback of Windows sessions. The executable has a GUI interface for requesting these actions. Most session capture and playback logic, therefore, resides in the DLL. The executable merely instructs the library to perform actions by using supplied information, such as input/output file names.

WinCapT API

WinCapT's DLL (WCTHOOK.DLL) provides four API functions for programs that want to capture and play back sessions:

- WctStartRecordSession(), which immediately starts recording mouse movements and keystrokes. It also enables the <PrintScreen> recording of window states.
- WctStopRecordSession() terminates the recording, saving the results (session and window state information) in files.

- WctStartPlaybackSession() starts playing back the specified session, saving playback window states in the provided file. It also supplies a window that the DLL will inform (via a custom Windows message) when the playback is done.
- WctStopPlaybackSession() cleans up after a session playback is complete. It is not designed to stop a playback in midstream. An application should call it only after the DLL reports that playback is finished.

Journaling Hooks

The DLL's main purpose is to implement a pair of Windows hook functions. Once registered, hooks receive control on certain events by Windows. WinCapT uses Windows' journaling hooks designed specifically for capture and playback systems.

Windows Hook Functions

One of the most powerful features of Microsoft Windows is the hook function. Windows allows applications to register hook functions that will be called when particular system events occur. For example, one can register hooks to get control whenever Windows creates or destroys a main (unowned) window (the WH_SHELL hook).

WinCapT uses the journaling hook functions. One (WH_JOURNALRECORD) will be called every time Windows processes a message from the system queue (i.e., handles a keyboard or mouse message). Another hook function (WH_JOURNALPLAYBACK) can substitute for the system queue, in that Windows disables the physical devices and obtains keyboard and mouse messages from the hook function instead. These functions, therefore, serve the recording and playback aspects of WinCapT.

One sets up a hook function by calling SetWindowsHookEx(), a Windows API call. It indicates the type of hook to set (e.g., WH_JOURNALRECORD), what the function is, etc. To turn off a hook function, call UnhookWindowsHookEx().

Note that some hook functions, such as the journaling ones, must reside in a DLL. Others can be in either an executable or a DLL.

In WctStartRecordSession(), the following call sets up the recording hook function for WinCapT:

```
hOldHook=SetWindowsHookEx(WH_JOURNALRECORD,
                          (HOOKPROC)WctRecordHook,
                          hMyInstance, NULL);
```

WctRecordHook() is the actual hook function called on each user interface event. hMyInstance is the instance handle for the DLL (cached from LibMain()). hOldHook will hold on to the old hook function of this type (if any). WinCapT uses it to unhook WctRecordHook() when recording is done.

In WctStartPlaybackSession(), the following call sets up the playback hook function:

```
hOldHook=SetWindowsHookEx(WH_JOURNALPLAYBACK,
                          (HOOKPROC)WctPlaybackHook,
                          hMyInstance, NULL);
```

Here, WctPlaybackHook() is used for the hook function.

From WinCapT's point of view, there are four types of events:

- Keystrokes
- Mouse movements
- Mouse button clicks
- Screen capture notices

The last type of event is triggered in WinCapT by the <PrintScreen> key. WctRecordHook() processes normal keys by simply recording which one was pressed and when. The <PrintScreen> key is used to record state information about the current window under the mouse cursor.

Mouse information not only involves the type of action (e.g., left mouse button click), but also the location. WinCapT considers clicks to be aimed against a **window**, so it records the **relative** mouse position for the window being clicked on. The window's name is also recorded. Upon playback, WctPlaybackHook() finds a window of the same name and "warps" the mouse to click on it in the same relative position. One can thus use WinCapT in situations where the windows can move.

Table 11.2 outlines the information saved for each type of event.

Table 11.2 Information Saved for Window Events

Window Event	Event Code	Information Saved
<PrintScreen>	B	Nothing
Other Keystrokes	K	Event structure
Mouse Clicks	M	Window title; event structure, modified for window-relative coordinates
Mouse Movements	V	Event structure, modified to capture delta of movement from last position

---

An event structure, as mentioned in Table 11.2, refers to the event information provided to the recording hook function from Windows, indicating what occurred. It has the following general layout:

```
typedef struct {
    UINT uiMessage;
    UINT uiLoParam;
    UINT uiHiParam;
    DWORD dwTime;
}
```

For those unfamiliar with Windows conventions, all types are typedef'd in WINDOWS.H. No base C data types are directly referred to elsewhere. UINT maps to unsigned int, and DWORD maps to a 32-bit unsigned value (unsigned long on 16-bit machines, unsigned int on 32-bit machines).

For mouse movements, the two arbitrary parameters refer to the coordinates of the new position. Since WinCapT works relative to windows, these need to be saved as actual movements—the pixel delta between the new position and the last recorded one. Similarly, for mouse clicks, WinCapT changes the position information from screen coordinates to coordinates for the application window under the mouse cursor. The window name is also recorded, so during replay WinCapT can transform window coordinates back into screen coordinates.

WinCapT records all this information by using a subsystem called the Windows Memory Dump. Direct access to a file (via fopen()) appears to be problematic in a hook function. The Windows Memory Dump provides a convenient means for "stuffing" event information into a memory buffer. It can later save it to disk all at once when recording is over. Before playback begins, the event information is loaded into memory so the playback hook can obtain events without incurring a file I/O.

Windows Memory Dump

The recording and playback functions of WinCapT, since they are Windows hook functions, must work quickly. Ideally, one would simply use the ANSI C file I/O functions (e.g., fopen()). However, speed is a concern, so it is desirable to work solely in memory while the hook functions are processing. The entire buffer should be transferred to and from disk outside these functions.

In Windows NT, one could use the memory-mapped file I/O functions. They give the illusion of working directly in memory even though they involve a file. The actual file access for writing occurs asynchronously with respect to the writer; reading is cached similarly.

Since WinCapT is to run under Windows 3.1 and memory-mapped file I/O is not part of the universally available Win32s API, a similar approach was needed. This led to the Windows Memory Dump (WMD) subsystem, found in the \WMD directory on the disk. It provides API functions that set up data streams for reading or writing. During writing, the data goes to an in-memory buffer, which WMD writes to disk when the stream is closed. Similarly, for reading, WMD reads the entire file into memory up front, then parcels it out upon request. A C++ implementation could support ANSI stream objects (e.g., iwinstream and owinstream).

Appendix B describes the API for this subsystem.

Screen State Capture

The output of a WinCapT session, either for recording or for playback, is a text file listing the states of all dialog controls on windows captured via <PrintScreen> (and their parent windows, etc.). When the user presses the <PrintScreen> key in recording mode, the recording journal hook function records a capture event, in addition to storing the current window states. Upon replay, when the playback journal hook function sees a capture event, it records the state of the same windows and proceeds to the next keyboard/mouse event.

To record the window states, the hook functions first determine what window is presently under the mouse cursor. It could be an application window, a dialog, or even a dialog control, such as a field or button (since they too are windows). The hook functions call WctSaveWindow() for the window under the cursor, plus all its parent windows. The parents are included because the cursor could be on a field; it is presumed that users are probably aiming for the whole dialog.

WctSaveWindow() looks through all child windows of the supplied window and determine which are dialog controls, since it is such controls (buttons, fields, etc.) for which we wish to record the state. The dialog controls are then sorted by control ID (a fixed value from run to run, so controls appear in largely the same order), and their states are captured in a Windows Memory Dump. Table 11.3 outlines the information captured for each control.

Table 11.3 Control State Information Recorded by WinCapT

Control Type	Information Recorded
Push Button, Radio Button, Check Box	ID, checked state, text
Listbox	ID, contents (and which were selected)
Combobox	ID, contents (and which were selected), dropped state
Edit (fields), Static (labels)	ID, text

Below is the source for WctSaveWindow(), which saves the state of a window (and its parent windows) during recording or playback:

```
void WctSaveWindow(HWND hWindowToSave)
{
    HCURSOR hCursor;
    char szLine[80];
    char szText[64];
    WCT_CHILDENUMINFO rEnum;
    int i;

    hCursor=SetCursor(LoadCursor(NULL, IDC_WAIT));
    GetWindowText(hWindowToSave, szText, 64);
    sprintf(szLine, "\015\012Window: %s\015\012", szText);
    WmdAppend(hResults, szLine, strlen(szLine));
```

```
        rEnum.iNextToUse=0;
        EnumChildWindows(hWindowToSave, WctChildEnum, (LPARAM) &rEnum);

        if (rEnum.iNextToUse)
        {
            qsort(rEnum.ahChildWnd, rEnum.iNextToUse, sizeof(HWND),
                   WctDlgIDCompare);
            for (i=0;i<rEnum.iNextToUse;i++)
            {
                WctDumpChildWindowInfo(rEnum.ahChildWnd[i],
                                             hWindowToSave);
            }
        }

        SetCursor(hCursor);

        return;
    }
```

After changing the cursor to a "wait" (hourglass) cursor, this function sends information about the window itself to the output stream. Then, it uses the Enum-ChildWindows() Windows API function to find all the children in this window. If there are any, they are sorted by ID and sent separately to the output stream. Finally, the normal cursor is restored.

Unfortunately, this approach will miss some controls. WinCapT only knows about the built-in Windows controls, with window classes of Edit, Button, ListBox, ComboBox, and Static. There are other controls that subclass existing ones, such as Borland's BorBtn (a part of the Borland Windows Custom Controls). There is no convenient way to find out that a window of class BorBtn behaves like a Button window; WinCapT simply ignores BorBtn windows. One can always modify the WctGetControlType() function in WCTHOOK.DLL to recognize other control types.

Here is the source for WctGetControlType():

```
WCT_CONTROLTYPES WctGetControlType(char *pszClass)
{
    if (strcmp(pszClass, "Edit")==0)
    {
        return(WCT_EDIT);
    }
    else if (strcmp(pszClass, "Button")==0)
    {
        return(WCT_BUTTON);
    }
    else if (strcmp(pszClass, "ListBox")==0)
    {
        return(WCT_LISTBOX);
    }
    else if (strcmp(pszClass, "ComboBox")==0 ||
                strcmp(pszClass, "ComboLBox")==0)
    {
        return(WCT_COMBOBOX);
    }
    else if (strcmp(pszClass, "Static")==0)
    {
        return(WCT_STATIC);
    }
    return(WCT_UNKNOWN);
}
```

One can add support for Borland's custom button class (BORBTN) by adding another test in the if-elseif chain:

```
    else if (strcmp(pszClass, "BORBTN")==0)
    {
        return(WCT_BUTTON);
    }
```

If there were special traits of Borland's button that should be tracked in the state output, another enumeration value (WCT_BORBTN) could be added and WctDumpChildWindowInfo() modified accordingly.

User Interface

WinCapT has a GUI front end for the three major actions of recording, stopping recording, and playback. This is simply a small Windows application, linked to the WCTHOOK.DLL library for the WinCapT functions. For simplicity, it uses a modal dialog as its main window, rather than a full-fledged application window.

This dialog and its buttons were created by means of Borland's Resource Workshop and use the Borland Windows Custom Controls for the bitmapped buttons.

Dialogs as Main Windows

In Windows 3.1, one usually creates an application window that serves as the "main window" for the overall program. This involves registering a window class, creating and opening a window, implementing a message loop, etc. It is far easier, particularly for single-window applications, to use a task-modal dialog. Since it is task-modal, it will not tie up the whole system. Since there are no other windows for this application, the fact that the main window is modal has no effect.

Setting up a program using a dialog for a main window is easy. After creating the dialog/main window by using the resource editor of one's choice, one must simply call DialogBox() or an equivalent function to open the dialog in WinMain(), as in the sample below:

```
int PASCAL WinMain(HANDLE hInstance, HANDLE hPrevInstance,
LPSTR lpszCmdLine, int iCmdShow)
{
    if (DialogBox(hInstance, "Main", NULL, MainDialogProc)==-1)
    {
        MessageBox(NULL, "Could not open main window!",
                   "MyApp",
                   MB_APPLMODAL | MB_ICONSTOP | MB_OK);
    }
    return(0);
}
```

Obviously, one still needs to implement a message-handling function, called MainDialogProc in the above example. It will primarily worry about the controls on the dialog. Also, it should follow two other rules:

- It should return TRUE if the message was processed by the function and FALSE otherwise.
- It should call EndDialog() when the dialog is to be closed (e.g., on the system menu or an Exit button).

When the user clicks the record button, the WinCapT GUI uses the GetSaveFileName() common dialog API function to obtain file names for the event recording and the window state file. Assuming the user did not cancel out of either of those, it calls the WctStartRecordSession() function to start recording.

When the user clicks the stop recording button, the WinCapT GUI simply calls the WctStopRecordSession() function, providing the filenames obtained earlier. The filenames are stored in static variables between the start and stop recording button clicks. Otherwise, inquiring for filenames when the user clicks the stop button would mean that all mouse movements and keystrokes in filling out the two Save As dialogs would also be recorded.

Here is the source for WctStopRecordSession():

```
int _export WctStopRecordSession(LPSTR lpszLogFile,
                                 LPSTR lpszResultFile)
{
    char cQuit='Q';

    WmdAppend(hEvents, &cQuit, sizeof(char));
    WmdWriteToFile(hEvents, lpszLogFile);
    WmdWriteToFile(hResults, lpszResultFile);
    WmdTerm(hEvents);
    WmdTerm(hResults);

    UnhookWindowsHookEx(hOldHook);

    return(0);
}
```

After writing an event to the log to indicate that the script stops, both the event log and the states are written out to disk. The hook function is then detached before the function returns.

Finally, when the user clicks the playback button, WinCapT asks the user to select an event recording file to play back, along with a file to store the new window states. The GUI then calls the WctStartPlaybackSession() function to begin playback.

The window must also respond to the WM_USER message, which the DLL sends once playback is complete. The GUI calls the WctStopPlaybackSession() function to save the window state file and clean up after the playback session. This cannot be automatically done by the playback hook function because of the file I/O restriction noted above.

11.6 Future Directions

WinCapT, while simple, provides more power than the Microsoft Recorder application bundled with Windows. There is certainly room for improvement, however. Below are features that would make WinCapT even more powerful.

Recording Images

Presently, WinCapT records only state information about dialog controls. This is insufficient for applications, such as drawing tools, which have "state" information not contained in controls. For such situations, a full-window bitmap capture would be more appropriate. WinCapT would have to be able to record bitmaps on session recording and playback. Users would also need a bitmap comparison tool to determine the differences between windows.

Support More Complicated Scripts

Like Microsoft's Recorder, WinCapT records a straight user session. The playback is exactly what the user recorded, with no loops or branches. There are situations where a finer level of control would be useful. For example, for stress testing an application, it would be useful to have the tool play back data entry for 10,000 records, even though only 10 were entered, before continuing with the next phase.

One way to provide such control would be to build a scripting language that can move cursors, press keys, etc. The recording end of the session capture would merely build a script. The script, if played back verbatim, would result in the original session being played back, just as it is now. It would also be possible to hand-modify the script to include loops or branches based on external conditions. Some commercial tools provide the capability by using Microsoft's Visual Basic as the host language. Of course, UTCLang could also serve this purpose.

Automated Playback

WinCapT has one major drawback for serious regression testing—no automated playback of test suites. Each test to be played back must be manually requested. There is no means for providing a list of tests to run, in a given sequence, with all results captured. This feature would allow a batch of tests to run overnight, with the team examining the results in the morning.

Alternative Window Identification System

Presently, WinCapT stores events targeted to a specific window (keystrokes and mouse clicks) with the window's title as its identifier. When playback is done, WinCapT finds a window with the same name and directs the events against it.

The problem, of course, is that one cannot test multiple windows with the same title at the same time because during playback WinCapT might grab the wrong one. This is a serious limitation. Unfortunately, there is no built-in identification scheme that remains constant between runs of the program. While windows have unique handles that can serve as IDs, those values might change in a later run.

11.7 Summary

Just as automation will help in regression testing subsystems via something like UTCLang, it can make regression testing user interfaces easier. Such automation typically comes in the form of session capture/playback tools, which monitor a human tester's actions and faithfully replicate them on demand later. Although such tools can be created for most user interfaces, GUIs add challenges that make them difficult to create ad hoc.

WinCapT is a session capture/playback tool for 16-bit Windows. It records user events and window states as requested. On playback, the events are rerun and the same states captured. Those states, in the form of ASCII reports, can be compared to identify differences between the results.

CHAPTER 12

Putting It All Together

This book has discussed quality assurance techniques and tools used from development through unit and system testing. However, there are two major gaps in the coverage:

1. What should one do after the software has been shipped to the user, and what tools, if any, can help in this final phase?
2. How can one combine all the tools into a cohesive quality assurance plan?

12.1 Quality after Delivery

Completing system test and deploying an application are certainly cause for celebration. However, it is not the end of concerns about quality, let alone the end of the project as a whole. One must apply the same SQA techniques here as in the other phases.

Bug Tracking

Much to everyone's dismay, nearly all applications wind up shipping with at least one fault. Having stringent, effective quality control programs will reduce the number of shipped faults. However, it will not eliminate them all.

Compounding the problem is that the definition of a "bug" differs by audience. End users define one as anything that does not work as expected or prevents them from achieving their goals. Developers typically define one as something identifiably wrong with the application as defined in the design. This difference can cause problems, such as:

- Low-quality documentation can cause many reports of bugs from users, more because they cannot understand how the application is supposed to work than from fault in the code.
- Users frequently have their own ideas of how the application should work. Many problem reports will be where users expect different behavior. This will be in spite of the fact that the requirements and design call for precisely what the program delivers. This is the source of the "that's not a bug—that's a feature" comment heard all too frequently.
- Users may report problems the developers cannot reproduce, because of differences in hardware, installed system software, data, etc.

Technical support should satisfy the users and deal with their concerns. In addition, the staff should be working toward improving the current product and the process for creating future ones. To do this, the staff must track problem ("bug") reports from users. This is true for any size team, ranging from one employee to 100,000.

Several problem-tracking packages are available. For those with database programming experience, creating a simple, custom database is not difficult. It must track the proper information and be rigorously used. In situations involving a technical support staff, having a shared repository of problem-tracking data (e.g., in a table on a file server) is important. Users frequently call about a past report; more than likely, someone else took that original call.

A problem-tracking database should capture the following information:

- **People:** who received the call, who is responsible for checking the problem, who is responsible for making repairs
- **Status:** when the problem was first discovered, when it was positively identified, when it was repaired, when the users were informed
- **Catalog Information:** what product the report is about, the version/patch-level, the severity of the problem, the part of the application with the problem
- **Notes:** General comments regarding each customer contact, since no technical support call quite fits the templates a bug-tracking tool provides

Continuous Improvement

The faults reported by users must be tracked and solved. For maximum effect, however, the information must be fed back into the system to support a continuous improvement mechanism. Continuous improvement, as introduced earlier, refers to the notion that quality control should not merely improve the end product but also the process by which products are made. It allows knowledge to be transferred to subsequent generations of developers. In doing so, it reduces the likelihood of shipped faults in the future.

Ideally, all faults detected in system testing should have been caught earlier. Part of the continuous improvement process is to modify the development system to better prevent or detect bugs. Obviously, faults that make it into the shipped product are particularly glaring—surely they should have been found and eradicated earlier. When the faults have been isolated and identified, the analysis should figure out how they got through testing. There are many possible ways this can happen, some of which are outlined below.

Inadequate QC Enforcement

The software development process may be fine but not implemented properly. Unfortunately, corners often are cut and the team ignores the proscribed process. Perhaps the quality team is not analyzing the results of coverage analysis tools properly. Perhaps some code walkthroughs were skipped due to lack of time. The list of potential breakdowns in the process can be long.

All one can do about this is to try to prevent such organizational breakdowns. Perhaps not everyone believes in the quality control effort. For others, quality is a concern but is less important than meeting deadlines or adding features. Somehow the project as a whole must recognize the importance of preventing faults from being shipped to users. Only when everyone is working toward that goal will breakdowns become a thing of the past.

Steps to take include the following:

- Ensure that failure to follow QC rules is reflected in reviews and compensation decisions.
- Get key developers to buy into the concept of strong SQA and let them apply peer pressure to change the team's attitudes.
- Create incentive plans based on number of reported faults from end users.

Gaps in the Process

The tools or procedures may be inadequate to catch particular types of faults. For example, path coverage might have detected a missed set of unit test cases (one of which would have found a bug), but other metrics said the suite was complete. Ideally, the approach here is to improve the tools to detect gaps. While some may balk at the cost of better tools, catching just a few bugs that might have gotten into the users' hands would more than pay for the extra expense.

Where tools cannot be augmented, the best approach is to improve the code walkthrough or inspection process. Some things to do include the following:

- The project can maintain a "Hall of Fame" of discovered faults, particularly those that might be missed by the rest of the process. Inspectors can look for these situations while reviewing the code. Unfortunately, this relies on the unreliable human inspection process. At best, it can reduce the chance of shipping certain classes of bugs. There are no guarantees that it will prevent them all.
- Divide the inspection process among the reviewers, rather than have everyone look out for faults and bad constructs universally. Some roles that Yourdon [16] recommends include a "user representative" who focuses on end-user concerns and a "standards bearer" who focuses on compliance with the coding style guide.

Improper Exception Handling

The fault may be the result of a failure to detect or deal with a system exception, such as being out of memory or unable to open a file. If the code assumes that such resource requests succeed, the application will work only so long as these assumptions are valid. Unfortunately, the assumptions are likely to fail in some real-world circumstances and users will wind up with a bug.

Exception handling ideally would be an integrated part of the overall application. Any request, from any possible operation, that might not be fulfillable would throw an exception and cause the system to unwind gracefully before shutting down. This avoids forcing developers to check for failures manually and reduces the probability of dealing with the exception incorrectly. However, such an all-encompassing, exception-handling system is difficult to find or create.

In a more traditional environment, checking code and ensuring thorough exception handling should be done during a code inspection or walkthrough. One could create tools to help (e.g., break out fragments of code containing calls that are known to be fallible, like malloc()), but it still will be a largely manual effort.

12.2 Tools Integration: Quality Plan

This book has outlined many tools and techniques to improve one's SQA efforts. While the focus has been on the six tools included in the book, a number of others have been described. One topic not covered is how to combine them into an integrated whole.

The concept of integrating tools has been tangentially discussed as part of the topic of continuous improvement. As noted, continuous improvement is a mechanism for improving the SQA process. To have such a process virtually requires a quality plan for the project. It is a document that outlines what the project hopes to achieve. It also enumerates how the work will be done, both in general terms and in specifics for each phase of the development life cycle. A quality plan serves as a guidebook for developers and SQA staff members for coordinating the overall quality effort.

Contents of Quality Plans

A quality plan must be practical. If it is to serve as a guidebook for team members, it must offer concrete rules or tasks that need to be accomplished. While managerial-level "hand-waving" or detailed mathematical analyses of quality approaches are all well and good, there needs to be something for team members to work with.

Here are a few things that could go into a quality plan.

Statement of Goals

All plans of any sort should have a goals statement. It should summarize what the plan hopes to achieve or what the overall process is supposed to accomplish. It should set down scope and desired outcomes. The outcomes can range from "soft" results like customer satisfaction to "hard" ones like specific fault rates (faults per 1000 lines of code, for example).

The statement should describe the foundation upon which the quality plan is based. Everything else in the plan should have a demonstrable impact on the project's ability to meet its goals.

Development SQA Tasks/Rules

Typically, a quality plan does not address phases in the software development life cycle before coding. The reason is the lack of solid procedures or tools for the earlier phases. Hence, the first major set of "rules" this document should contain refers to programming practices.

One popular component is a coding style guide. It is a set of rules by which programs should be written. Typical style guides include commenting conventions, exhortations against certain constructs (e.g., global variables), and makefile templates. This section might also mandate certain programming approaches, such as exception handling or numeric error codes as return values from functions. The idea is that the style guide will collect simple-to-apply rules that have been found to prevent certain classes of programming errors.

Another component will be mandatory steps to take or tools to apply to the code written. One might have rules regarding the use of assertions, pre-/post-conditions, or class invariants. One might mandate a version control system and means for using it. One could also state a policy for tracking resources (e.g., using a library such as ResTrack). These steps and tools should be justified in terms of expected benefit to the project. This will help reduce the negative reaction to "bureaucracy" that such rules often engender in developers.

Also, the plan should spell out the criteria for defining the end of programming and the beginning of unit testing. The criteria are either fixed (such as deadlines) or content-based (when all the functionality slated for a phase is completed). The most important thing is that they are provided in a clear, unequivocal fashion to those who will be judged by them.

Testing SQA Tasks/Rules

Similarly, the quality plan should discuss what the team should do in the testing phases, both unit/integration testing and system testing. Once again, the goal is to provide a concrete description of what the organization expects and, in general, the procedures to follow.

A key section of this component is a description of how to conduct unit- and system-level tests. The document can outline what mechanisms developers should use for each (e.g., what unit test framework to follow, such as UTCLang). If test plans or results are to be formally written up, templates can be provided so they are formatted in a standard way. This section should clarify what outcomes are expected from the testing phases.

This section, like the one for the development phase, can also describe steps to take or services to employ during testing. It should include a test condition catalog, if one is to be used during either unit testing (like the one UTCGen uses) or system testing (to outline different things to try in a GUI, for example). It should also outline the metrics testers should capture, ranging from lines of code to coverage metrics, along with an outline of the tools to measure them.

Finally, this section also must discuss the criteria for success. A project can use a fixed deadline, if there is a "hard and fast" delivery date that must be met. Alternatively, testing can continue until certain coverage metrics have been achieved or until the faults per tester-day have fallen below some threshold value. Whatever the criteria are, the testers must be aware of them, so they know what to aim for and can project how long it will take to get there.

Additional Material

A quality plan certainly can contain other sections as well, such as:

- Quality tasks after system testing, such as a description of acceptance testing, an overview of the fault-tracking tools to use, etc.
- What knowledge should be captured during the SQA steps that one can feed back into the process via continuous improvement
- Other standards that must be met, such as GUI "look and feel" guidelines

Types of Quality Plans

Quality plans come in three major varieties, based on their life span and scope. Each is perfectly valid, and any is better than no plan at all. Some documents take more work and have additional benefits over others, however.

Ad hoc Plans

An ad hoc quality plan is slightly better than nothing at all. It means that a project "tosses together" a combination of documents and word-of-mouth to transfer SQA knowledge among team members. There might be a coding style guide or a GUI style guide as separate documents. Knowledge about available tools probably comes in the form of memos or discussions among team members.

As "ad hoc" suggests, this form of quality plan is not well organized and would not meet any typical external requirements. However, it is the cheapest to produce, given that there is nothing from which to start.

Formal Project Plans

A formal project plan would look like the one described in the previous section, containing goals plus techniques and criteria for each SQA phase. The team would compile it into a single document, in a format similar to a design document or other major project deliverable. Such a formal plan can be presented to outsiders, in addition to serving the team's needs directly.

The major drawback to this approach is the overhead involved in formalizing the document versus just getting by with ad hoc materials.

Organization "Living Documents"

While a formal quality plan is geared toward a single project, one could also set up one that states an organization's objectives. It would be useful for all projects. Special sections or appendixes would cover platform-specific issues; projects might also create their own separate addendums for anything else that is project-specific.

This is the most painful of the three to produce up front, particularly for larger organizations, since more people will want to offer input. Not only must the plan be written, but it must also be maintained to reflect changes in methodologies, targeted platforms, or available tools. Hence, there is considerable centralized cost (time and money) involved in such a "living document."

There are three main advantages, however, to this approach:

- Since several projects can use the central plan, the amount of work any one project needs to invest is minimal, sometimes even less than with the ad hoc approach.

- An organization-wide plan will increase consistency and compatibility between projects, as well as leverage major expenditures, such as high-priced SQA tools.
- A long-lived quality plan is the best mechanism for continuous improvement, described in the next section.

Quality Plans and Continuous Improvement

Continuous improvement dictates that knowledge from each project's SQA efforts should somehow modify the process for future projects. There must be a feedback loop that succeeding generations of project teams will honor. This can be done on an ad hoc basis, via memos, "brown bag" discussion lunches, or simple office chatter, but this will not guarantee that knowledge gleaned from SQA work will have any effect down the road.

A better approach is to incorporate the SQA information into new revisions of an organization-wide quality plan. Since everyone uses the plan and follows its prescriptions, changes made to improve the SQA process will certainly affect all future projects. Also, the quality plan already has a structure into which new information can be added. For example, if it contains a "Hall of Fame" of classic faults, teams can add new ones and have immediate impact.

There are costs, of course. During a project's ongoing quality work, the team must take time to work with the central quality plan's coordinator. They must provide input for changes or confirmation of a prior round of modifications. This increases the overall cost of both a central quality plan and continuous improvement in general. However, the potential benefits over a scattershot method are so great that it is difficult to conceive of a continuous improvement process without a central quality plan.

12.3 Where to Go from Here

The following sections outline various ways of getting more information about SQA tools and techniques

Internet Resources

The Internet is currently in its greatest growth phase. Originally serving only the educational and research communities, it is now moving into the mainstream. Both commercial enterprises and average people are using it for everything from home shopping to investment analysis to playing games.

With regard to software quality and testing, there are resources one can use to get questions answered and find out more about available tools and techniques. These are discussed below. Bear in mind that the Internet is constantly changing!

Usenet Newsgroups

The newsgroups are daily feeds of questions and answers posted by anyone around the world. Usenet offers many of them, ranging in subject matter from object-oriented programming to the last known whereabouts of Elvis Presley. Their advantage is the culture of *quid pro quo* in which most questions that are posted receive a reply, either via electronic mail or as another posting.

For software testing, the main newsgroup is `comp.software.testing`. A hundred or so postings, discussing SQA, metrics, etc., occur each week. If one has questions related to a specific operating system or language, there is a good chance there is also a newsgroup for it (such as `comp.os.msdos.programmer` or `comp.lang.c`).

One accesses Usenet newsgroups through a tool called a newsreader. Newsreaders frequently come from the Internet service provider. People who have Internet access but no newsreader should contact others in their organization or the service provider about obtaining one for their platform.

Anonymous FTP Sites

FTP is a file transfer package that allows one to move files on the Internet. One needs to log in to a remote machine, using a valid ID and password, as if one were trying to log in to it directly. However, many locations offer files via anonymous FTP, which can be accessed by anyone in the world with FTP client software. These sites carry everything from academic papers to the latest shareware PC games.

Few anonymous FTP sites exist solely for software testing. A few researchers put their papers out on FTP sites for public access, but finding out where the papers are located requires special contacts. There is no common repository or index for all files available via FTP.

Currently, the best anonymous FTP site is Brian Marick's at `cs.uiuc.edu` (an FTP server provided by the University of Illinois). The `pub/testing` directory contains a number of resources maintained by Marick, including:

- A list of SQA and related tools, both commercial and freely available
- The Generic Coverage Tool, a free C/Unix coverage analysis package (described in Chapter 9 on UTCCover)
- Papers on software testing, particularly coverage analysis and subsystem testing

Other anonymous FTP sites may spring up over time. Announcements about them typically appear in the `comp.software.testing` newsgroup.

To access files via anonymous FTP, one needs FTP client software. It typically comes with one's TCP/IP network software (required for Internet access).

Other Internet Information Sources

There are information sources on the Internet, such as Gopher and the World Wide Web. The latter in particular is rapidly gaining popularity because of its hypertext nature and graphics capability. Right now, there is little on these resources related specifically to SQA, although this will undoubtedly change with time.

Other Tools

This book provides a taste of the tools that are available to assist in software quality assurance. Many tools and libraries included here have commercial equivalents; there are other types as well. Hence, one should surely investigate what tools are available for the platforms the project is using.

The major SQA tool vendors advertise in the popular programming magazines and journals, such as *Dr. Dobb's Journal* or *C/C++ Users Journal*. Buying copies of them at the newsstand is a good starting point for identifying tools.

Another resource is the list maintained by Brian Marick at his anonymous FTP site (see above). It lists both commercial and public domain tools. Commercial tools typically include the name and telephone numbers of the publisher. Public domain tools come with information about obtaining them, typically via anonymous FTP.

Obviously, the standard techniques for finding out about any software, such as searching CD-ROM indexes or the *Microcomputer Index* of magazine articles, will also work. Also, many publishers and organizations are publishing their papers via CD-ROM, ranging from *PC Magazine* through the OOPSLA conferences.

12.4 Conclusion

Software will always have faults—that is merely a statement of our fallibility. The key to success is, of course, to minimize the number of faults that affect anyone outside the development team by preventing faults up front or by catching them during testing.

This book has focused on SQA tools and how they can aid a development team in achieving higher levels of quality. One can apply tools to improve quality during all phases of software development, particularly coding and testing. Almost as important is the ability to take the information gained from these tools to improve the process of writing software, to better prevent or detect faults in the future.

12.5 Story Conclusion

"We, of course, are extraordinarily pleased with the work done by the TurboChem team on their most recent release, which has allowed us..."

Midearth Chemicals' chairman has a tendency to drone on interminably, Sam concluded. He was at the annual shareholders' meeting. Moreover, he was seated at the main conference table as a special guest. The chairman wanted to introduce Sam to the shareholders (as a public relations gesture, Sam allowed) and for Sam to "say a few words" about TurboChem's most recent release. Sam, of course, was hating every minute of it, being a fairly private person.

On the other hand, it could have been much worse, Sam admitted to himself. TurboChem finally had a reasonably bug-free release. It worked on all platforms, performed well, and did not crash regularly, as had its predecessors. Not that it was perfect, mind you, but it was much better than it had been.

The droning continued, "...with a 25% increase in the number of designer chemicals created per year, Midearth is now in a position to..."

The bulk of the credit went to the project team, as they did an excellent job getting the release out on time and in one piece. However, he did feel that his early work in organizing the quality assurance effort had paid off. The whole team concerned itself with the quality of TurboChem, but not to the ridiculous, inefficient levels of the previous team. They particularly worked hard on automation to leverage the computers themselves to help prevent, identify, and diagnose problems.

For example, the test drivers the team created for the subsystems were priceless when TurboChem was ported to new platforms. The regression testing went very quickly, as the drivers generated reports that could be automatically compared for differences. Without those, Sam thought, the project would never have delivered on time.

Moreover, the SQA efforts centered around creating a quality plan, not only for this release of TurboChem but for future use as well. Sam hoped that the "continuous improvement" philosophy that he tried to instill would carry forward to the next generations of project teams. That will be the only way for the success of TurboChem to have an impact beyond the application itself.

"And so, I would like to present to you, Sam Ramgee, TurboChem project leader!"

Sam swallowed hard, before getting up to the podium. The shareholders' applause was heartfelt and boisterous as he prepared to say his "few words." Even though he hated public speaking, he did have a glow in his heart for the quality job he and his team had done.

THE END

APPENDIX A

About the Disk

This book comes with a 3.5" high-density floppy disk, containing the source code for all the tools, along with selected executables for DOS or Windows 3.1. This appendix describes the disk and how to install it.

A.1 Installing the Disk

The disk contains three files:

- README.TXT, late-breaking notes regarding the rest of the disk
- QTOOLS.ZIP, a compressed archive of the files for the tools
- UNZIP.EXE, a DOS program for expanding the ZIP archive

DOS, Windows, and OS/2 Users

To install the files from the floppy, simply do the following:

1. Create a directory on the hard disk where the files are to reside.
2. Make that directory the current working directory.
3. Run UNZIP from a DOS command line, providing QTOOLS.ZIP as a parameter.

For example, to install the files from the A drive to H:\QUALITY, execute the following statements at the DOS prompt:

```
MD H:\QUALITY
H:
CD \QUALITY
A:UNZIP A:QTOOLS.ZIP
```

If you use PKZIP to unpack the archive, include the -d switch to expand the directory tree.

Users of Other Platforms

The UNZIP program on the disk is Info-ZIP's portable free ZIP file extractor. Versions exist for many platforms, including most flavors of Unix. Many sites already have it available; check with your system administrator.

If you need to obtain UNZIP, you can obtain copies through the Info-Zip World Wide Web page at `http://quest.jpl.nasa.gov/Info-Zip/Info-Zip.html.`

Once you have UNZIP, follow its instructions to unpack the QTOOLS.ZIP archive to the desired directory.

A.2 Contents of the Archive

The archive will expand into several subdirectories (see Table A.1). Each contains the source for a single tool or subsystem.

Table A.1 Directory Contents of the Included Disk

Directory	Contents
ADDRLITE	Address Lite sample application, including generated MFC code
ASSERT	AssertLib: assertion library
COVER	UTCCover: coverage analysis library and tool
GC	Garbage collection subsystem, used by UTCLang
LIST	Linked-list C++ classes, used by various tools
MKPROTOB	C function prototypes generator utility, used by UTCCover and useful for UTCGen
REGEX	Regular expression parsing library, used by UTCGen

Table A.1 Directory Contents of the Included Disk (Continued)

Directory	Contents
RESTRACK	ResTrack: memory allocation diagnostic library
UTCGEN	UTCGen: Unit test condition generator
UTCLANG	UTCLang: Scripting language library
UTIL	Various utility functions, used by various tools
UTILDLG	Windows utility dialogs, used by WinCapT
WINCAPT	WinCapT: Windows session capture/playback tool
WMD	Windows Memory Dump subsystem, used by WinCapT
XBASE	X-Base library and test driver, used by Address Lite

Each directory has a FILELIST.TXT file describing the contents of each file. Also, be sure to check the main README.TXT file (on the floppy disk) to see if there are notes about a particular directory's contents.

APPENDIX B

Library and Framework APIs

This book provides several libraries for development use as "official" testing tools and related subsystems. While the interfaces (APIs) for each are described in their respective chapters, this appendix outlines the public functions.

This chapter also describes the two main frameworks provided in the book: UTCLang and the garbage collection subsystem. It outlines behaviors provided by the framework classes and ones that must be implemented in concrete subclasses.

B.1 AssertLib

All the functions/macros shown below are in _ASSERT.H.

Assert(int bValue)

Parameters

bValue: Value to be asserted (0=failure, non-zero=success)

Purpose

Raises an assertion if the provided value is zero. The intent is to wrap it around an expression that tests a condition. The actual representation of the assertion (e.g., dialog, logged to file) will be determined by a compiler macro definition.

AssertAction(int bValue, <expr>)

Parameters

bValue: Value to be asserted (0=failure, non-zero=success)

<expr>: C expression to be inserted into code

Purpose

Raises an assertion if the provided value is zero. If the assertion style is one that allows processing to continue (i.e., log to file or dialog), the action provided as the second parameter will also be executed on failures. For example, this can be used to terminate the current function.

AssertMsg(int bValue, char *pszMsg)

Parameters

bValue: Value to be asserted (0=failure, non-zero=success)

pszMsg: Message to be displayed to user indicating what assertion failed

Purpose

Also raises an assertion if the provided value is zero. Rather than displaying the expression, however, this macro displays the message. Again, the message will be shown via a mechanism determined by a compile-time macro definition.

AssertMsgAction(int bValue, char *pszMsg, <expr>)

Parameters

bValue: Value to be asserted (0=failure, non-zero=success)

pszMsg: Message to be displayed to user indicating what assertion failed

<expr>: C expression to be inserted into code

Purpose

Raises an assertion if the provided value is zero. If the assertion fails, the message will be shown, rather than the expression text. Also, if the assertion mode supports continued processing after a failure, the provided expression will be executed.

B.2 Garbage Collection Framework

This framework, part of the UTCLang scripting language, provides simple garbage collection. Objects allocated through it do not need to be explicitly freed. Instead, one can request that "garbage" memory be reclaimed; the framework itself will destroy objects no longer referenced by the application.

The following sections outline the public classes provided in this framework and how they can be used or subclassed.

GcSpace

GcSpace()

Constructor for GcSpace. Simply creates a new object space with no generations and no objects. An instance must be provided to all created objects (GcObject instances).

~GcSpace()

Destructor for GcSpace. Also destroys all generations and objects the space holds on to.

void FullGC()

Requests a full garbage collection, implemented as collection of all generations.

void FullSweep(GC_SWEEP_FN pfnSweep, void *pData)

Applies the provided sweep function and data pointer to all objects in the space. Useful for enumerating instances of a particular class, etc.

virtual unsigned int GetMaxGenCount() = 0

Must be implemented by subclasses to return the highest generation number to use in promoting objects that survive collection. Primarily controls the storage used in the GcObject subclass for the generation number (e.g., unsigned short versus unsigned long).

virtual int IsFreeSpaceLow() = 0

Must be implemented by subclasses to return true (1) if available memory is deemed to be low. Determination of low space is typically a function of the operating system or other memory access mechanism.

unsigned long ObjectCount()

Returns the number of objects in the space, including garbage instances not yet collected. After a FullGC(), this value represents the total number of live instances.

void QuickGC()

Requests a fast garbage collection, implemented as a collection of the most recent generation.

GcObject

Note: All the pure virtual member functions except SweepChildren() are handled automatically by the GcSimpleObject class. This class uses plain data members to hold the information. If one needs a more space-efficient mechanism, subclass GcObject and implement all the pure virtual functions.

GcObject(GcSpace *pSpace)

Constructor for GcObject. Takes an object space as a parameter, indicating the space in which the object will operate. Any subclass of GcObject should call the GcObject constructor as part of the subclass constructor.

virtual ~GcObject()

Destructor for GcObject. Should not be called directly by an application. So long as the application lets go of the object, the space will call the destructor and free the memory when needed.

void AddChild(GcObject *pChild)

Informs the subsystem that a new child has been added. Used for generation management: The child will move to the generation of the parent, if the parent is older.

virtual unsigned int GetGeneration() = 0

Returns the generation number for this object, representing its age. Must be implemented in subclasses. See GcSimpleObject for a sample implementation.

GcSpace *GetSpace()

Returns the object space in which this object operates—the same value that was set in the constructor.

virtual int IsHeld() = 0

Returns true (1) if the object is held by the application (e.g., is a root, in garbage collection terms). This must be implemented in subclasses and can be a simple data member. See GcSimpleObject for a sample implementation.

virtual int IsReached() = 0

Returns true (1) if the object has been reached during the current garbage collection scavenging operation. This must be implemented in subclasses and can be a simple data member. See GcSimpleObject for a sample implementation.

virtual int IsSwept() = 0

Returns true (1) if the object has been swept during the current sweep of objects. This must be implemented in subclasses and can be a simple data member. See GcSimpleObject for a sample implementation.

virtual void MarkAsHeld(int bState) = 0

Marks the object as being held by the application (e.g., indicating that it is a root). This must be implemented in subclasses and can be a simple data member. See GcSimpleObject for a sample implementation.

virtual void MarkAsReached(int bState) = 0;

Marks the object as being reachable from a root during this garbage collection scavenge. This must be implemented in subclasses and can be a simple data member. See GcSimpleObject for a sample implementation.

virtual void MarkAsSwept(int bState) = 0;

Marks the object as being swept as a part of this object sweep. This must be implemented in subclasses and can be a simple data member. See GcSimpleObject for a sample implementation.

void RemoveChild(GcObject *pChild);

Indicates to the subsystem that the child is no longer held by the object. Presently is a no-operation, but might be required in other GC implementations.

virtual void SetGeneration(unsigned int uiGeneration) = 0

Sets the generation number for the object. Must be implemented in subclasses. See GcSimpleObject for a sample implementation.

virtual void SweepChildren(GC_SWEEP_FN pfnSweep, void *pData) = 0

Must be implemented by subclasses to iterate over the children held by the object and call the provided sweep function for each. The sweep function takes two parameters: the child object and the provided data pointer. Examples appear in various subclasses of UtcObject in UTCLang.

B.3 ResTrack

ResTrack redefines the malloc(), free(), and strdup() functions in _ALLOC.H. The rest of the public API, shown below, appears in RESTRACK.H.

MemCheckListIntegrity()

Parameters

None

Purpose

Walks the list of allocated blocks and checks each one's header for corruption. The function raises an exception if corruption is found. It can be added to code to detect serious overwriting or underwriting of memory.

MemDumpUnfreed()

Parameters

None

Purpose

Writes to RESTRACK.OUT a list of all buffers allocated via MemMalloc() or MemStrDup() but not freed. Frequently used as an atexit() function to ensure it gets executed as the application terminates.

MemFree(void *pBuffer)

Parameters

pBuffer: Buffer allocated by MemMalloc() or MemStrDup() to be freed

Purpose

Releases storage; also detects overwrites/underwrites and raises assertions in case of problems. Do **not** use it to free memory not allocated via either MemMalloc() or MemStrDup().

MemIsValidPointer(void *pBuffer)

Parameters

pBuffer: Pointer to memory to be determined if still usable

Purpose

Returns true (1) if the supplied pointer points to memory allocated by MemMalloc() or MemStrDup() that has not yet been freed. Otherwise, returns false (0). It can be used to test pointers suspected of having been previously freed.

MemMalloc(unsigned int uiSize)

Parameters

uiSize: Size of block to allocate, in bytes

Purpose

Similar to malloc(), except that it also tracks allocations in a master list, which is used to determine what has not been freed. It also allocates space around the application's requested block, for use in storing block information and detecting overwrites and underwrites. The pointer returned by this function points to a block of memory of the requested size.

MemStrDup(char *pszOriginal)

Parameters
pszOriginal: String to be copied

Purpose
Copies a string to another buffer on the heap. Works like strdup(), except that it uses MemMalloc() to track memory allocation. This means that buffers returned by it are also tracked for leaks.

B.4 UTCCover

UTCCover consists of three parts:

- Logging function and macros
- Library of routines for processing the log files to generate results
- Shell executable to process log files indicated on a command line

The logging function and macros are described in the text; the shell executable simply uses the library routines. The following sections describe each of the API functions and how to use them to generate coverage statistics.

UtcFreeHandle(COV_HANDLE hHandle)

Parameters
hHandle: Handle to a set of coverage statistics for log files

Purpose
Releases all storage held by the handle, including information about coverage results. The handle is unusable afterward.

UtcGetFirstEntry(COV_HANDLE hHandle, UTC_COVERINFO *prInfo)

Parameters
hHandle: Handle to a set of coverage statistics for log files
prInfo: Information about a single coverage situation, including the location, type of coverage (e.g., loop), and whether it succeeded

Purpose
The coverage handle, after parsing the log file, contains a list of coverage situations and their results. Retrieves the first entry from the results list. The UTC_COVERINFO structure contains the following information:

- int iType: Type of coverage (values defined in an enumeration in UTCCOVER.H)

- char szFilename[]: File containing the source for this coverage situation
- unsigned long ulLine: The line number in the source for this coverage situation
- int bPassed: Flag indicating whether the situation passed the coverage metric (true=1) or failed (false=0)
- char szDescription[]: Single text line describing the missed coverage, contains an unusable string if bPassed is true

UtcGetNextEntry(COV_HANDLE hHandle, UTC_COVERINFO *prInfo)

Parameters

hHandle: Handle to a set of coverage statistics for log files

prInfo: Information about a single coverage situation, including the location, type of coverage (e.g., loop), and whether it succeeded

Purpose

Retrieves the next entry from the list of results held by the coverage handle. See UtcGetFirstEntry() for more information about the result list and its contents.

UtcGetSourceForCurrentEntry(COV_HANDLE hHandle, char **apszLines, unsigned int uiBuffSize, unsigned int uiLines, char **ppszActualLine)

Parameters

hHandle: Handle to a set of coverage statistics for log files

apszLines: Array of strings into which to copy source file lines

uiBuffSize: Size of each string in apszLines

uiLines: Number of strings in apszLines

ppszActualLine: Pointer to the string from apszLines that represents the actual location of the coverage situation

Purpose

For reporting purposes, it is frequently useful to show a snapshot of code around a coverage situation. This function provides such a snapshot for the current coverage situation (as set by UtcGetFirstEntry() and UtcGetNextEntry(), described above). The caller must provide the space into which to copy lines of source code (apszLines). The function centers the coverage situation line in the array; an array of five lines thus will have the actual coverage situation as the third line. This line is also pointed to by ppszActualLine.

UtcInitHandle(COV_HANDLE *phHandle)

Parameters

phHandle: Pointer to handle to a set of coverage statistics for log files

Purpose

Allocates initial storage for coverage information to be collected for log files. This storage should be released by UtcFreeHandle() when the handle is no longer needed.

UtcNameForType(int iType, char *pszName, unsigned int uiBuffSize)

Parameters

iType: Type of coverage (values defined in an enumeration in UTCCOVER.H)

pszName: Buffer to hold name for this type of coverage

uiBuffSize: Size of pszName buffer

Purpose

For reporting purposes, it is useful to have a name for a type of coverage metric rather than merely the number returned in the results. This function will return a name for a given coverage type number, copying it into the supplied buffer.

UtcParseLogFile(COV_HANDLE hHandle, char *pszFilename)

Parameters

hHandle: Handle to a set of coverage statistics for log files

pszFIlename: Log file to be parsed and results collected

Purpose

Takes the raw log information contained in the provided log file and determines where coverage situations exist and which have passed/failed. Afterward, UtcGetFirstEntry() and UtcGetNextEntry() can be used to review the results.

B.5 UTCGen

Although UTCGen is largely a tool, its main processing functions are encapsulated into a separate library. The front end provided here serves as a command-line shell, but other user interfaces can be created by writing to the API in the same way.

UtcFreeHandle(UTC_HANDLE hFunction)

Parameters

hFunction: UTCGen handle to a function's results, from UtcProcessFunction()

Purpose

Releases storage allocated by UtcProcessFunction() when determining the unit test conditions for this function. This function should be called on all handles allocated by UtcProcessFunction()

UtcGetCondition(UTC_HANDLE hFunction, int iParm, int iCondition, char *pszBuffer, unsigned int uiBufferSize)

Parameters

hFunction: UTCGen handle to a function's results, from UtcProcessFunction()
iParm: Index (0-based) of function parameter for which to obtain condition
iCondition: Index (0-based) of condition to obtain for the function parameter
pszBuffer: Buffer to store text of unit test condition from catalog
uiBufferSize: Size of buffer pointed to by pszBuffer

Purpose

Obtains the text for a unit test condition for a given parameter of a function. Typically used inside a loop, with the number of iterations controlled by UtcGetConditionCount(), to obtain all conditions for a parameter.

UtcGetConditionCount(UTC_HANDLE hFunction, int iParm)

Parameters

hFunction: UTCGen handle to a function's results, from UtcProcessFunction()
iParm: Index (0-based) of function parameter for which to obtain condition

Purpose

Returns the number of conditions logged for this parameter in this function. Typically used to control the indexes passed to UtcGetCondition().

UtcGetFunctionName(UTC_HANDLE hFunction, char *pszBuffer, unsigned int uiBufferSize)

Parameters

hFunction: UTCGen handle to a function's results, from UtcProcessFunction()
pszBuffer: Buffer to store text of function name
uiBufferSize: Size of buffer pointed to by pszBuffer

double GetValueAsDouble()

Returns the value of the number as a C double, even if the value is integral.

virtual int IsNumber()

Returns true, indicating that the object is a number. Also implemented on UtcObject, so all objects respond to it appropriately.

int IsTrue()

Returns true (1) if the object represents the logical "true" condition in the language.

int IsFalse()

Returns true (1) if the object represents the logical "false" condition in the language.

UtcString

UtcString(GcSpace *pSpace, char *pszStart)

Creates a new string object, given a C string as the value. The space (pSpace) should come from an existing object or the handle, via the GetSpace() function. Do not create a new space, as it will not be managed by the interpreter.

B.7 Utility Dialogs

A pair of Windows utility dialogs, used by Address Lite, are in a separate library. One dialog allows the user to enter a single line of text; the other allows the user to select an entry from a list. They are "canned" dialogs, in that a single API call invokes them. No additional application code is required, other than linking to the utility dialog DLL.

TextDialogBox(LPSTR lpszTitle, LPSTR lpszResult, int iSize)

Parameters

lpszTitle: Informational message to user about what should be entered

lpszResult: Buffer to hold string typed by user

iSize: Size of provided buffer

Purpose

Brings up a dialog containing the title, a single entry field, and OK/Cancel buttons. The entered string is returned in lpszResult (up to iSize bytes) if OK is clicked.

ListDialogBox(LPSTR lpszButtonName, LPSTR *alpszContents, int iCount, int *piSelection)

Parameters

lpszButtonName: Name of selection button

alpszContents: Array of strings to go into listbox

iCount: Number of strings in array

piSelection: On return, holds the index of the selected string

Purpose

Dialog contains a listbox and a button to indicate that the selection has been made. The button's label is set by lpszButtonName, and the listbox is filled with the strings provided by alpszContents. The index of the string (0-based) selected by the user is returned in piSelection. The Windows constant LB_ERR is returned in piSelection if the user closes the window without making a selection.

B.8 WinCapT

Like many of the other tools, WinCapT consists of a user interface (WINCAPT.C) and a back-end processing library (WCTHOOK.C). This is particularly important here, as Windows mandates that journaling hook functions, used for recording and playing back events, be placed in a DLL instead of in an application itself.

WctStartPlaybackSession(LPSTR lpszLogFile, LPSTR lpszResultFile, HWND hCallingWnd)

Parameters

lpszLogFile: File containing event information from prior recording session

lpszResultFile: File to use for storing control states for comparison

hCallingWnd: Window handle of the UI requesting the playback

Purpose

Seizes control of the mouse and keyboard from the user and begins playing back the recorded events, stored in lpszLogFile. At the points in the script when the user requested window states to be captured, the states will be recaptured and stored in lpszResultFile. Barring a major system failure, control will not return to the user until the playback is complete. The provided window will be sent the WM_USER message when the playback session ends.

WctStartRecordSession()

Parameters

None

Purpose

Starts recording all user actions, both keystrokes and mouse movements, storing the information in an internal buffer (see Windows Memory Dump, below). When the user presses <PrintScreen>, WinCapT will also capture state information about the window under the mouse cursor and its parent windows. Recording continues until WctStopRecordSession() is called.

WctStopPlaybackSession()

Parameters

None

Purpose

To be called by the UI after receiving the WM_USER message from the WCTHOOK DLL. Concludes a session playback and allows the DLL to clean up allocated memory, etc. Should only be called when WM_USER is sent from the DLL.

WctStopRecordSession(LPSTR lpszLog, LPSTR lpszResult)

Parameters

lpszLog: File in which to store event information

lpszResult: File in which to store window state information

Purpose

Stops the recording session already started by WctStartRecordSession(). The information retained by the DLL (mouse/keyboard events and window state results) will be written to files. A subsequent WctStartPlaybackSession() call can use the lpszLog event file.

B.9 Windows Memory Dump

This subsystem allows one to implement file I/O to a memory buffer. The buffer can then be written to disk or restored from it. Used in situations where a "stream"-style interface is useful for reading to and writing from a memory buffer, without having to be manually resized as it needs to grow.

WmdAppend(HGLOBAL hDump, LPSTR pszData, UINT uiLength)

Parameters

hDump: Stream of data for writing, created by WmdInit()
pszData: Buffer to append to stream
uiLength: Size of buffer (note: NULL terminator ignored)

Purpose

Adds the data block to the stream, expanding its storage if needed.

WmdExtract(HGLOBAL hDump, LPSTR pszData, UINT uiLength)

Parameters

hDump: Stream of data for writing, created by WmdInitFromFile()
pszData: Buffer to hold data pulled from the stream
uiLength: Size of buffer and the number of bytes to pull from the stream

Purpose

Given a stream for reading, obtains data and copies it to the provided buffer. Fails if there is less than the requested amount of data available.

WmdInit(HGLOBAL *phDump, DWORD dwStartSize)

Parameters

phDump: Pointer to a handle to represent the stream
dwStartSize: Size in bytes to use for the stream at the outset

Purpose

Initializes a stream for writing, preallocated to the requested size. The stream will grow as needed if the starting size is exceeded. Data can be added to the stream via WmdAppend().

WmdInitFromFile(HGLOBAL *phDump, LPSTR pszFileName)

Parameters

phDump: Pointer to a handle to represent the stream
pszFileName: File to read into memory

Purpose

Initializes a stream for reading, using the provided file as the source. Data can be pulled from it via WmdExtract().

WmdTerm(HGLOBAL hDump)

Parameters
hDump: Stream of data for writing, created by WmdInitFromFile()

Purpose
Frees the memory associated with the stream. The handle is unusable afterward. If data was appended, it will be lost if not saved by WmdWriteToFile() or other means.

WmdWriteToFile(HGLOBAL hDump, LPSTR pszFileName)

Parameters
hDump: Stream of data for writing, created by WmdInitFromFile()
pszFileName: File to hold stream data on output

Purpose
Writes the contents of the stream to the named file for later restoration via WmdInitFromFile(). Nothing is put in the file beyond the raw data provided by the application, so it can be modified by other applications without danger of corrupting later use by the Windows Memory Dump.

APPENDIX C

Testing the Sample Code

This appendix outlines plans for the X-Base library's unit test and Address Lite's system test.

C.1 X-Base Library

The sample code provided here includes a library for accessing X-Base database files. The library can open and close files, retrieve records and fields within records, etc. It can serve as a simple database manager and is used as such by Address Lite.

This library has been unit tested for inclusion in this book. The UTCGen tool was used to help generate test conditions described below. A test driver was constructed to implement cases based on the conditions. The test suite was then run, using UTCCover.

The following sections outline the steps in the implementing the unit test.

Unit Test Conditions

Unit test conditions record aspects of a function that should be tried. They represent atomic items that have concrete expected outcomes. Test cases are then constructed from the conditions.

UTCGen-Generated

Table C.1 lists test conditions generated by UTCGen, based on the header files. Ones deemed irrelevant (e.g., accessing strings as arrays) are not included. Also, reasonable interpretations were substituted for the raw output as needed.

Table C.1 UTCGen-Generated Conditions

#	Function	Condition
1	XblOpen()	phHandle is NULL
2	XblOpen()	phHandle is not NULL
3	XblOpen()	pszFilename is NULL
4	XblOpen()	pszFilename is not NULL
5	XblOpen()	pszFilename is a zero-length string
6	XblOpen()	pszFilename is a 1-character string
7	XblOpen()	pszFilename is longer than 1 character
8	XblSeek()	ulRecNum = 0
9	XblSeek()	ulRecNum > 0
10	XblGetFieldAsString()	uiFieldNum = 0
11	XblGetFieldAsString()	ulFieldNum > 0
12	XblGetFieldAsString()	Zero-length string value
13	XblGetFieldAsString()	Single-character string value
14	XblGetFieldAsString()	Multiple character string value
15	XblGetFieldAsInt()	uiFieldNum = 0
16	XblGetFieldAsInt()	uiFieldNum > 0
17	XblGetFieldAsInt()	plResult is NULL
18	XblGetFieldAsInt()	plResult is not NULL
19	XblGetFieldAsFloat()	uiFieldNum = 0
20	XblGetFieldAsFloat()	uiFieldNum > 0
21	XblGetFieldAsFloat()	pdResult is NULL
22	XblGetFieldAsFloat()	pdResult is not NULL
23	XblPutFieldAsString()	uiFieldNum = 0
24	XblPutFieldAsString()	ulFieldNum > 0
25	XblPutFieldAsString()	Zero-length string value

Table C.1 UTCGen-Generated Conditions (Continued)

#	Function	Condition
26	XblPutFieldAsString()	Single-character string value
27	XblPutFieldAsString()	Multiple character string value
28	XblPutFieldAsString()	pszBuffer is NULL
29	XblPutFieldAsString()	pszBuffer is not NULL
30	XblPutFieldAsInt()	uiFieldNum = 0
31	XblPutFieldAsInt()	uiFieldNum > 0
32	XblPutFieldAsInt()	lValue = 0
33	XblPutFieldAsInt()	lValue > 0
34	XblPutFieldAsInt()	lValue < 0
35	XblPutFieldAsFloat()	uiFieldNum = 0
36	XblPutFieldAsFloat()	uiFieldNum > 0
37	XblPutFieldAsFloat()	lValue = 0
38	XblPutFieldAsFloat()	lValue > 0
39	XblPutFieldAsFloat()	lValue < 0
40	XblFieldNameFromNum()	uiFieldNum = 0
41	XblFieldNameFromNum()	uiFieldNum > 0
42	XblFieldNameFromNum()	pszFieldName is NULL
43	XblFieldNameFromNum()	pszFieldName is not NULL
44	XblFieldNumFromName()	pszFieldName is NULL
45	XblFieldNumFromName()	pszFieldName is not NULL
46	XblFieldNumFromName()	pszFieldName is a zero-length string
47	XblFieldNumFromName()	pszFieldName is a 1-character string
48	XblFieldNumFromName()	pszFieldName is longer than 1 character
49	XblFieldNumFromName()	puiFieldNum is NULL
50	XblFieldNumFromName()	puiFieldNum is not NULL

Table C.1 UTCGen-Generated Conditions (Continued)

#	Function	Condition
51	XblFieldType()	uiFieldNum = 0
52	XblFieldType()	uiFieldNum > 0
53	XblFieldType()	pcType is NULL
54	XblFieldType()	pcType is not NULL
55	XblFieldLength()	uiFieldNum = 0
56	XblFieldLength()	uiFieldNum > 0
57	XblFieldLength()	pucLen is NULL
58	XblFieldLength()	pucLen is not NULL
59	XblFieldDecimals()	uiFieldNum = 0
60	XblFieldDecimals()	uiFieldNum > 0
61	XblFieldDecimals()	pucDec is NULL
62	XblFieldDecimals()	pucDec is not NULL

Manually Generated

Table C.2 outlines unit test conditions created by a manual inspection of the source code, without assistance from UTCGen. If an API function does not appear in any tables, no conditions were generated for it.

Table C.2 Manually Generated Conditions

#	Function	Condition
63	XblOpen()	malloc() of XBL_DBINFO succeeds
64	XblOpen()	malloc() of XBL_DBINFO fails
65	XblOpen()	Requested file exists
66	XblOpen()	Requested file does not exist
67	XblOpen()	File header is legal
68	XblOpen()	File header is illegal
69	XblOpen()	malloc() of field structures succeeds
70	XblOpen()	malloc() of field structures fails

Table C.2 Manually Generated Conditions (Continued)

#	Function	Condition
71	XblOpen()	malloc() of record succeeds
72	XblOpen()	malloc() of record fails
73	XblSeek()	Record number too high
74	XblDelete()	Record is presently deleted
75	XblDelete()	Record is presently not deleted
76	XblIsDeleted()	Record is presently deleted
77	XblIsDeleted()	Record is presently not deleted
78	XblGetFieldAsString()	Field number is valid
79	XblGetFieldAsString()	Field number is invalid
80	XblGetFieldAsString()	Field type is string
81	XblGetFieldAsString()	Field type is number
82	XblGetFieldAsString()	Field type is date
83	XblGetFieldAsString()	Buffer size is valid
84	XblGetFieldAsString()	Buffer is too small
85	XblGetFieldAsInt()	Field number is valid
86	XblGetFieldAsInt()	Field number is invalid
87	XblGetFieldAsInt()	Field type is string
88	XblGetFieldAsInt()	Field type is number
89	XblGetFieldAsInt()	Field type is date
90	XblGetFieldAsInt()	Field value is negative
91	XblGetFieldAsInt()	Field value is zero
92	XblGetFieldAsInt()	Field value is positive
93	XblGetFieldAsInt()	Field value is integral
94	XblGetFieldAsInt()	Field value has fractional component
95	XblGetFieldAsFloat()	Field number is valid

Table C.2 Manually Generated Conditions (Continued)

#	Function	Condition
96	XblGetFieldAsFloat()	Field number is invalid
97	XblGetFieldAsFloat()	Field type is string
98	XblGetFieldAsFloat()	Field type is number
99	XblGetFieldAsFloat()	Field type is date
100	XblGetFieldAsFloat()	Field value is negative
101	XblGetFieldAsFloat()	Field value is zero
102	XblGetFieldAsFloat()	Field value is positive
103	XblGetFieldAsFloat()	Field value is integral
104	XblGetFieldAsFloat()	Field value has fractional component
105	XblPutFieldAsString()	Field number is valid
106	XblPutFieldAsString()	Field number is invalid
107	XblPutFieldAsString()	Field type is string
108	XblPutFieldAsString()	Field type is number
109	XblPutFieldAsString()	Field type is date
110	XblPutFieldAsString()	New value fits within field size
111	XblPutFieldAsString()	New value longer than field size
112	XblPutFieldAsInt()	Field number is valid
113	XblPutFieldAsInt()	Field number is invalid
114	XblPutFieldAsInt()	Field type is string
115	XblPutFieldAsInt()	Field type is number
116	XblPutFieldAsInt()	Field type is date
117	XblPutFieldAsFloat()	Field number is valid
118	XblPutFieldAsFloat()	Field number is invalid
119	XblPutFieldAsFloat()	Field type is string
120	XblPutFieldAsFloat()	Field type is number

Table C.2 Manually Generated Conditions (Continued)

#	Function	Condition
121	XblPutFieldAsFloat()	Field type is date
122	XblPutFieldAsFloat()	New value is integral
123	XblPutFieldAsFloat()	New value has fractional component
124	XblFieldNameFromNum()	Field number is valid
125	XblFieldNameFromNum()	Field number is invalid
126	XblFieldNameFromNum()	Name buffer size is valid
127	XblFieldNameFromNum()	Name buffer is too short
128	XblFieldNumFromName()	Request name of first field
129	XblFieldNumFromName()	Request name of middle field
130	XblFieldNumFromName()	Request name of last field
131	XblFieldNumFromName()	Use invalid name
132	XblFieldType()	Field number is valid
133	XblFieldType()	Field number is invalid
134	XblFieldLength()	Field number is valid
135	XblFieldLength()	Field number is invalid
136	XblFieldDecimals()	Field number is valid
137	XblFieldDecimals()	Field number is invalid
138	XblFieldDecimals()	Field type is string
139	XblFieldDecimals()	Field type is number
140	XblFieldDecimals()	Field type is date
141	XblFieldDecimals()	Field has no decimal places
142	XblFieldDecimals()	Field has one or more decimal places

Unit Test Cases

Negative Test Cases

Negative cases are expected to fail, via either an assertion or an error code. They are easy to write, since only one condition can appear (a negative one). The case is simply the steps needed to try the negative condition.

Tables C.3 and C.4 are two sample negative test cases that arose from the conditions outlined above.

Table C.3 Test Case: Invalid Buffer for XblGetFieldAsString()

Step	Expected Result
Call XblOpen() with a valid handle pointer and filename (file must not be empty)	Function returns 0, file is opened
Call XblSeek() with the opened handle and a record number of 1	Function returns 0
Call XblGetFieldAsString() with the opened handle, a field number of 1, and a NULL buffer pointer	Failed assertion on NULL buffer pointer
Call XblClose() with the opened handle	Function succeeds

Table C.4 Test Case: Seek Past End-Of-File

Step	Expected Result
Call XblOpen() with a valid handle pointer and filename (file must not be empty)	Function returns 0, file is opened
Call XblSeek() with the opened handle and a record number of 2^31	Function returns XBL_ILLEGAL_RECNUM
Call XblClose() with the opened handle	Function succeeds

Positive Test Cases

Positive cases, on the other hand, are expected to succeed. Several positive test conditions can be combined to create cases. The script must describe each step to try the positive conditions, along with the expected results. Tables C.5 and C.6 are two sample positive test cases for the X-Base library.

Table C.5 Test Case: Retrieve One Record from Single-Record File

Step	Expected Result
Call XblOpen() with a valid handle pointer and filename. Filename must be of file containing single record with known values in the fields.	Function returns 0, file is opened
Call XblSeek() with the opened handle and a record number of 1.	Function returns 0
Iterate over columns and call XblGetFieldAsString() for each, passing the opened handle, appropriate column number, and a buffer big enough to hold any columns. Compare the values against the expected ones.	XblGetFieldAsString() returns 0 for each call. Each column/value pair matches, except for possible trailing blanks
Call XblClose() with the opened handle.	Function succeeds

Table C.6 Test Case: Seek Each Record, Reverse Order

Step	Expected Result
Call XblOpen() with a valid handle pointer and filename. Filename should point to database file containing several rows, each with a single numeric column. The column should contain the record number as it is in the database (e.g., the first record's column's value is 1).	Function returns 0, file is opened
Call XblRecordCount() to get the number of records in the file; compare against expected value. Use the handle opened in the prior step.	Function returns expected record count

Table C.6 Test Case: Seek Each Record, Reverse Order (Continued)

Step	Expected Result
For each record in the file, iterating in reverse numerical order, call XblSeek() with the opened handle and the record number. Then call XblGetFieldAsInt() with the opened handle, a column number of 1, and a valid pointer to a long integer. Compare the field value against the record number.	XblSeek() and XblGetFieldAsInt() both return 0; the record number and column value match
Call XblClose() with the opened handle.	Function succeeds

C.2 Address Lite

To thoroughly test Address Lite, one needs a set of system test matrixes. They will help identify what has to be tested, cross-referenced to the cases that try the conditions. The matrixes will help testers define the cases; the cases then can be implemented to perform the actual system test.

For most applications, the most important system test matrix is the requirements matrix. It ensures that all requirements for the application have been tried at least once. If certain features are required, they must be ensured to work. Since Address Lite did not stem from a set of requirements, we have no requirements matrix.

Instead, two other matrixes were developed (Tables C.7 and C.8). One, for the GUI elements in Address Lite, ensures that all features are exercised at least once. The other is for major data operations, designed to ensure that basic application functionality performs properly. These conditions also test how well Address Lite works with the X-Base library for storing addresses.

Tables C.7 and C.8 list the conditions for each matrix. Formal matrixes would cross-reference the conditions with the cases that implement them. However, the roster of system test cases is too large to reprint here, so the tables list only the conditions.

Note that all conditions for child window controls (e.g., fields) and data operations must be tried both with one file open and with more than one open. This will help ensure that Address Lite does not mix up records between files, etc.

Table C.7 GUI Conditions for Address Lite System Test

Main Window	Moves, minimizes, maximizes, resizes, system menu operates (including close)
Child (MDI) Window	Moves, minimizes, maximizes, tiles, cascades, system menu operates; both one and several child windows work
Entries Drop-Down List	Drops, selects, keeps names in sorted order, tabs to first line of street
Street Field (line 1)	Allows text entry, cuts/copies/pastes, tabs to second line of street
Street Field (line 2)	Allows text entry, cuts/copies/pastes, tabs to city
City Field	Allows text entry, cuts/copies/pastes, tabs to state
State Field	Allows text entry, cuts/copies/pastes, tabs to ZIP code
ZIP Code Field	Allows text entry, cuts/copies/pastes, tabs to phone
Phone Field	Allows text entry, cuts/copies/pastes, tabs to FAX
FAX Field	Allows text entry, cuts/copies/pastes, tabs to entries list
Icon Button	Clicks to show "about box"
About Box	OK button clicks to close dialog
Menu	All items select, all hotkeys and accelerator keys work

Table C.8 Data Conditions for Address Lite System Test

Creating Files	Create with new name, create and overwrite existing file, can close new file without adding entries
Opening Files	Open empty file, open non-empty file, cannot open nonexistent file, cannot open invalid file (e.g., a flat ASCII file)
Adding Records	Can add one/several to empty file and restore, can add one/several to non-empty file and restore, can set values for all fields

Table C.8 Data Conditions for Address Lite System Test (Continued)

Deleting Records	Can remove one/several from a file that leaves file empty, can remove one/several from a file that leaves records in file
Changing Records	Can change data in one record and restore, can change data in several records and restore, can change values in all fields except name

APPENDIX D

Tool Unit Tests and Compatibility Notes

The author would be remiss if he failed to document the testing performed on the tools provided here. This appendix outlines the six tools and how they were tested.

D.1 General

For all compilers except Watcom, makefiles are provided in the tools' main directories to build an executable. For library-based tools (AssertLib, ResTrack, and UTCLang), the executables are test versions for running the unit tests. For executable-based tools (UTCGen, UTCCover, and WinCapT), the makefiles create the executable itself. Exceptions are noted in the sections on each tool.

Watcom handles makefiles awkwardly through the IDE, and their use is inadequately described in the on-line documentation. Watcom project files are included for each tool instead.

Some of the tools have been crudely ported to Linux. GNU *make* under Linux appears to follow different rules than the ones used by the major PC compilers. For those tools that have been ported, a simple *bash* shell script is supplied (typically called *build*) to create them.

Each makefile is named MAKEFILE.<ext>, where <ext> depends on compiler and target platform. Table D.1 lists the extensions.

Table D.1 Compilers, Platforms, and Makefile Extensions

Compiler	16-bit DOS	32-bit DOS	16-bit Windows	32-bit Windows	OS/2
Borland C++	BD1	BD2	BW1	BW2	—
Microsoft Visual C++	MD1	—	MW1	—	—
Symantec C++	SD1	SD2	SW1	SW2	—
Metaware High C/C++	—	—	—	—	HO

D.2 AssertLib

The unit test for AssertLib had to try all its functionality, both actions (i.e., assertions and invariants) and results (e.g., logging to file, ANSI-standard assertions). To do so, a single test program (TEST.CPP) was written to exercise the main operations. It was compiled on each platform for the following assertion modes:

- No assertions (production code)
- Log assertions to file
- Log assertions to file and quit
- Assertion dialog (Windows only)
- ANSI-standard assertion

Makefile-driven Builds

The makefiles (MAKEFILE.*) support the selection of the assertion mode from the *make* command line. All supported implementations of the *make* utility allow one to define makefile macros there. To specify a makefile mode, simply declare the ASSERT_MODE macro to be the desired compilation macro. For example, to build the 16-bit DOS test program using assertions sent to a file when using the Borland compiler, one would execute:

```
make -f makefile.bd1 -DASSERT_MODE=ASSERT_FILE
```

This makes it easy to build an executable using a specified assertion mode.

Symantec

For 16-bit Windows "console-mode" applications, Symantec supplies the WINC library, akin to QuickWin from Microsoft and EasyWin from Borland. However, WINC's abort() function causes its window to close immediately. Both QuickWin and EasyWin terminate the program but leave the window visible until the user closes it. Using the assertion modes other than the normal ANSI assert() macro helps significantly. In particular, one can still determine the assertion from a dialog or log file. With the assert() macro, the window closes before the developer can read it.

Watcom

Watcom's IDE provides a means for specifying macros to declare; this was used rather than direct makefile modification. Hence, one must modify the settings in the IDE to try each assertion mode in addition to recompiling the test executable.

Unit testing under Watcom showed that it handles non-console Win32 API calls differently than do Borland, Microsoft, and Symantec. Under their compilers, one could use ASSERT_DIALOG mode for NT console applications—the program popped up assertion dialogs as expected. Watcom did not support this; instead, the MessageBox() calls for the dialog displayed nothing. Although the program still ran, it provided no notification for failed assertions.

D.3 ResTrack

ResTrack's test executable (TEST.C) exercises MemMalloc() heavily to ensure that it captures all leaks appropriately and does not report false ones. Tests were run with one and several "leaked" buffers, mixed with regular freed allocations, to check the built-in linked-list management of the resources. The other key APIs, except MemCheckListIntegrity(), were also tested. MemCheckListIntegrity(), to fail, requires serious damage to the resource linked list, which is difficult to simulate.

The output of the test program is a roster of each run and the results from RESTRACK.OUT and ASSERT.LOG (assertion to file is selected). That way, a simple inspection of the test results should indicate what went wrong. Moreover, since the values are deterministic, one can run file-comparison utilities (such as *diff*) to detect changes.

Microsoft

When compiling the test executable under Visual C++, one gets spurious warnings about how it calls specific test functions. These warnings can be ignored because they do not affect the results. Moreover, no other compiler complained.

Watcom

The function to release ResTrack-allocated memory had to be renamed to MemRelease(), because MemFree() is a function Watcom uses internally.

D.4 UTCGen

UTCGen is a file-based tool, in that it does not link with another application and does not require direct user input. Hence, it was unit tested by creating catalog files and C header files to be processed. The files cover the major operations to be performed by UTCGen (e.g., obtain conditions for a function parameter). In particular, care was taken to try both successful and failed operations. For example, function parameters were selected that both generated conditions and failed to do so.

UTCGen uses C standard output via printf() for its results. This is typically redirected to a file. A batch file called UNITTEST.BAT (with corresponding UNITTEST.CMD OS/2 command file) executes the entire test suite. All results are redirected to UNITTEST.OUT, with each test's results appended to the last set. In addition, tags were sent to this file via the echo command to label the results. A master set of results is in UNITTEST.MST.

Note that although UTCGen has been ported to Win16, its usefulness in this environment is questionable. The results cannot easily be redirected to a file and, depending on the standard I/O replacement used by the compiler, might be truncated due to lack of buffer space. A 16-bit DOS version should be used instead. On Windows NT, a console mode application will work fine.

Two restrictions on the function prototype syntax are worth repeating here:

- All pointers (*) must have a space between the asterisk and the parameter name. MKPROTO does this appropriately.
- There is no support for variable arguments, in the form of an ellipsis (...) as the last function "parameter." UTCGen's internal parser ignores this "parameter," so one cannot set up catalog entries to report it.

D.5 UTCLang

UTCLang was tested by a series of scripts, which can be executed either by the plain UTCLang driver or by an extended driver (e.g., the X-Base test driver). The scripts exercise the key components of the language and provide reasonable coverage over the code.

A batch file (or command file or shell script, for each environment) executes all scripts and concatenates their output to a single result file (UNITTEST.OUT). It can be compared to a master copy (UNITTEST.MST) to check for discrepancies from run to run.

D.6 UTCCover

To test this tool, a sample source file (TEST.C) exhibiting the various types of coverage situations was created. When compiled, it uses branches, loops, and functions singly and in conjunction to show all different types of complete and incomplete coverage. By instrumenting it with UTCCover and examining the results, one can determine if UTCCover caught all missed coverage and properly ignored passed coverage.

Like UTCGen, UTCCover sends its output to C standard output via printf(). This is typically redirected to a file. A batch file called UNITTEST.BAT (with corresponding UNITTEST.CMD OS/2 command file) executes the UTCCover unit tests. The results are redirected to UNITTEST.OUT, with a master set of results in UNITTEST.MST.

As mentioned in the test, UTCCover cannot be used in a Win16 environment, because the system() function is not natively supported there by most compilers. It is used to execute the MKPROTO program to parse a C source file to obtain a list of functions and their locations. Win16 programs can be instrumented with UTCCover, however, to collect coverage statistics. The results can be examined only by a command-line program, such as a 16-bit DOS program. Given the nature of UTCCover's reporting tool, a Win16 version would have been of questionable utility over a DOS version even if this limitation did not exist.

Also, note that the MKPROTO program must be in the current working directory or along the PATH for UTCCover's reporting program to work properly. MKPROTO should also be compiled for the proper environment. Using a DOS version of MKPROTO from an OS/2 version of UTCCover, for example, does not work.

D.7 WinCapT

WinCapT, due to its nature, is difficult to test. One cannot easily apply another capture/playback tool upon it, so all testing must be done manually. Also, due to the high volume of processing done by the hook functions, it was not possible to employ coverage (for the same reasons the Windows Memory Dump was created; refer to Chapter 11 on WinCapT for details).

As a result, the WinCapT testing was ad hoc, exactly the style this book denounces as inadequate. The goal was to ensure that the playback faithfully reproduced the events from the original recording and that the window state capture routines worked in all situations.

APPENDIX E

Coding Style Guide

A coding style guide is a model for all programmers, experienced and novice, to follow when writing C/C++ code. If everyone follows it, quality will improve. This is in part due to consistency, as it will be easier to maintain code that all looks the same. More important, the rules in the guide transfer knowledge from generation to generation of developers. Following them will help prevent many types of faults.

This appendix outlines a condensed style guide, the one used for the code accompanying the book. It can serve as a starting point for projects wishing to create their own guides.

E.1 Hungarian Notation

Hungarian notation is described in the section on Address Lite at the beginning of the book. It essentially is a scheme for using prefixes on variable names to identify their type. This helps reviewers and maintainers keep track of what the variables hold.

Table E.1 outlines the prefixes used in this book. Note that there is no "official" set of prefixes.

Table E.1 Hungarian Notation Prefixes

Prefix	Data Type	Example
c	char	cFieldType
d	double	dVelocity
f	float	fMonetaryValue
h	handle	hMainWindow
i	int	iXOffset
l	long	lDelta
pfn	pointer to function	pfnCallback
psz	string (dynamic)	pszName
r	structure ('r'ecord)	rBook
s	short	sYear
sz	string (automatic)	szTitle
ui	unsigned int	uiFieldNum
ul	unsigned long	ulBlockSize
us	unsigned short	usIndex

In addition, a lowercase p indicates a pointer to the specified data type. A variable named prBook would represent a pointer to a structure; pprBook would be a pointer to a pointer to a structure.

The difference between psz and sz lies in where the space for the string is declared. Automatic strings (i.e., ones allocated on the stack) have the sz prefix. Ones allocated from the heap use psz. Also, any string passed as a parameter has "psz" as a prefix.

E.2 Rules for C Code

The following sections outline style guidelines that apply to both C and C++ code.

Function Names

Function names should follow a consistent pattern. They should be distinct from the names of variables and other types, so functions can easily be identified by their names.

Each function name should begin with a prefix, from two to four characters long, that identifies the subsystem. For example, XblOpen() has a prefix of "Xbl," since it is a part of the X-Base library. This makes it easy to tell at a glance where the function is defined.

The rest of the name should consist of words (or common abbreviations). Each "word" should be capitalized (e.g., XblGetFieldAsString()), and underscores are prohibited. The exception is a leading underscore for diagnostic functions (e.g., _MemMalloc()) that should not be used in a production environment. This is one of the most readable styles available and is the one used for most of the OS/2 API.

Variable Names

Variables should have names based on Hungarian notation prefixes. That convention will help developers keep track of their data types. The base part of the name should be structured like that of a function name. It should consist of words (or common abbreviations), each capitalized and without underscores. Hence, function names and variable names will look alike, except that functions use a capitalized prefix by subsystem and variables use a lowercase one by type.

Table E.1 lists examples of valid variable names.

Formatting

More so than anything else in C coding, indentation schemes and other formatting styles are a personal selection. Many "religious" debates have raged over how loops should be indented, whether braces should be used for single-line loop bodies, etc. In general, attempts to create a rigid standard will cause open revolt among programmers.

However, the following rules regarding formatting are less controversial:

- Although indentation schemes can vary, each programmer should be consistent within his or her own code. Code reformatting tools are available to change format later.
- Divisions between functions should be clearly marked by a few blank lines, along with a comment (see below).
- Liberal whitespace should serve to set off logical blocks. For example, each loop (including initialization statements) should have blank lines on either

side. Blank lines should also separate local variable declarations and the final return statement from the rest of the code.

Comments

Comments are key for readers to have any idea what the code does. Even the most readable source in the world can be incomprehensible to one who lacks experience with the domain, types, subsystems, etc.

Each file should have a comment box at the top, containing the following information:

1. Name of the file
2. Subsystem to which it belongs
3. Copyright notice and other required legal statements
4. If a version control system is used, a version history (version number and description)

Similarly, each function should have a comment, that provides its name and purpose. This should come on the lines immediately preceding the actual code.

Each variable declaration (global or local) should be described via an end-of-line comment. With a C++ compiler, the // syntax is ideal. All these comments should begin in the same column so they are left-aligned.

Other comments should be sprinkled in functions as needed to clarify the code. Any obscure function calls, strange loops, or other unusual structures should be commented.

Macros

All significant constants should be defined as macros. This helps readability, as the macro name typically means more to a reader than the value would. Also, it helps maintainability, since changes can be made in one spot. Not every constant needs to be so defined — one need not define the zero used to initialize for() loops, for example. Names of macros representing constants should be in all uppercase to distinguish them from functions and variables.

Macro functions are a popular device, as they provide the syntax of a function with less overhead. They can be problematic, however, since many debuggers will not "step into" them. This makes them difficult to debug. The best solution is to initially implement them as true functions, then make them into macros after they have been confirmed to work. Other rules to follow with macro functions include the following:

- Name them like regular functions (e.g., subsystem prefix plus base name).

- Have them work syntactically like regular functions. In other words, they should require either a semicolon or the rest of an expression to follow the macro "call."
- Wrap definitions inside parentheses to ensure that they are evaluated intact. Otherwise, when the macro is expanded, the rest of the expression might alter the way it operates.

Types

All structures should also be set up as user-defined types with a typedef statement. This makes their declarations easier to read (no extra "struct" keywords). Also, it hides the implementation somewhat: The structure could be replaced by a union or C++ class later.

Other important types used in the application should also be set up with typedefs, particularly when their definitions might change. There are several reasons why a type might change over time, including the following:

- Strings might be replaced by C++ String class instances.
- Types where size (in bits) is important might have to change to fit the target architecture. Windows does this to maintain compatibility between Win16 and Win32, for example.

Types should take all uppercase names to distinguish them from built-in ones. Portions of a name within a type can be separated by underscores (e.g., XBL_ERR_CODES), since mixed case cannot be used. Although types and macros have the same naming style, they are rarely used in the same places, so this should not cause a problem.

Also, the type should contain a subsystem prefix to denote where it is defined. The prefix should be the same as the one for the function names, except for case. For example, the X-Base library uses "Xbl" for a function prefix and "XBL_" for types.

Variable Scope

Global variables should be avoided because they cause problems in multithreaded environments. If they are used, ensure that they are properly protected if the environment requires it. All globals that can be initialized at application startup should be initialized to ensure that they always have a defined value. Ones that cannot be initialized easily (e.g., structures) should be initialized by a special subsystem initialization function. Also, all globals should be marked as static, so that they can only be accessed within the source file where they are defined. Code from other files should not be manipulating the globals directly; instead, define accessing functions for that purpose.

Static variables within functions should be avoided for the same reasons as globals. They should also follow the same rules (e.g., initialize at startup when possible).

E.3 Rules for C++ Code

All rules for C code are also valid for C++. The following sections describe additional rules related to C++ classes.

Class Names

Classes should be named like C functions. Hence, they should have a subsystem prefix, followed by words (or common abbreviations), with each word capitalized.

Public/Private/Protected Members

With the exception of constructors and destructors (which usually must be public), the default should be to make all class members protected or private. Only those that must be public should be. In particular, no data members should be public. Instead, define member functions to perform all supported operations on the data. This provides much greater control and reduces the probability of misuse of the class.

The distinction between protected and private is important for class frameworks, where others are expected to create subclasses. One should still aim to defend as much of the class as possible against misuse, even though subclasses have a much more intimate tie with their superclasses than does anything else. Hence, the default should be to mark all members private unless they are specifically needed by subclasses. In particular, make all data members private and provide manipulation functions for subclasses.

Member Function Names

Member functions should be named like regular functions, minus the prefix. Since they are always evaluated within some scope, it should be clear what subsystem they belong to. Also, this makes for a more natural reading of class behaviors, with names that follow the object models more closely.

Function Definitions

One can define member functions either in the class declaration or in a separate file. For most compilers, using the class declaration means that the function will be inlined. This is frequently done for performance reasons, since an inlined function will execute faster than one "hidden" by a call. However, putting functions in class declarations hampers maintainability, for several reasons:

- It violates encapsulation, as other developers can readily see some of the inner workings of the class.
- If the function must change behavior, all files that include the class definition must be recompiled. Normally, only the one containing the function would need to be recompiled. This can dramatically increase build times.
- Some debuggers have difficulty stepping into inlined functions, just like they do with macro functions.

As with macro functions, the best approach is to build the member functions normally first, then inline ones where it makes a significant difference in performance.

APPENDIX F

UTCLang Implementation Notes

The following sections describe the use of UTCLang, including creating interpreted classes and the inner workings of its C++ implementation.

F.1 Interpreted Classes and Methods

The focus of creating a UTCLang driver is on adding compiled classes to attach to a subsystem. One can also add classes in a script. They are called **interpreted** classes because they are entirely defined within interpreted code.

Creating a new class is simple: Send the AddClass message to the System global object. At a minimum, the message takes the name of the class as a string parameter. If the class is to subclass something other than Object, the superclass name is the second parameter.

The examples used here will create a class, called Book, that represents a book pulled out of a database of books.

The following statement adds an interpreted class named Book:

```
System.AddClass "Book"
```

If we needed specializations of books, such as a PaperbackBook, we could create as follows:

```
System.AddClass "PaperbackBook" "Book"
```

At this point, one can create instances of either class by sending it the New message. However, since the classes have no behaviors associated with them (beyond those inherited from Object), there is not much one can do with them.

One can then add instance variables to the class definition. They are logically equivalent to data members of C++ classes, in that they represent the data held on to by instances.

In the example of a Book class, we would want to give it instance variables like "Title", "Author", and "Price". They represent the data that comprises a book record in the database.

To add an instance variable to a class definition, send the AddInstVar message to the class, with its name as a string parameter. All instances created from this point forward will have the instance variable. Of course, the class will also inherit instance variables from its superclass.

In the following script, we both create the Book class and add the desired instance variables to it:

```
System.AddClass "Book"
Book.AddInstVar "Title"
Book.AddInstVar "Author"
Book.AddInstVar "ISBN"
```

All instances of Book will now have the three instance variables. Note, however, that one can only access them from within a method on this class (see below).

The final step is to add methods to the interpreted class. It will inherit methods known to its superclass (which means at least the ones in Object). Any new ones defined for this class will have access to the instance variables defined for the class itself.

To define a new method, send the AddMethod message to the class. There must be at least one parameter: the name of the method. Other tokens following the name are interpreted as being parameters to be passed to the method when called. Following the AddMethod line comes the text of the method itself, written like any other portion of a UTCLang script. The difference is that the lines will not be executed immediately. Instead, they will be stored under the method name and executed when it is invoked. The method definition is terminated by the EndMethod statement.

The following fragment adds a method to the Book interpreted class. The method populates a Book from a DbfRecord object.

```
Book.AddMethod "LoadFromRecord" aRecord
Title.Assign aRecord.Get "TITLE"
Author.Assign aRecord.Get "AUTHOR"
ISBN.Assign aRecord.Get "ISBN"
^aRecord
EndMethod
```

As shown in the above example, a method can indicate the object to be returned via the ^ symbol in front of it. By default, the method will return the receiver (i.e., the instance sent the message that triggered it).

Suppose we execute the following script, after creating the Book class and the LoadFromRecord method:

```
| file book rec |

file.Assign DbfFile.New
file.Name "..\on_hand.dbf"
file.Open

book.Assign Book.New
rec.Assign {book.LoadFromRecord {file.GetRecord 1}}
Log.Print rec

file.Close
```

The Log contains a single line:

```
Database record
```

The script assigns the result of the LoadFromRecord message to the rec temporary.

There is one other noteworthy difference in using interpreted methods. Frequently one needs to send the "current" object a message from within a method. In C++, one uses the "this" magic variable, which represents the object currently processing the member function. UTCLang takes a different approach: Sending a message to "nothing" (i.e., nothing to the left of the dot) means send the message to the current object.

Here are two more methods for the Book class:

```
Book.AddMethod "Display"
Log.Print Author ", " Title " (" ISBN ") "
EndMethod

Book.AddMethod "LoadAndDisplay" aRecord
| aRec |
aRec.Assign .LoadFromRecord aRecord
.Display
^aRec
EndMethod
```

The Display method simply dumps the book on to the Log. LoadAndDisplay wraps around the LoadFromRecord and Display methods, calling each.

Here is another example of class, one that implements Euclid's algorithm for computing the greatest common divisor of two numbers:

```
| gcd result |
System.AddClass "GCD"
GCD.AddInstVar "Numerator"
GCD.AddInstVar "Denominator"

GCD.AddMethod "SwapValues"
| temp |
temp.Assign Numerator
Numerator.Assign Denominator
Denominator.Assign temp
EndMethod

GCD.AddMethod "UpdateValues"
(Numerator < Denominator).IfTrue [.SwapValues]
Numerator.Assign (Numerator - Denominator)
EndMethod

GCD.AddMethod "Evaluate" n m
Numerator.Assign n
Denominator.Assign m
[Numerator > 0].WhileTrue [.UpdateValues]
^Denominator
EndMethod
```

```
gcd.Assign GCD.New
result.Assign {gcd.Evaluate 13 (13*5)}
Log.Print "GCD = " result
```

This script implements a class, GCD, which knows how to evaluate the greatest common denominator. Its primary method is Evaluate, which accepts two integers and returns the greatest common divisor. Internally it uses two methods, SwapValues and UpdateValues, for the processing.

One of UTCLang's limitations is that a code block ([] expression) can contain only a single statement. That is why we need the SwapValues and UpdateValues methods: the logic called for multiple actions after an IfTrue or WhileTrue statement.

Note the sending of messages to the GCD object itself in the Evaluate and UpdateValues methods, inside the code blocks. This is how one passes control to other methods implemented in the same object.

F.2 How UTCLang Works

More so than other tools and libraries provided here, UTCLang is easier to use and understand if one sees its inner workings. There is quite a bit to the implementation of this language framework, from source interpretation to garbage collection. Although readers do not need to understand the details, a description may help explain why things are set up the way they are. This section will go into detail to describe how UTCLang works.

UTCLang, like the other programs, consists of a library with a replaceable user interface. The command-line shell opens requested script files and passes them to the driver. It takes the result (in the form of a string) and writes it to standard output. Obviously, one could create a GUI front end if desired; one could also embed a UTCLang-derived language in another application.

The following sections describe how to use the UTCLang library in practice and what services it provides. They also discuss many advanced features of UTCLang, such as exception handling.

Driver Instances

UTCLang avoids almost all global variables within the library. Most of the data is held by a handle. Inside the library, the handle is an instance of the UtcHandle class. This class can perform several actions, including the following:

- Find local and global script variables.
- Raise exceptions.
- Execute script code.

- Perform garbage collection.
- Handle system initialization.

To allow UTCLang to be driven by a C (rather than C++) front end, UTCLANG.CPP exports a C API. There are four main functions front ends will use if subscribing solely to this API:

- UtcInitDriver() creates an instance of UtcHandle, returning it as a UTC_HANDLE (void *) to the front end.
- UtcTermDriver() destroys a handle, shutting down that driver instance.
- UtcExecuteStatements() provides a script to be executed and gets back a buffer pointing to the results (as captured by the Log object).
- UtcFreeResultsBuffer() frees the buffer returned by UtcExecuteStatements().

Frequently, a custom driver must add compiled classes to the system; this is done by using the UtcAddCompiledClass() API function. The function, however, is available only from a C++ front end, since it deals with classes and objects.

System Initialization

When an instance of UtcHandle is created, it performs some system initialization for that driver. Each instance is set up in the same way, using three functions:

- InitCompiledClass() logs a new script class implemented as a C++ class. The name of the class and an instance-creation static member function are provided as parameters. Given this information, the driver can now allow scripts to create new instances. This is the function behind the UtcAddCompiledClass() API function.
- AddGlobal() creates a new global object reference, either for the nil object or for another created object. For example, UtcHandle, during initialization, creates the true and false globals to be the numbers 1 and 0, respectively.
- ExecuteStatements() is the function that executes script code. The driver uses it to perform global assignments that are more conveniently implemented as scripts rather than inline C++ code.

Below is the implementation of UtcHandle's constructor, illustrating the actions described above:

```
UtcHandle::UtcHandle()
{
    UtcObjectReference *pRef;

                           /* log classes          */
    InitCompiledClass("_System", UtcSystem::New);
    InitCompiledClass("_Log", UtcLog::New);
                           /* use static New 'constructor' */
    InitCompiledClass("String", UtcString::New);
    InitCompiledClass("Number", UtcNumber::New);
                           /* add globals  */
    AddGlobal("nil", new UtcUndefinedObject(GetSpace()));
    AddGlobal("System", GetNil());
    AddGlobal("Log", GetNil());
    AddGlobal("true", new UtcNumber(GetSpace(), 1L));
    AddGlobal("false", new UtcNumber(GetSpace(), 0L));
                           /* execute script to init globals */
    ExecuteStatements("System.Assign _System.New");
    ExecuteStatements("Log.Assign _Log.New");
}
```

Custom drivers must perform more system initialization, done after creating the driver instance by using UtcInitDriver(). Presently, UTCLang has API functions to add compiled classes (UtcAddCompiledClass()) and to execute script statements (UtcExecuteStatements()). This should be sufficient for most purposes.

Interpreted Classes

All interpreted classes (i.e., ones defined in the scripts themselves) are instances of the C++ class UtcInterpretedClass. Each UtcInterpretedClass holds on to the following:

- Its name, used to set it up as a global object
- A list of instance variable names that belong to it
- A dictionary of source methods, keyed by name (selector)

Source methods are instances of UtcSourceMethod and contain the text of a method that a script adds to a class.

Scripts create interpreted classes by sending the AddClass message to the System global. Internally, the method simply creates a new instance of UtcInterpretedClass and adds it to the roster of globals. At this point, the script can send messages to the class object like any other global, such as sending it New to create a new instance.

When a new instance of an interpreted class is made, the C++ object is an instance of UtcInterpretedObject. This object holds a pointer to its interpreted class object, so each object can access its class. In addition, the interpreted class tells the interpreted object all the instance variable names associated with it. The object uses them to populate a dictionary, keyed by name, of the variables themselves (initialized to the global nil object).

Dictionaries

A "dictionary" is a type of collection, frequently found in C++ class frameworks (such as the Standard Template Library, or STL). It is a keyed collection, in that it stores a series of pairs of key and value. It is optimized for searching by key, much like an index. Typical operations one would perform on a dictionary would be to return or set a value for a particular key.

UTCLang employs a dictionary C++ class, subclassed off the List class, found in the \LIST subdirectory. While UTCLang could have used one of the standard collection class frameworks, it would have reduced portability, as there is no ANSI standard for such classes.

The definition for the Dictionary class is:

```
class Dictionary : public List
{
public:
    void *At(char *pszKey);
    int AtPut(char *pszKey, void *pItem);
    void *GetFirstValue();
    void *GetNextValue();
protected:
    DictionaryEntry *EntryAt(char *pszKey);
};
```

DictionaryEntry is a private class used to hold the key/value pairs in the normal linked list. Note that the class is not optimized for searches by key. If a UTCLang driver executes scripts too slowly, one can replace Dictionary's implementation with something faster. This can be done without affecting the rest of UTCLang, so long as the same member functions are provided.

UTCLang executes the following code when a new instance of an interpreted class is created (in UtcInterpretedClass::PerformMethod()):

```
UtcInterpretedClass *pClass=this;

pInst=new UtcInterpretedObject(pHandle->GetSpace(), this);
AssertValid(pInst);

while(pClass->IsInterpretedClass())
{
    pszInstVarName=pClass->InstVars.GetFirstEntry();
                                        /* give it instvars      */
    while (pszInstVarName)
    {
        pInst->AddInstVar(pszInstVarName, pHandle);
        pszInstVarName=pClass->InstVars.GetNextEntry();
    }
    pClass=(UtcInterpretedClass *)pClass->GetSuperclass(pHandle);
}
```

After creating the instance of UtcInterpretedObject, each class in the class hierarchy, starting with the current one, puts its instance variables into the instance. This is done by executing the AddInstVar() member function on the interpreted object itself. Note that once a non-interpreted class is reached (e.g., UtcObject), no more instance variables will exist and the loop stops.

One side effect is that instance variables added to a class will not affect existing instances!

When a message is sent to an interpreted object, it asks its class for the source method for that selector. If the class does not have one by that name, the object walks the class hierarchy (asking its class for the superclass, etc.) until it finds a match or runs out of interpreted superclasses. If no match is found, the interpreted object passes control to UtcObject, which handles messages common to all UTCLang objects (such as PrintString). If a source method was found, however, it is used to perform the action requested by the message (described in the next section).

Below is the PerformMethod() used for interpreted objects:

```
UtcObject *UtcInterpretedObject::PerformMethod(char *pszName,
                                               UtcObjectList &Parms,
                                               UtcHandle *pHandle)
{
    UtcSourceMethod *pCode;
    UtcInterpretedClass *pClass=pMyClass;
    UtcObject *pSuper;

    while (pClass) /* spin through class hierarchy      */
    {
        AssertValid(pClass);
        pCode=pClass->MethodFor(pszName);
        if (pCode) /* if found, evaluate it             */
        {
            return(pCode->Perform(Parms, pHandle, this));
        }
                  /* find superclass of class */
        pSuper=pClass->GetSuperclass(pHandle);
        if (pSuper && pSuper->IsInterpretedClass())
        {
            AssertValid(pSuper);
            pClass=(UtcInterpretedClass *)pSuper;
        }
        else
        {
            break;
        }
    }
                  /* chain to Object to process msg    */
    return(UtcObject::PerformMethod(pszName, Parms, pHandle));
}
```

Starting at the interpreted object's immediate class, each class is searched for a method with the provided name. If one is found, it is executed and its result is used as the return object. Otherwise, control chains to UtcObject.

Note the following limitation of the UTCLang implementation: All interpreted subclasses have Object (UtcObject) as their superclass. It is not possible to create an interpreted subclass of any other compiled class.

Methods and Blocks

As mentioned above, UTCLang holds source methods as instances of UtcSourceMethod. Source methods hold on to two pieces of data: a list of statements (strings) that form its code and a list of parameter names.

When a source method is executed, it is passed a list of parameter objects. The method sets up new local variables, using its parameter names and the provided objects, so the code of the method can access those values. It then uses an interpreter object to evaluate the source code held by the method itself. The result object is returned to the caller of the source method after the parameter references are destroyed.

A subclass of UtcSourceMethod is UtcCodeBlock, the object sitting behind script-level code blocks (e.g., [anObj aMessage]). By and large, UTCLang views code blocks as being just like methods, with two main differences:

- Instead of being held on to by an interpreted class, code blocks are passed around as UTCLang script-level objects. When one is evaluated, the result from executing it is returned. Syntactically, it is like an immediate expression (messages enclosed in braces). It simply evaluates later, on demand.
- Blocks cannot take parameters, unlike methods.

Variable Scoping

Just as in most structured languages, variables have a specific scope, meaning that not all declared ones are addressable from every point in the script. Global variables are universally accessible. However, each method can declare local variables that are accessible only from within it, not from methods called by it. In addition, each interpreted class instance can have instance variables, which are accessible only by methods on that object's class. One cannot make instance variables public, like C++ data members.

Another distinction between variables in C++ and UTCLang is the lifetime of objects. In C++, automatic variables are lost upon return. The only way to have data persist between functions is to mark it static or allocate it on the heap. In UTCLang, all data is held in heap-based objects. Objects stay alive until nothing else addresses them (variables or other objects), at which point they are destroyed, as described in the next section. All UTCLang variables "point" to objects, much as C++ pointers "point" to heap-allocated objects.

To handle this, UTCLang has the UtcObjectReference class, instances of which represent variables in the script. Each object reference has a name and a UtcObject value. UTCLang represents global variables as a list of object references held by a UtcHandle. Instance variables are object references held on to by objects.

Table F.1 Variable Scoping Rules for UTCLang

Variable Scope	Declaration	Visibility
Global	Send System the AddGlobal message, with the global's name as a string parameter	Visible to all script code *following* the declaration
Temporary	Enclose the variable in vertical bars within a script (typically at the beginning of a method)	Visible to all script code within the declaring area (e.g., the method or all non-method code in a script)
Parameter	Part of the method declaration	Visible within that method only
Instance Variable	Send the AddInstVar message to the class to hold the instance variable	Visible to all instances of that class created *after* the instance variable was added

Local Variables and Method Parameters

When a new object is created, it is not necessarily assigned to a variable. When one is so assigned, UTCLang places the object into an object reference. All objects pointed to by all object references in the system are the "live" objects. All others are inaccessible and can be destroyed. Whenever variables are assigned to, the new assignment overlays the older value in the object reference, creating new garbage if nothing else was pointing to the original object.

When a method is called, UTCLang creates a new "execution context," an instance of UtcContext. This object holds on to object references to parameters or temporaries for this particular invocation of the method. If it was called with parameters, they are placed into object references at the start. When temporaries are declared, new references pointing to the global object nil are created.

When a variable is referenced within a script, the value is found by searching the name space in the following order:

- instance variables of the receiving object
- temporaries or parameters (in the current execution context)
- globals

Blocks are treated like methods, with their own execution context; they can also access the temporaries and parameters of the method they are in. Figure F.1 illustrates the search order.

Figure F.1 Variable Search Order

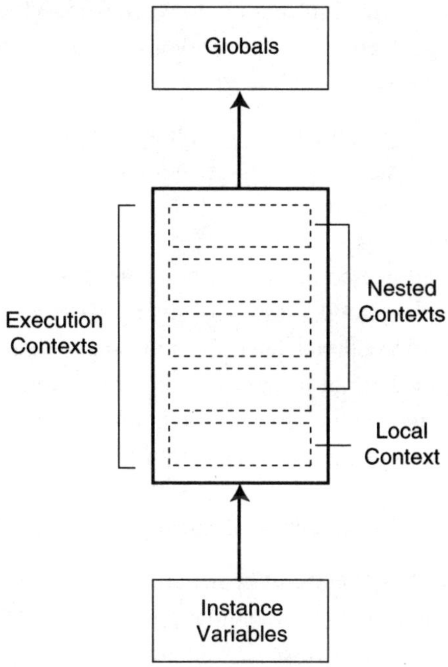

When a method or block completes, UTCLang destroys the object references for that context (and the context itself). Other objects created by the method that are not referenced elsewhere are "garbage" and will be reclaimed soon, as described below.

Garbage Collection

In normal C/C++ systems, every piece of allocated memory must be manually released. Failure to do so causes memory leaks, the problem that ResTrack detects. Applications with garbage collectors, however, can recognize memory that nobody is referencing or holding on to anymore. That memory is considered to be garbage and can be reclaimed periodically. Rather than forcing programmers to track each piece of memory they allocate, the garbage collector does this "bookkeeping."

Garbage collection is far from perfect; otherwise, all languages would implement it. Problems with it include the following:

- Creating and debugging a garbage collection subsystem is difficult; any bugs in it can easily affect all portions of an application using it.

- The garbage collection engine knows little about how the application works and therefore has limited information to work from when determining what memory is garbage. Hence, it might reclaim memory later than a programmer would be able to free it manually.
- The search algorithms that a garbage collector uses to identify garbage are time-consuming, particularly for large memory spaces. Creating a fast garbage collector is challenging.

UTCLang uses garbage collection for script-level objects. C++ does not have a built-in means for garbage collection. However, one can construct a framework, whereby certain application classes have their instances managed in this way. The system is incomplete, in that not all application classes are necessarily part of the garbage collection mechanism, let alone non-classes like allocated strings. Also, the framework will require significant developer effort.

UTCLang's Garbage Collection System

UTCLang's garbage collection classes are in a separate subsystem (found in the \GC subdirectory), since it can serve other purposes. There are two main classes: GcObject and GcSpace. A third class, GcGeneration, is only used by GcSpace and is not directly manipulated by application programmers.

GcObject is the abstract class for all classes managed by the garbage collection engine. GcSpace represents an "object space"; all GcObjects belong to one and only one space. The space actually holds the objects in linked lists managed by GcGeneration objects. Figure F.2 illustrates that structure.

Figure F.2 Garbage Collection Structure

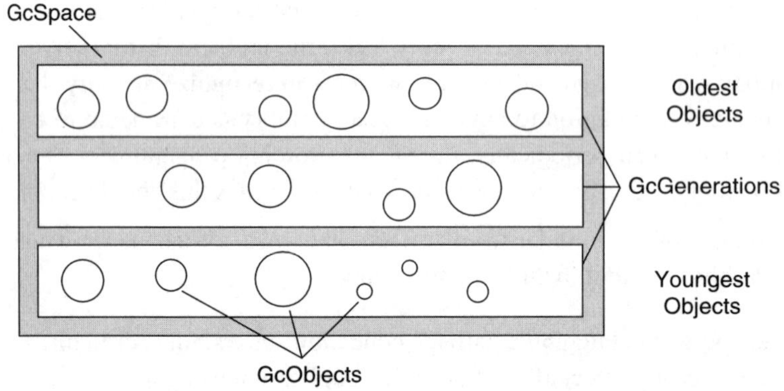

All concrete subclasses of GcObject must be able to perform certain actions, via overriding pure virtual functions. Another class, GcSimpleObject, is provided by the GC subsystem and implements some of these actions. For example, UtcObject, the superclass for all UTCLang objects, is a subclass of GcSimpleObject, so all UTCLang objects are managed by the garbage collection engine. Table F.2 outlines the requirements for subclasses of GcObject.

Table F.2 Virtual Member Functions for GcObject

Member Function	Purpose	Handled by GcSimpleObject
GetGeneration()	Returns the GcGeneration for the object	Y
SetGeneration()	Sets a new generation that holds on to the object	Y
IsHeld()	Returns true (1) if the object is being held by something in the application (e.g., the stack)	Y
MarkAsHeld()	Sets the held state to true (1) or false (0)	Y
IsReached()	Returns true (1) if the object has been reached during the current garbage collection	Y
MarkAsReached()	Sets the reached state to true (1) or false (0)	Y
IsSwept()	Returns true (1) if the object was touched during the current sweep of objects	Y
MarkAsSwept()	Sets the swept state to true (1) or false (0)	Y
SweepChildren()	Applies the provided function to all GcObjects the object holds on to	N

Similarly, GcSpace is abstract and must have virtual functions implemented in a concrete subclass. One such virtual function, IsFreeSpaceLow(), returns true or false depending on whether memory is deemed to be tight. This controls the scope of a garbage collection; if space is low, all generations are scavenged. The other, GetMaxGenCount(), returns the maximum number of generations to use. Once an object reaches the maximum generation, it will not be promoted any further. Hence, globals and other long-lived objects will tend to gather in the top generation. The maximum count may reflect memory considerations or the way in which the generation number is stored in objects (e.g., max of 65,536 if an unsigned short is used).

Objects that are created are logged to the object space, which puts them in the "youngest" generation. The different generations track the age of the objects; everything starts out in the youngest generation. Most objects will not make it out of that generation before becoming garbage. By collecting that generation more frequently than older ones, one should have a more effective garbage collection system.

The constructor for GcObject is:

```
GcObject::GcObject(GcSpace *pSpace)
{
    pMySpace=pSpace;
    pSpace->AddObject(this);
#ifdef GC_DEBUGMODE
    bCollected=0;
#endif
}
```

As the object is created, it immediately informs its object space of its existence. The space turns around and adds it to the newest generation, reflecting its age.

The bCollected flag is used in debug mode with the garbage collection engine. To confirm that garbage collection is working properly, one can define the GC_DEBUGMODE macro when compiling an application. Instead of memory being released when an object is no longer referenced, the bCollected flag is set instead. The AssertValid() macro will check for this setting. If an application ever can touch an object that has been collected, then it is telling the garbage collection subsystem about all reachable objects.

In production, AssertValid() turns into a no-operation statement, and garbage is truly freed rather than just marked as collected.

When objects are referenced by ones **not** managed by the garbage collection system, they must be marked as "held," so they (and their children) will not be garbage collected. In UTCLang, held objects include:

- Globals
- Method and block parameters while their methods are in progress
- Result object from a block/method invocation

As objects are added as children to other garbage-collectible objects (i.e., instance variables), the object space must be given a chance to examine the new relationship. If the holding object is older (i.e., in an older generation) than the newly held object, that object and its children are automatically "aged" to match the holder. If the holding object is younger or of the same age as the newly held object, nothing is done. This ensures that when a generation is garbage collected, all objects *reachable* from that generation are *in* it.

For example, in UTCLang, instance variables in interpreted objects are represented by a dictionary of object references. When a new value is set, the object reference is informed of the change. Not only will the reference update its referent object, but it will also inform the garbage collection system that the old one is no longer referenced, while the new one is. If nothing else is holding on to the old instance variable value, that object will be garbage and will be collected sometime.

When garbage collection is requested, the scavenger marks all objects that are held as reachable; their children are marked as reachable as well. Anything remaining that has not been reached must, by definition, be garbage—these objects are then deleted (by firing their destructors). The remaining objects are moved up to the next generation. Since most garbage collection focuses on the younger generations, the older objects are not scanned as frequently.

One can invoke garbage collection in three ways:

- If the object space detects a low-memory condition when adding an object, it will garbage collect as many generations as needed to rectify the problem.
- The application can request a full garbage collection, in which case all generations will be collected. UTCLang does this when terminating the driver session (i.e., destroying the driver handle).
- The application can request a quick garbage collection. In this case, only the youngest generation will be collected. In general, this generation is the most likely to have garbage. Instances of UtcHandle offer this capability as a CollectGarbage() member function.

UTCLang has each UtcHandle hold a GcSpace, representing the objects used in that instance of the driver. Each script-level object, both of compiled and interpreted classes, is a GcSimpleObject with suitable implementations of the required framework functions. After every statement in the script, UTCLang requests a quick garbage collection. When the script is complete, UTCLang performs a full collection.

Exception Handling

UTCLang is not immune to exceptions, any more so than any other language. A message might be sent with the wrong number of parameters; a parameter might be of the wrong type; etc. UTCLang has an exception handling mechanism to alert users to such problems and allow them to be handled programmatically, if desired.

When a compiled class encounters an exception condition, it raises the exception by executing RaiseException(), a member function of UtcHandle. This takes a string, the name of the exception, as a parameter. All exceptions of the same type should have the same name (e.g., all problems with an illegal type should be "BAD-TYPE").

One can raise exceptions in custom compiled classes only in member functions where a UtcObject pointer is returned, such as the implementation of a UTC-Lang method. The RaiseException() function may return an object which is to be the result of the code that raised the exception (described below).

To raise an exception from within a UTCLang script, send the System global object the RaiseException message, providing the name of the exception to raise.

The following statement raises an exception named Test.

```
System.RaiseException "Test"
```

The default action when an exception is raised is to print an error message to standard output and terminate the program, via the abort() function. The message comes from EXCEPT.TXT, a text file listing all exceptions and messages to show the user when each exception is raised. The text file simply contains two columns, one of exception names and one of messages.

Here is a sample entry from an EXCEPT.TXT file:

```
NOTFOUND:Message not found
```

The string "NOTFOUND" represents the name by which the exception is known in the script or C++ code. UTCLang will display the string "Message not found" to the user if a NOTFOUND exception is raised and there is no exception handler in the script for that exception.

One can opt to handle exceptions in other ways. By sending the System global object the AddExceptionHandler message, one can provide a code block that will get fired when a certain exception occurs. Rather than a message being printed and the program being terminated, the exception block will be evaluated and its result returned to the code that raised the exception.

The following script implements an exception handler, one that simply sends a message to a global object to handle the problem:

```
System.AddExceptionHandler "DbError" [MasterDb.RollbackTransaction]
```

For exceptions raised in C++ code, the exception handling mechanism returns an object. It is the value of the exception handler block, assuming a handler is found (otherwise, the script ends with an abort()). In the above example box, the Log object would be returned if C++ code raised the "Test" exception. Typically, the C++ code should return this object as a result of whatever operation it was doing. Exceptions are typically raised in the context of processing some script-level message; the object returned from the exception handler should be returned as the result of that message. This allows exception handlers to inject objects into the main script, if needed.

Acronyms

API	Application programming interface
CASE	Computer-aided software engineering
DBF	Database file (file extension for X-Base or dBASE files)
DLL	Dynamic-link library
GC	Garbage collection
GUI	Graphical user interface
IDE	Integrated development environment
K&R	Kernighan and Ritchie, referring to the C coding style promoted in their book, *The C Programming Language*
MDI	Multiple document interface
MFC	Microsoft foundation classes
OOPSLA	Conference on Object-Oriented Programming Systems, Languages, and Applications
SQA	Software quality assurance
UI	User interface

Glossary

Acceptance test Test phase when the application is evaluated by clients or users for suitability.

Assertion A statement in a program that validates something the programmer believes to be true. Embedding assertions into a program allows it to continuously check the validity of assumptions and inform the developer if they fail.

Beta testing Term applied to releasing early versions of an application to a small set of users, to try out and report their experiences.

Black-box conditions Conditions identified by looking solely at the interface to a function.

Boundary conditions Conditions that test the boundaries between partitions of input values (see also **equivalence partitioning**).

Bug rate The number of faults detected per unit time. Sometimes used to determine when a test phase is complete—low bug rates suggest that additional effort may not be cost-effective.

Continuous improvement The philosophy that quality assurance should not only solve today's problems but should also try to prevent tomorrow's problems. This is done by constantly modifying the quality assurance process itself, based on how effectively it is preventing or identifying faults.

Coverage A measurement of the quality of a test suite, created by determining how much of an application (or subsystem) it executed. The precise mechanism for calculating this metric depends on the specific type of coverage used.

Driver Subsystem that exercises the API of another subsystem, used in unit and integration testing.

Equivalence partitioning The act of dividing the set of inputs to a function according to the different types of outputs it can return. Done for unit testing to select test conditions: Each partition should have at least one condition.

Exception An external event that causes a software failure.

Fault A coding or design error that causes the application to fail to work in the expected fashion. Fault and "bug" are synonymous here.

Guard bytes Bytes used to identify overwrites and underwrites of memory buffers. They are added to either side of an allocated buffer and set to specific values. If the values change, the application must have tried writing past a bound of the buffer.

Handle A piece of data that, to the user, has no inherent meaning. It is just a "black box" passed to functions that require it. Used for information hiding, akin to using private data members in a C++ class.

Hungarian notation A standardized prefix scheme for naming variables and function parameters. The prefix indicates the type of the variable.

Instance variables Term used for data members of a UTCLang interpreted class.

Invariant A statement of something about an object that should not change over its life span. An example is "A window object will hold onto a valid window handle at all times."

McCabe's cyclomatic complexity A metric for measuring the complexity of a function or subsystem, based in part on its size and number of decision points.

Message A means of invoking behavior in a UTCLang object. Sending a message is akin to executing a member function in C++.

Method An implementation of a behavior in a UTCLang class. A method is like a member function in C++.

Postconditions Rules that define the state of the component and results after an interface is through executing.

Preconditions Rules that define the state of the component before an interface is actually executed.

Regression testing The act of rerunning prior tests and comparing the results to see if anything changes. The technique can be applied for unit or system testing.

Regular expression A string that serves as a pattern against which to match other strings.

Software contract An agreement between developers as to the nature of the interfaces between their subsystems. Serves as the basis for determining what assertions to use.

Statistical process control Concept that process improvement can be attained by first getting the process under control, then improving the result.

Stubs Do-nothing libraries with the same interface as existing subsystems. Stubs are used in place of real libraries during unit testing to isolate one subsystem from its partners.

Temporaries Term used for variables local to a method in a UTCLang interpreted class.

Test case A description of a series of conditions to try as a group in a unit or system test. It also describes all steps needed to try the conditions, along with the expected results.

Test condition A statement of a single item to be tried in a unit test. Test conditions typically refer to states of individual parameters. An example would be "try passing a NULL pointer for the pszName variable."

Waterfall Software development methodology that has all design work done before development begins. Similarly, all programming is completed before testing begins.

White-box conditions Conditions determined by examining the implementation of a function. Contrast with **black-box conditions**.

X-Base Database file format popularized by dBASE.

References

[1] Beizer, B. 1990. *Software Testing Techniques*, 2nd ed. New York: Van Nostrand Reinhold.

[2] Brocka, B., and M. Brocka. 1992. *Quality Management.* Homewood, IL: Business One Irwin.

[3] Crosby, Philip B. 1979. *Quality Is Free.* New York: McGraw-Hill.

[4] Deming, W. Edwards. 1986. *Out of the Crisis.* Cambridge, MA: MIT Center for Advanced Engineering Study.

[5] Glass, Robert. 1992. *Building Quality Software.* Englewood Cliffs, NJ: Prentice Hall.

[6] Hetzel, Bill. 1988. *Complete Guide to Software Testing*, 2nd ed. Wellesley, MA: QED Information Sciences, Inc.

[7] Howard, Robert. 1993. "The Eiffel Programming Language," *Dr. Dobb's Journal*, October.

[8] Kernighan, Brian, and Dennis Ritchie. 1988. *The C Programming Language*, 2nd ed. Englewood Cliffs, NJ: Prentice Hall.

[9] Maguire, Steve. 1993. *Writing Solid Code.* Redmond, WA: Microsoft Press.

[10] Mosley, Daniel. 1993. *Handbook of MIS Application Software Testing.* Englewood Cliffs, NJ: Yourdon Press.

[11] Myers, Glenford. 1976. *The Art of Software Testing.* New York: John Wiley & Sons,

[12] Richter, Jeffrey. 1992. *Windows 3.1: A Developer's Guide.* New York: M&T Books.

[13] Royer, Thomas. 1993. *Software Testing Management.* Englewood Cliffs, NJ: Prentice Hall PTR.

[14] Spuler, David. 1994. *C++ and C Debugging, Testing, and Reliability.* Englewood Cliffs, NJ: Prentice Hall.

[15] Thielen, David. 1992. *No Bugs!* Reading, MA: Addison-Wesley.

[16] Yourdon, Ed. 1977. *Structured Walkthroughs.* Englewood Cliffs, NJ: Yourdon Press.

Index

A

D

E

F

G

H

I

J

K

L

R

S

T

U

V

W

X

Y

LICENSE AGREEMENT AND LIMITED WARRANTY

READ THE FOLLOWING TERMS AND CONDITIONS CAREFULLY BEFORE YOU PROCEED. THIS LEGAL DOCUMENT IS AN AGREEMENT BETWEEN YOU AND PRENTICE-HALL, INC. (THE "COMPANY"). BY ENTERING "YES" TO RECEIVE ACCESS TO THE SOFTWARE, YOU ARE AGREEING TO BE BOUND BY THESE TERMS AND CONDITIONS. IF YOU DO NOT AGREE WITH THESE TERMS AND CONDITIONS, ENTER "NO" OR "ESCAPE" AND YOU WILL NOT HAVE ACCESS TO THE SOFTWARE AND ALL ACCOMPANYING ITEMS.

1. **GRANT OF LICENSE:** The Company grants to you a nonexclusive, nontransferable right to use and display the software being transmitted to you (hereinafter the "SOFTWARE") so long as you comply with the terms of this Agreement. The Company reserves all rights not expressly granted to you under this Agreement.

2. **USE RESTRICTIONS:** You may not sell, license, transfer, or distribute copies of the SOFTWARE or the Documentation to others. You may not reverse engineer, disassemble, decompile, modify, adapt, translate, or create derivative works based on the SOFTWARE or the Documentation without the prior written consent of the Company.

3. **TERMINATION:** This license is effective until terminated. This license will terminate automatically without notice from the Company if you fail to comply with any provisions of this license. All provisions of this Agreement as to warranties, limitation of liability, remedies or damages, and ownership rights shall survive termination.

4. **MISCELLANEOUS:** This Agreement shall be construed in accordance with the laws of the United States of America and the State of New York and shall benefit the Company, its affiliates, and assignees.

5. **LIMITED WARRANTY AND DISCLAIMER OF WARRANTY:** Because this SOFTWARE is being given to you without charge, the Company and the author of the SOFTWARE make no warranties about the SOFTWARE, which is provided "AS-IS." THE COMPANY DISCLAIMS ALL WARRANTIES, EXPRESS OR IMPLIED, INCLUDING WITHOUT LIMITATION, THE IMPLIED WARRANTIES OF MERCHANTABILITY AND FITNESS FOR A PARTICULAR PURPOSE. THE COMPANY DOES NOT WARRANT, GUARANTEE, OR MAKE ANY REPRESENTATION REGARDING THE USE OR THE RESULTS OF THE USE OF THE SOFTWARE. IN NO EVENT SHALL THE COMPANY OR ITS EMPLOYEES, AGENTS, SUPPLIERS, OR CONTRACTORS BE LIABLE FOR ANY INCIDENTAL, INDIRECT, SPECIAL, OR CONSEQUENTIAL DAMAGES ARISING OUT OF OR IN CONNECTION WITH THE LICENSE GRANTED UNDER THIS AGREEMENT INCLUDING, WITHOUT LIMITATION, LOSS OF USE, LOSS OF DATA, LOSS OF INCOME OR PROFIT, OR OTHER LOSSES SUSTAINED AS A RESULT OF INJURY TO ANY PERSON, OR LOSS OF OR DAMAGE TO PROPERTY, OR CLAIMS OF THIRD PARTIES, EVEN IF THE COMPANY OR AN AUTHORIZED REPRESENTATIVE OF THE COMPANY HAS BEEN ADVISED OF THE POSSIBILITY OF SUCH DAMAGE.

SOME JURISDICTIONS DO NOT ALLOW THE LIMITATION OF IMPLIED WARRANTIES OR LIABILITY FOR INCIDENTAL, INDIRECT, SPECIAL, OR CONSEQUENTIAL DAMAGES, SO THE ABOVE LIMITATIONS MAY NOT ALWAYS APPLY. YOU MAY HAVE RIGHTS WHICH VARY IN ACCORDANCE WITH LOCAL LAW.

ACKNOWLEDGMENT

YOU ACKNOWLEDGE THAT YOU HAVE READ THIS AGREEMENT, UNDERSTAND IT, AND AGREE TO BE BOUND BY ITS TERMS AND CONDITIONS. YOU ALSO AGREE THAT THIS AGREEMENT IS THE COMPLETE AND EXCLUSIVE STATEMENT OF THE AGREEMENT BETWEEN YOU AND THE COMPANY AND SUPERSEDES ALL PROPOSALS OR PRIOR AGREEMENTS, ORAL OR WRITTEN, AND ANY OTHER COMMUNICATIONS BETWEEN YOU AND THE COMPANY OR ANY REPRESENTATIVE OF THE COMPANY RELATING TO THE SUBJECT MATTER OF THIS AGREEMENT.

Should you have any questions concerning this Agreement or if you wish to contact the Company for any reason, please contact in writing at the address below.

Robin Short
Prentice Hall PTR
One Lake Street
Upper Saddle River, New Jersey 07458